Credits

Author
Michael J.R. Whitehead

Reviewer
Alan Sutton

Technical Editors
Nanda Padmanabhan
Rushabh Sanghavi

Editorial Manager
Dipali Chittar

Development Editor
David Barnes

Indexer
Ashutosh Pande

Proofreader
Chris Smith

Production Coordinator
Manjiri Nadkarni

Cover Designer
Helen Wood

About the Author

Michael J. R. Whitehead is a leading authority on the design and implementation of Customer Relationship Management (CRM) systems. Michael's experience and expertise spans a thirty year career in software architecture, design, and development as well as business management and ownership of multiple technology organizations. Among many other accomplishments Michael is the contributing author of the SugarCRM Open Source User Guide.

Michael has authored this book for entrepreneurs and small/medium business leaders, like himself, to help propel the success of their businesses through the disciplined application of CRM best practices. More than just a practical guide for the implementation of SugarCRM, this book explores and explains the business implications—and benefits—of customer relationship management for the small/medium business.

Michael is currently the founder and President of The Long Reach Corporation (`www.thelongreach.com`). Long Reach blends real-world CRM expertise with commercial open-source technologies to design, develop, and deliver cost-effective CRM solutions for small/medium business and divisions of large enterprises. Long Reach offers a full range of SugarCRM implementation, customization, and training services. Long Reach is also the developer of Info At Hand, a complete, commercial-grade, customer-centric business management solution built on SugarCRM Open Source.

To the Whitehead Family: Rennie, Nesta, Maureen, Andrew, Katherine & Suzanne.

For the help and encouragement they have all given me through the years, and during this project, each in their own special way. They have taught me all the important things.

I'd like to thank John, Clint, and Jacob for having the courage and skills to create the wonderful SugarCRM platform, and David Barnes for having the vision to recognize its importance at such an early stage.

About the Reviewer

Al Sutton has worked for several years in systems design, development, and deployment for large corporations such as Reuters and Chase Manhattan Bank, smaller organizations, and start-ups, from which he has gained a wide experience of many types of IT environment. He is currently working with Argosy TelCrest on its security software.

Table of Contents

Preface

In 1999, a company named Salesforce.com changed the rules for Customer Relationship Management (CRM) tools. Once exclusively the domain of multi-million dollar solutions designed to be used by large organizations, Salesforce.com revolutionized the capabilities and price points of CRM so that it was usable and affordable by much smaller firms.

In 2004, a further paradigm shift took place, when a Silicon Valley startup by the name of SugarCRM released its first version of software that made the benefits of effective CRM available to firms as small as home-based businesses (and as large as several thousand employees).

I have been involved with the SugarCRM Open Source project since its very early days. I remember my first thoughts after seeing it—thinking how good the user interface and performance were, and wondering why there was no user documentation. One of the first contributions I made to the project was the Open Source User Guide—a basic reference guide to the system's operation.

With *Implementing SugarCRM*, my goal was to bring more perspective to the topic of CRM technology and its role in small/mid-size businesses today, and to illustrate those possibilities with a detailed introduction to SugarCRM Open Source. I also wanted to give small/mid-size businesses the benefit of the experience I have gained from carrying out over 30 SugarCRM implementations just during the course of writing this book.

This book is intended to help you on two fronts:

- Learning about the recent game-changing advances in the field of Customer Relationship Management for small to mid-size businesses, using a step-by-step guide to modern CRM capabilities illustrated by worked examples and images from SugarCRM Open Source—today's leading open-source CRM solution.
- Leading you though the business analysis process of understanding how your organization is different from other firms, and therefore how your CRM should be customized so it best fits your needs and business processes.

I have tried to write a book that will engage you at your current level of knowledge, whether you already have some familiarity with CRM principles, or with the details of SugarCRM itself, or would like to gain familiarity with the CRM field from the bottom up. It will deliver in-depth understanding of CRM concepts, SugarCRM capabilities, and advanced applications, and the business context to apply CRM to your real-world challenges.

From the initial blank sheet of paper you face when first considering a CRM implementation for your business, through the detailed business and technology considerations of creating the right CRM solution for you, to the challenges of deploying and introducing the CRM into your business, this book will lead you each step of the way.

During the course of this book, I will demonstrate and explain how to improve your business processes, business performance, and quality of life using CRM tools created specifically for managing small and mid-size businesses. By the end of the book you will be doing business—better!

What This Book Covers

Chapter 1 introduces you to CRM and shows how CRM systems such as SugarCRM can increase your business's productivity and profitability, and lead to richer, even more pleasurable business relationships. You'll also meet Doc, the proprietor of our case study business—*RayDoc Carpets*.

Chapter 2 provides the critical business analysis process you need to work your way through to identify, understand, and satisfy the special CRM needs of your business. The business analysis for the RayDoc case study is presented in worksheet format, and then you mark up an analysis worksheet for your own business.

Chapter 3 makes a break from the theoretical, and gets down to the practical considerations of deploying your CRM system, explains the options you have to choose from, and ends with your new system up and running.

Chapter 4 helps you take your new CRM for a test drive, providing a step-by-step introduction to CRM concepts and usage, illustrated with a task-oriented series of worked examples in SugarCRM. This hands-on approach lets you get a real feel for the information held in a CRM and how easy it is to find it and keep it up to date.

Chapter 5 takes you beyond the basic CRM information, and explains the Sugar Open Source features you may not have realized were part of a CRM—marketing campaigns, project management, document management, RSS news feeds, linking to external websites, and sending email.

Chapter 6 discusses commercial and Open Source add-ons for SugarCRM. Some important CRM capabilities may be found in Open Source and commercial add-ons, including the ability to prepare quotes, receiving email within the CRM, security and access control, standard and custom report generation, sales forecasting, wireless handheld browser access, wirelessly synchronizing CRM data with handheld devices, HR management, and service contract management.

Chapter 7 is a guide to managing your CRM implementation. How do you make sure that your new CRM will be the right fit for your business, and that users will embrace it? This chapter deals with the key issues of setting goals and requirements, involving all areas of the business throughout the entire process, managing the development of any customizations, and then system training and rollout—making sure it becomes a welcome part of the new office routine.

Chapter 8 explains how to link SugarCRM with your customers. Outside the walls of your business, there is an entire world of integration opportunities for your CRM. This chapter explores the creation of automated lead capture from your public website, and integration of Sugar Open Source with a customer self-service web portal based on the Mambo portal.

Appendix A details the step-by-step process of installing SugarCRM on a Linux server.

Appendix B explains the relatively simple process of installing SugarCRM on a Windows server.

Appendix C shows you in detail how to get your valuable data out of your old contact manager or CRM, and into SugarCRM.

Appendix D explains the role and responsibilities of the system administrator—at the time of initial system installation, as well as for ongoing support and maintenance.

Conventions

In this book, you will find a number of styles of text that distinguish between different kinds of information. Here are some examples of these styles, and an explanation of their meaning.

There are three styles for code. Code words in text are shown as follows: "We can include other contexts through the use of the `include` directive."

A block of code will be set as follows:

```
$_POST['status'] = "New";
$_POST['refered_by'] = "Lead Capture Webpage";
$_POST['email_opt_out'] = empty($_POST['email_opt_in']) ? 'on' : 'off';
```

When we wish to draw your attention to a particular part of a code block, the relevant lines or items will be made bold:

```
$_POST['status'] = "New";
$_POST['refered_by'] = "Lead Capture Webpage";
$_POST['email_opt_out'] = empty($_POST['email_opt_in']) ? 'on' : 'off';
```

Any command-line input and output is written as follows:

```
/echo "0,10,20,30,40,50 * * * * cd /<path-to-sugar>;
<path-to-php> ./scheduler.php" | crontab -u apache/
```

New terms and **important words** are introduced in a bold-type font. Words that you see on the screen, in menus or dialog boxes for example, appear in our text like this: "clicking the Next button moves you to the next screen".

> Warnings or important notes appear in a box like this.

Reader Feedback

Feedback from our readers is always welcome. Let us know what you think about this book, what you liked or may have disliked. Reader feedback is important for us to develop titles that you really get the most out of.

To send us general feedback, simply drop an email to `feedback@packtpub.com`, making sure to mention the book title in the subject of your message.

If there is a book that you need and would like to see us publish, please send us a note in the SUGGEST A TITLE form on `www.packtpub.com` or email `suggest@packtpub.com`.

If there is a topic that you have expertise in and you are interested in either writing or contributing to a book, see our author guide on `www.packtpub.com/authors`.

Customer Support

Now that you are the proud owner of a Packt book, we have a number of things to help you to get the most from your purchase.

Downloading the Example Code for the Book

Visit http://www.packtpub.com/support, and select this book from the list of titles to download any example code or extra resources for this book. The files available for download will then be displayed.

> The downloadable files contain instructions on how to use them.

Errata

Although we have taken every care to ensure the accuracy of our contents, mistakes do happen. If you find a mistake in one of our books—maybe a mistake in text or code—we would be grateful if you would report this to us. By doing this you can save other readers from frustration, and help to improve subsequent versions of this book. If you find any errata, report them by visiting http://www.packtpub.com/support, selecting your book, clicking on the **Submit Errata** link, and entering the details of your errata. Once your errata have been verified, your submission will be accepted and the errata added to the list of existing errata. The existing errata can be viewed by selecting your title from http://www.packtpub.com/support.

Questions

You can contact us at questions@packtpub.com if you are having a problem with some aspect of the book, and we will do our best to address it.

1

Doing Business—Better

On the face of it, you have to wonder why we do it. Why we work all the long hours, often making a less than comfortable income, and dealing with seemingly endless problems in all different areas of the business. Handling internal staffing issues, supplier problems, customer complaints, government paperwork, and technology challenges—some days it never seems to stop!

Of course, we do it because we love it, because being a vital part of a small or mid-size business allows us to accomplish so much and to have such a significant influence on the performance of the business. Helping to realize a vision of a business we believe in gives us so much satisfaction that we are prepared to put up with everything else it entails. But we're not crazy—if we could find a way to reduce the pressure and workload that comes with being part of a dynamic small or mid-size business, we would likely embrace it. And if it helps the business grow, and makes our customers happier—that would be quite something.

However—while there are many technologies that profess to deliver these benefits, typically the solutions and systems available are too expensive, too complicated, or too poor a match to the specific requirements of our business for them to deliver salvation.

Well, not to raise your hopes unduly, I believe help is on the way. I too am a small business person, having bought and sold small businesses including an art gallery, a women's clothing store, a computer retail store, a couple of software development companies, and several computer manufacturing companies. I have created new businesses, and purchased and revived other people's businesses. I have held management positions in operations, technology, sales, and marketing. I have been the boss, and I have worked for bosses with a wide variety of skill sets. Perhaps like you, along the way I have made money, and sometimes lost it. But it has always been worth it to me—the tradeoff between the burden of responsibility, pressure, and stress for the relative freedom to pursue your own vision of how a business or a department should be operated.

This book is about being a part of a small or mid-size business. The principal constituencies within a **Small** or **Mid-Size Business (SMB)** addressed by this book include **senior management** (an owner, partner, shareholder, or manager), the **Information Technology group** (the CTO, or an IT manager, specialist, or advisor), the **Sales department** (Sales Manager or quota-bearing sales executive or representative), as well as the **Administration** (both, the managers of finance, and administration, as well as the rank and file employees). The objective of this book is to demonstrate and explain how to improve your business processes, business performance, and quality of life using **Customer Relationship Management (CRM)** tools created specifically for managing small and mid-size businesses.

The Business Benefits of CRM Technology

As someone who owned his first micro-computer (a Sol-20 from Processor Technology) in 1977, I have always made a point of using technology to lighten the load of managing a small business and with the recent advances in the field of CRM for small and mid-size businesses, so can you. Until recently, smaller businesses typically could not afford management tools of this type, and even when they could, those tools were more oriented towards larger businesses, and they found them impractical and unwieldy.

Throughout the book I will endeavor as much as possible to deal with CRM from a business, not technical, perspective. However, the later chapters do become quite technical, explaining how to customize your CRM, and link your CRM to external portals and lead capture mechanisms. We (you and I, that is) will be using a leading open-source CRM tool, SugarCRM, a good example of the very capable yet affordable CRM tools that are now available now, and focus on the needs of smaller businesses.

In this book we will not just discover the specifics of installing and implementing SugarCRM although we will cover those issues in detail. We will also explain the business context, and describe a broader business perspective on the generic issues of CRM implementations in smaller businesses. What it can do for your business. How best to implement it. And how should it be customized to maximize your business benefits. By the end of the book, you too will be doing business—better.

Small and Mid-Size Businesses: The Good, the Bad, and the Ugly

Let's just stop a moment to consider and clarify our definition of a small or mid-size business, as it covers a wide range of organizations. While the Gartner Group may have one definition, and the Meta Group another, for our purposes here a small or mid-size business falls into these categories:

- **Home-based business with a proprietor**: The proprietor may or may not work with other people on a regular basis. If others are involved, they may be outsourced contractors, commissioned salespeople or agents, or one or more partners who also work from their homes. These businesses vary widely—some involving lots of travel, and some requiring very little. This is very relevant, as travel is a frequent cause of lack of good information flow within an organization, and lack of good communication with customers. These businesses tend to have a headcount in the range of 1-10 employees and partners, and annual sales under 2 Million USD.
- **Small services businesses**: These would usually have office premises that deal directly with businesses and retail consumers. Perhaps in the field of financial or legal services, real estate, graphics services, doors and windows replacement, home renovation, carpet cleaning, or catering—a multitude of businesses. Often these businesses have mobile staff making customer site visits in company vehicles. These firms are often in the 5-50 range in terms of employees, with sales in the 0.5 to 10 Million USD range.

- **Small-to-medium product or services businesses**: These usually have shop-front premises that deal with businesses and consumers. This can include almost any retail sales and service activity with an average sale value high enough to merit tracking customers or clients individually. These firms are usually in the 10-100 range in terms of employees, with sales in the 1 to 20 Million USD range.

If your business has more than 100 employees, you are on the verge of becoming, or have already become, a more sophisticated, complex, and (let's face it) wealthier organization with different needs and budget from those businesses described above. If your business falls under the 100 employee level, this book is definitely for you.

However, while businesses with less than 100 employees are classified as small or mid-size businesses, there is nothing small about the job of administering and managing these businesses! While being your own boss (of the organization, or of a department within it) often means there is no boss around to tell you what to do—it merely means that you have to tell yourself to do far too many things. In a typical small business, the owners and managers wear multiple hats—one minute running finance, the next minute sales, and then on to customer service and support, binding a proposal, arguing with the landlord, and so on.

Running a smaller business also means having to be careful and smart with cash. Administration is almost always understaffed, as the lack of scale in a smaller business makes business infrastructure and administration relatively more expensive. Overworked book-keeping clerks and part time accounting resources are frequently the order of the day. All this unfortunately has also meant that too many businesses have, until now, been effectively disenfranchised from the club of those able to afford the best management tools.

Typical Small Business Needs

A glance at the income statements for a typical smaller business reveals a need to lower administrative costs. If it doesn't, that usually means the owner's quality of life is pretty low, as he or she is likely doing it all by themselves. Or it can indicate that administration is being very poorly executed. Unfortunately, even though administration costs are usually high, the administration resources that exist are typically overworked, and struggling to meet the workload. This usually doesn't get much better until the 100 employee milestone is passed.

Another key need for those managing smaller businesses is the need to get out of the office more—get out of the office just to get home and spend some time with the family, to win new customers and service existing ones, or just to see different scenery without having the whole house of cards falling apart. But instead, the usual day spent managing a smaller business consists of:

- An endless stream of visits from employees with questions
- Shouting instructions across the open office
- Dropping by the various departments for an update
- Spending half the day on the phone
- Firing off emails to contacts stored in Microsoft Outlook
- Staying late to bring paperwork up to date

Getting out of the office often means traveling some distance on business, and this highlights another need—the need to get business information while traveling, on laptops and handhelds, offline and online. This kind of connectivity and flexibility is what it takes to compete in today's increasingly demanding and cost-conscious business environment—and most of the smaller businesses just don't have these tools. What tools they have are typically client-server based—meaning that some software is loaded on a shared server computer, and more software is loaded on the PC of each person allowed to use the system. This can get expensive, with license fees typically being charged on the per-user model, and time consuming and potentially costly maintenance and updates required for each PC quite frequently. It also tends to keep people in the office, where the PCs with this software loaded on them are located.

A web-based CRM, by way of contrast, has no user software to load on each PC—all that is needed is a browser like Internet Explorer, Mozilla Firefox, or Apple's Safari. While the server software is still often licensed on the per user basis, these users can be anywhere (including at home or traveling to see customers) and still have access to the system and all the information it holds. And an open-source CRM like **Sugar Open Source** is best of all, as it has no licensing fees of any sort.

A web-based small business CRM directly addresses all the needs listed above. It lets you get out of the office, yet stay in touch. It lets you see your family or win more business without dropping you out of the organization's information loop. It reduces administrative load and costs by ensuring that the company and customer information only needs to be keyed in once, and is well-organized and easily accessible. And it is accessible not only by home PCs and road-warrior laptops, but even by handheld devices such as the Treo and BlackBerry, as even these smaller devices contain a web browser (see Chapter 6 for details of handheld information access, and wireless synchronization).

What is Customer Relationship Management?

If you are going to consider implementing a CRM, it is probably important that we first go over what a CRM really is, and how it compares to some tools you may already be familiar with.

A CRM or a Customer Relationship Management System, is just that—a system that manages information and processes around your relationship with your customers, not only the sales aspect of that relationship but also the ongoing service and support aspects. The system should provide at least basic information about the companies you are doing business with, and the people you work with at those companies. Typically these are referred to as **Accounts**, and **Contacts**. Accounts can be your customers, but may also be your suppliers, your partners, or your sub-contractors.

You are likely to be familiar with one or more simple contact management systems—such as Microsoft Outlook, ACT!, or GoldMine. Let's talk a bit about Microsoft Outlook as it is the one most people have seen and used. While it is used mostly as an email client, Outlook is also a contact manager. It keeps track of the people you know—often both personal and business contacts in one system. It lists for each person their phone number(s), email address(es), mailing address(es), and personal information such as their birthday, and anniversary. It also records the organization they work for as one of the data fields on their record. If you have a second person you know, who also works at that company, Outlook has functions that let you copy the first person's information, so as not to have to re-enter all the company-related information.

Unfortunately, if that company moves, or changes its fax number, that information is duplicated on the contact record for everyone you know at that company, and you will have to chase them all individually to correct them.

By contrast, one of the minimum features offered by a CRM is that the company, or account, has information kept on it as an independent entity, and then has people you know, or contacts, linked to it. In this way, the company information only gets changed in one place when it needs updating, and yet each contact record easily brings up the information of the account with which it is associated.

Also, in Microsoft Outlook there is no attempt to automatically link upcoming meetings, telephone calls, or tasks with the contact or account to which these activities relate, or to keep an organized history of past account activity including emails and notes. Essentially any CRM can do this.

These features (maintaining account records separate from contact records, and maintaining account and contact history) are two of the fundamental features you should expect to see in any CRM, but there are many more, including:

- **Sales-force automation**: This includes lead capture and the promotion of leads to Opportunities.
- **Opportunity tracking**: This tracks the sales stage and percentage likelihood.
- **Sales pipeline tracking**: This uses graphical charts that offer drill-down from the bar or segment of the chart to the data that underlies it.
- **Definition of sales teams and territories**: This helps in managing information sharing and tracking sales performance by territory.
- **Lead source analysis of sales and opportunities**
- **Product catalog management:** It also takes care of tracking sales inventory, corporate assets, and client products covered by support contracts.
- **Creating quotations for clients**
- **Flexible reporting**: This extracts precisely the information you want to see.
- **Service case tracking**: There are also other service/support capabilities such as tracking software bugs, and managing support contract renewals.
- **Corporate calendar management**: This can be used for arranging meetings.
- **Corporate directory**: This can be used for contacting fellow employees.
- **Interface consolidation**: This brings additional everyday needs into the CRM environment in order to make a company website that employees can *live in*. This includes news feeds, views of financial metrics, integration of external web links and applications, and integrated web-based email.
- **Document management and revision control**: This helps in managing and retaining reference copies of important corporate documents.

A well-conceived CRM must also have a truly outstanding user interface, as the whole purpose of the system is to make the organization's information accessible quickly, easily, and naturally. As the CRM software field has matured, many CRM systems have come to adopt similar solutions for navigating through the CRM. Let's have a look at what it feels like to use a CRM with a state-of-the-art user interface, by having our first look at SugarCRM.

What is SugarCRM?

SugarCRM is both a company, and an Open Source project. SugarCRM the company was created as a commercial Open Source company, and funded by Silicon Valley venture capital firms (three rounds of financing and 25 Million USD to date). Its business model is to not only develop an open-source CRM product, which will benefit from broad adoption and feedback from the user community, but also to develop enhanced versions of it that it can sell. The open-source product is called **Sugar Open Source**, and the commercial products are called **Sugar Pro** and **Sugar Enterprise**. In this book we will deal primarily with Sugar Open Source, because, as William Shatner was once paid to remark on a commercial for a large chain of grocery stores, "By Gosh, the Price is Right!".

The SugarCRM Open Source project has its official home at http://www.sugarforge.org/. The SugarCRM Open Source project was established on April 23, 2004, and so is of quite recent vintage! But the founders of SugarCRM (both the company and the Open Source project) are veterans of CRM implementations at several other organizations, notably Epiphany (recently purchased by SSA Global), Aurum Software, Baan Software (also purchased by SSA Global), and BroadVision, and were able to turn their experience into a relatively fully functioned CRM system in a remarkably short time span. SugarCRM 1.0 was released on August 4, 2004. SugarCRM 2.0 was released on November 3, 2004; SugarCRM 3.0 came out on April 30, 2005, and SugarCRM 3.5 was introduced on August 15, 2005. SugarCRM 4.0 (the current revision at time of writing) was introduced on December 15, 2005.

It is worth noting that the nature of Open Source is such that if one day (perish the thought), SugarCRM the company was no more, SugarCRM the Open Source project would carry on, with the same or different individuals leading the project. The two are quite separate entities in law. So unlike many products from smaller companies, using SugarCRM should not make you worry about the stability of the vendor.

The history of the SugarCRM product is that SugarCRM 1.0 established the basic architecture of the product. With SugarCRM 2.0, the strong visual design was introduced. With SugarCRM 2.5, capabilities were introduced that enabled users to customize the CRM to a significant extent—adding new fields, removing unnecessary fields, rearranging screen layouts, changing options on drop-down lists, and so on. These customization capabilities are particularly relevant to a CRM, as CRM systems tend to need more tuning to the business adopting them than many other business applications.

In SugarCRM 3.0, the application added **document management**, **project tracking**, **marketing campaigns**, **user roles**, and several other new features. In 3.5 the Sugar architecture was strengthened significantly, enabling the addition of the **Module Loader** and **Upgrade Wizard**, **change logs**, and **collapsible sub-panels**. Numerous navigation enhancements as well as HTML email were also added at this time. SugarCRM 4.0 marked the beginning of an increasing gap between the Open Source and Pro versions of SugarCRM, and saw the introduction of such features as limited inbound email processing, limited access control capabilities, and workflow.

In the figure below, you see the SugarCRM Home screen. It is the first thing you will see (after the login screen) once you start using the system:

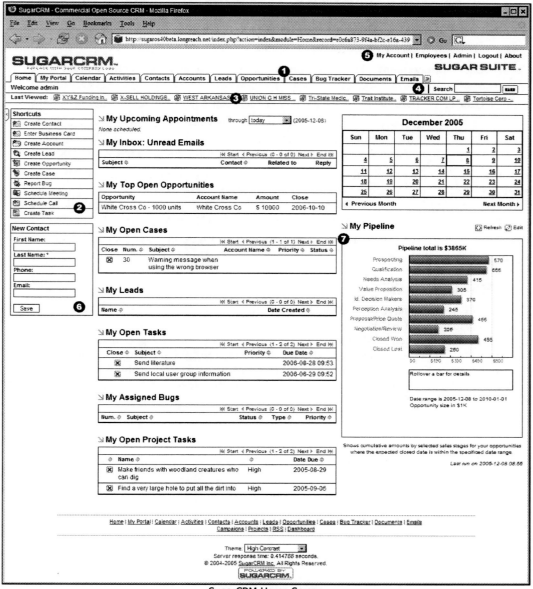

SugarCRM Home Screen

Various key elements of the screen layout overleaf have numbered highlights, as follows:

1. **Navigation Tabs**: Click to choose desired module

2. **Navigation Shortcuts Box**: Specific shortcuts useful within each module

3. **Last Viewed**: A remarkably handy trail of recent records you have viewed

4. **Search Box**: Search for a text string within all data held by SugarCRM

5. **User Management Links**: The Admin link is only available to users marked as administrators

6. **Quick New Item Box**: Quick data entry box to create a new item for the current module

7. **Main Screen Body**: On the Home tab, this includes My Upcoming Appointments, My Open Tasks, My Open Cases, My Assigned Bugs, and a monthly Calendar. My Top Open Opportunities, My Leads, and a Pipeline graph fill out the main screen body

In this image, the whole SugarCRM browser window is shown, including the Internet Explorer frame, and the SugarCRM copyright information at the bottom of the window. For all the other screen captures in this book, only the necessary portions of each SugarCRM screen will be shown. You should understand that each screen appears in a browser window like the one shown overleaf.

Scan across the navigation tabs, and the User Management Links, to get an idea of all the capabilities packaged together in this system.

The Beauty of CRM Navigation

SugarCRM is representative of the best CRM systems available in the market for the manner in which the systems are used, or navigated. There are tabs across the top for accessing the different types of information, such as Accounts, Contacts, Documents, Cases, Opportunities, and so on. More important, however, is how related items of information are linked together, and how the user follows those links. The figure opposite shows an Accounts screen within SugarCRM. This is fairly representative of similar screens in other leading commercial web-based CRM systems, such as Salesforce.com, NetSuite, and SalesLogix:

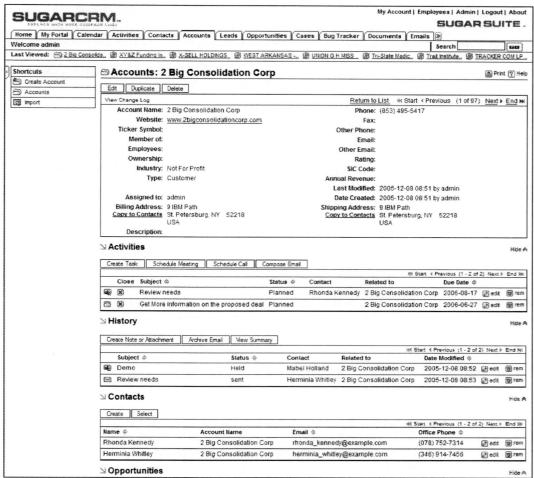

SugarCRM Account Detail Screen

We see that the top block of information (typically called a panel) displays the core information about the account—address, contact information, website, company email address, number of employees, ownership, industry classification, and so on.

The following blocks of information, or sub-panels, show information that is related to this account, such as ongoing account activities, a history of past account activities, contacts, leads, and opportunities within this account, plus ongoing cases (service issues) and projects within the account. Also shown are documents related to the account and any software bugs reported by the account (should that be relevant to your business).

The power of the system is the manner and speed with which it can be navigated. Once an account has been looked up and displayed, the user can click on a contact in that account to see the information associated with it. That contact record will include a list of related activities to be performed, and the user can click on those to update them. A related meeting may involve other contacts, and their information is listed, and the user can click on them to check current activities related to those contacts. Are there any ongoing cases? When was the last time we met with them? What products have they been buying from us?

Each of these questions is answered with a mouse click. And as more and more of the background information of an account, or contact, or opportunity is revealed, the user may have more and more little questions that come to mind—and each of them can be answered with a mouse click too. Because information can be obtained so quickly and easily, and because that information is related and linked in a manner so similar to the way the user's mind relates those items of information, employees now perform their tasks with a much higher level of knowledge about their customers.

One particularly handy feature of the SugarCRM user interface is Last Viewed, which is the list of items the user has recently accessed—making it quick and easy to return to an item after following links to information it relates to.

Marshall McLuhan was quite right—the medium is the message. In this case, the medium of web-based business applications, with many linkages between related items of information, makes that information so easy to obtain that it is as if somehow the overall quality of that information has been improved.

What are my CRM Options?

Depending on whom you talk to, CRM all started somewhere between the mid 1980's and the early 1990's with efforts from companies such as Oracle, PeopleSoft, Siebel Systems, and SAP. But true CRM involving not just the accumulation of static customer databases but a genuine enhancement to business processes began only recently, around the turn of the millennium. This evolution of CRM would not have been possible without the increasing influence of the Internet and the development of web services for connecting multiple business systems together despite their being in different locations and implemented in different technologies.

Originally, CRM systems from the big four companies named above were uniformly expensive, heavily customized, and unwieldy for any but the largest firms. In 2001 Siebel Systems had sales worth 2.1 Billion USD based on their model in which each customer spent millions of dollars. But their market share, and indeed gross sales, slipped in later years as the *built-for-the-web* generation of mid-size CRM systems came to market from firms such as Salesforce.com, NetSuite, Upshot, and SalesNet. Now Upshot has been purchased by Siebel Systems, and they seem to be somewhat on the upswing again.

With the introduction of SugarCRM in 2004, history will show that there has been yet another revolution in CRM, as even smaller firms gained cost-effective access to the latest in CRM technologies. For small-to-mid-size firms, NetSuite and some of the other mid-size generation are also becoming a viable option financially.

One trend easily visible above is that since about 2000, the market has been rapidly moving to web-based CRM tools as indeed it has in many other business application areas. The advantages are many—ubiquitous access, making the best use of expensive user licenses, and easier interfacing with other business systems via web services.

Some of the more highly-regarded CRM solutions available for smaller business today include:

- **NetSuite** (`http://www.netsuite.com/`): This firm offers both, NetSuite Small Business, a combination of accounting software and CRM, and NetCRM, its successful stand-alone CRM product.

- **Salesforce.com** (`http://www.salesforce.com/`): This firm is one of the key champions of the *software-as-a-service* model. While a popular solution, the Salesforce.com CRM is often perceived as one of the more expensive options. Salesforce.com has led the field in innovations such as end-user customization, and **Application Programming Interfaces** (**APIs**) for business process integration.

- **Microsoft CRM** (`http://www.microsoft.com/smallbusiness/products/mbs/crm/detail.mspx`): In spite of it not being one of the cheapest, or most highly regarded solutions, Microsoft CRM is still one to watch out for. It's Microsoft—known for never giving up on becoming number one in a market. If you use Microsoft Exchange and Small Business Server, it is a real option, but if you don't, it may not make sense for your business.

- **SalesLogix** (`http://www.saleslogix.com/`): Sage Software (formerly Best Software) produces this leading CRM for smaller businesses, as well as ACT!, the leading contact management software.

Deployment Options

In today's CRM market, there is not only a choice of vendors, but also a choice of deployment options. The options are:

- **On-Demand Model**: The On-Demand model (a phrase popularized by IBM advertising), formerly known as the **Application Service Provider** (**ASP**) model is the simplest (and often, the most expensive) way to implement and adopt a CRM. The CRM vendor simply hosts the CRM application, and provides the customer with a URL (Universal Resource Locator or a web address) at which to point their browser. No fuss over software installation, no messy application patching and maintenance, but also, no data on your premises—the vendor keeps it all on its system, a fact that makes many customers uneasy. Recent surveys show a full 50% of businesses are not prepared to adopt this model.

- **Application Pack**: The Application Pack option is the one the industry has practiced for years. The vendor licenses you its application software—often on an annual basis. You install the software on your own server, and take responsibility for your own data. You also take responsibility for maintaining the software as it evolves, for maintaining and backing up the server itself, and for the support of the network infrastructure to which it is attached. These are things you are not going to do without access to some fairly knowledgeable computer networking people—either on your staff, or whose services are retained on a regular basis.

- **Hosted Application Pack**: An intermediate version of these two models, which many businesses find attractive, involves licensing the software, but then hiring a hosting firm to provide and maintain the server on which it runs. Of course, the concerns about offsite corporate data remain.

- **Server Appliance**: The Server Appliance option involves purchasing a server pre-loaded with licensed software. This reduces concerns about installation problems, and the capacity and performance of the server you might use yourself, but leaves the bother of maintaining and updating the server and its software image, as well as backing up your data.

You should be aware that not every vendor supports all deployment options. Some of the best known mid-size vendors only support the On-Demand model, including Salesforce.com, NetSuite, and SalesNet. While all their talk (especially from Salesforce.com) of the 'No Software' model can sound attractive, you will want to balance that against costs of 65 to 130 USD per user per month, and having someone else holding on to all your customer data.

That being said, network technicians are not cheap either, and backing up your data regularly is not something every small business is set up to do well. Different models will appeal to different organizations—no doubt that is why this range of choices exists!

SugarCRM, for its part, offers Sugar Pro in all three deployment options: 239 USD per user per year to license the software as an application pack, US 39 USD per user per month as an On-Demand service, and a variety of server appliances (*Sugar Cubes*) at different prices. Sugar Enterprise is also available, at a price of 449 USD per user per year to license the software as an application pack, US 75 USD per user per month as an On-Demand service, and on server appliances of various capacities.

CRM Customization

If you are skimming this book thinking that CRM customization is an advanced topic and not applicable to you, stop right now and listen to some advice for a moment. Customization is a fact of life, and indeed a generally positive one, for most business applications. The negative aspect of it is that is can sometimes be long and involved, and frequently can be quite expensive. The positive side is that it takes an off-the-shelf shrink-wrapped software application, and adapts it to the way your business actually works.

CRM systems are known to need customization more frequently than other business applications. After all, the average Sales, Purchase, and General Ledger accounting system works pretty much the same way for any business—just set up your structure of initial account codes, and away you go. CRM systems are different!

CRM customizations fall into several classes:

- **Minor cosmetics:** Changing color schemes, adding company logo.

- **Minor user interface changes:** Suppressing certain features from being seen by certain or perhaps all users, rearranging screen layouts, adding and deleting fields from screens, changing field names, and editing the set of options presented on drop-down boxes.

- **Major application changes:** Adding whole new modules to the application, or making major changes to the business logic and function of existing modules.

- **Application integration:** Linking the CRM application with other business applications and processes, to more thoroughly automate and integrate your business operations.

Most advanced products make it easy to change minor cosmetics of the system. Historically, user interface changes were fairly difficult and expensive to perform, but all that has changed. With the release of the Customforce tool by Salesforce.com for customizing the user interface of its CRM, the bar was raised to a significant degree in this key area. Salesforce.com deserves recognition as an innovator in this field of technology, and it has caused nothing short of a revolution in CRM. Today, most important CRM vendors (including SugarCRM) offer this extremely important and useful capability.

Major application changes will always require a software consulting and development firm to perform them, unless you happen to have those resources in house. These changes involve tailoring a CRM to manage aspects of a business that are not uniform across the gamut of small businesses.

More recently, Salesforce.com has been at it again, and has introduced the Sforce API, which offers a well-documented and open programming interface to link other business applications to the Salesforce.com programs and data hosted by Salesforce.com for your business. This is creating a similar disruption in the CRM industry, and several firms are responding in kind. SugarCRM, for one, has its own (more limited) SOAP-based web service interface (using the Nusoap PHP library), which supports such handy capabilities as filing leads captured by forms on your public website into your SugarCRM lead database.

What Will a CRM Do for my Business?

A CRM system is to some extent a groupware application for managing your business. Groupware is a term used to describe computer software designed to help a group of people work together cooperatively. As such, a CRM helps everyone in the business (especially all those in direct contact with customers) to know the historical and planned activities of the business that involve a specific customer. This is clearly very useful to avoid miscommunications with the client resulting from lack of communication within the business. Everyone in the business can record all of their interactions with a client, helping all their co-workers understand the current state of any issues, sales opportunities, and so on.

Even more importantly, a CRM records all new business leads, and keeps track of promising qualified leads as specific opportunities. These opportunities are recorded with an expected date on which the business will be closed, the current stage of the sales cycle for this opportunity, and the percentage likelihood of closing the business currently assigned to this opportunity.

This information, aggregated across the business, provides a clear view of the organization's sales pipeline. Visual charts of this information are typically *live-linked*, making it easy to drill down to view the individual data items that were aggregated to build the chart. Classification of opportunities by sales person, by lead source, or by expected close date is a simple activity, easily performed and fantastically informative.

A properly implemented CRM used by all customer-facing staff will help you track the sales performance of your business more closely with less work. It will also help you see the future more clearly, and plan more effectively.

Just as the customer is the focus that ties all business activities together, your CRM can be the business tool that ties together all your business information, particularly with custom integration into other business systems such as your public website, and the creation of new customer self-service websites for building orders, creating and reviewing service cases, and managing their own information profile.

Another key area in which a CRM can help greatly is in customer communication. After all, a CRM knows who all your customers are, is connected to the Internet, holds all your key marketing documents in it, and can send (and often receive) email. There are very few tools that are as useful as a CRM when it comes to sending out customer newsletters on a monthly or quarterly basis, selecting only those customers who have purchased specific products, or keeping track of any customers who have indicated they do not want to receive marketing emails.

These powerful capabilities add up to make big changes at most businesses where they are adopted:

- **Sales are increased**: Using the new marketing communications capabilities to increase sales
- **Costs are reduced**:
  - Typing in information only once
  - Automatically sharing information with everyone instantly
  - Everyone in the business knowing right away where to find information without wasting time looking for it
- **Customers are happier**: Dealing with employees who now seem to know more about them and what's going on in their account is a big plus
- **Business is managed better**:
  - Sales pipelines are better understood
  - The most productive lead sources and sales staff are clearly identified
  - Any business downturn is visible well before it represents a commercial risk to the business

How Will This Book Help Me Get the CRM That Fits my Business?

This book is structured and written the way it is, specifically to accompany you on the journey of discovering what Customer Relationship Management is and what it can do for your business. Issues such as identifying the specific CRM needs of your business, implementing and adopting a CRM, and customizing the CRM to optimize its use within your business are all dealt with in detail.

As much as possible, the chapters of this book have been sequenced to mirror your own time sequence through the installation and adoption of SugarCRM. Some of the extended details of installing SugarCRM, and importing your data into it, were located in the appendices, to keep them from slowing down the plotline as you progress through the book.

This book is titled *Implementing SugarCRM: Introduce the leading Open Source CRM application into your small/mid-size business with this systematic, practical guide*, and SugarCRM is the practical focus of all our CRM examples in the book. But despite that, generic CRM principles and practices are detailed and explained at each stage to help you recognize when and if SugarCRM is ever insufficient for your needs, or requires some customization work to fit your business better.

Throughout this book we will not only refer to a specific tool, SugarCRM, but also to a specific (and mythical) company whose progress through the installation, adoption, and customization of a CRM we shall explore here. Our fictional case study will involve RayDoc Carpets, Doors, and Windows, and their wily fox of a leader Doc Newhart. (In actual fact, there are several real world Docs with whom SugarCRM was implemented throughout the writing of this book, to ensure that their real-world problems, issues, experiences, and comments were mirrored accurately in this volume.)

As this book progresses through the natural sequence of stages involved in the introduction of a CRM, at each stage the relationships between CRM theory and the practical experiences of Doc Newhart will be described and explained. The solution of real everyday business problems, gaps between CRM theory and practical benefits, and unexpected drawbacks and bonuses in live CRM implementations will all be dealt with in detail.

Our Case Study: RayDoc Carpets, Doors, and Windows

RayDoc Carpets, Doors, and Windows is a fairly average small business. It has slightly rundown commercial premises, with office space in the front, and workshops and carpet cleaning bays in the back. It has annual sales of about 3 Million Canadian dollars each year, and its staff is comprised of Doc, his wife Maureen who does the book-keeping and manages Kay the receptionist, a junior partner Andrew, and a staff of about 22 employees.

The name RayDoc once celebrated the teaming of Ray and Doc to create this business, but Ray is long gone, and Doc now runs things by himself. Well, by himself is not quite true. Maureen actually runs the office, except when Doc is in one of his moods, and between them Maureen and Kay take care of nearly all the paperwork and administration in the company.

Some of the services provided by RayDoc include carpet and upholstery cleaning at customers offices or homes, the provision of rotating supplies of clean carpet runners and boot trays for businesses during the Canadian winter, deep cleaning of large Indian and Persian rugs in the bays behind the offices, the sale and installation of replacement doors and windows, and general contracting and building services. RayDoc owns several vans and mini-vans, which are used by staff to get themselves and their equipment to jobs and to bring large carpets back to the office.

While some of RayDoc's customers have had only one transaction with RayDoc, much of their business is with existing customers: businesses that have their carpets cleaned on a regular basis, property management firms that always get their doors and windows repaired or replaced by RayDoc, and home owners who have come to count on RayDoc for a broad range of services over the sixteen years it has been in business.

Our Hero: Doc

Doc likes to focus on finding new business opportunities, and schmoozing new and existing customers. He also spends much of his time finding new suppliers of interesting new products, and making sure that the bigger jobs they get are always done to the customer's satisfaction.

A street-smart individual, Doc is somewhat bored by the rather mundane nature of much of his business after all the years he has been doing it, and he consciously ducks a lot of the everyday administrative work, searching for more interesting business opportunities, or just customers to talk to. Doc comes from a fairly rough blue-collar background, and just as well, as a lot of the young men doing the carpet cleaning are pretty rough themselves.

Doc prides himself on his business sense and to some degree on his marketing abilities. His main advertising expense is running an advert on the local cable TV Guide channel. As a boy, Doc didn't much care for academics, as he was too impatient to get on with living his life. Skilled with his hands, he has mastered many trades. But at 45, he knows he is doing a lot of things the hard way at RayDoc, and wants to get the company working smarter. Not in the least because he has hopes of taking more and more of a back seat in the business before too long, and he needs to put more business systems and processes in place before that can happen.

Doc has been hearing about CRM systems from some of his friends and customers for a few years now. Recently he had a long chat in a local bar with an old friend who owns another small business, who was extolling the virtues of being able to get at all his business information from home, while out of town, and even from his fancy Treo cell phone, all because of the new CRM he had purchased. That was it. Doc wasn't going to have his old friend be able to say he knew more about running a business than Doc did. He needed to find out about this CRM stuff, and quickly!

What Does the Future Hold for RayDoc?

RayDoc has been holding its own for several years now, neither growing nor shrinking. Making reasonable, but not exciting incomes for Doc and Maureen, and showing just enough promise for Andrew to stick around, hoping for Doc's retirement. Part of a younger generation of well-educated tradesmen, Andrew has often tried to encourage Doc and Maureen to adopt newer business management tools, but it has been difficult, as Doc resisted change, and Andrew's responsibilities kept him out of the office, supervising on-site employees nearly all the time. But he will be a willing and supportive ally for Doc in his CRM initiative.

An automated system that documents all of RayDoc's customers and their history with RayDoc is just as essential for Andrew's succession plan as it is for Doc's early retirement.

Summary

In this chapter we introduced the topic of Customer Relationship Management, and touched upon a number of important points:

- CRM applications have been evolving rapidly since the late 1990's, and are now delivering on their promise of enhancing business profitability, improving customer satisfaction and levels of service, and streamlining business processes.

- CRM applications, once highly priced, are now affordable even for smaller businesses.

- Smaller businesses typically have an administrative staff that is overloaded with work, and yet there is constant pressure to cut administrative costs.

- Most small businesses employ business systems that are not accessible outside the office, acting as a force that limits business communication with outbound workers, and tends to keep business managers in the office.

- Web-based CRM systems can lower administrative workloads and costs, and are accessible from PCs, laptops, and handheld PDA/mobile phones—anywhere, anytime.

- Contact management systems such as Outlook, ACT! and Goldmine are not CRMs, and lack many fundamental features of leading CRMs.

- SugarCRM is a web-based CRM introduced in 2004, available as a free Open Source version, or as a commercial Pro- or Enterprise-level version.

- Like many top CRMs, SugarCRM is quick and easy to use, making access to customer information a natural and even pleasant experience.

- For the smaller business, there are many valid CRM choices: NetSuite, Salesforce.com, Microsoft CRM, and SalesLogix among them. We have chosen SugarCRM Open Source as our example CRM for this book as it is free, and contains most of the latest features that make CRM adoption so compelling for small and medium businesses.

- CRMs may be deployed as On-Demand web-based services, as application software to be installed on your own servers, or as server appliances delivered pre-loaded and ready to run. The choice is yours, and involves some tradeoffs between cost and convenience.

- To truly deliver on their promises, CRM systems typically must be customized to suit your business. There are several levels of complexity to this customization, and the most recent CRMs help you do quite a bit of it yourself, rather than paying for expensive computer services staff to do it for you.

- CRMs can help you track the sales performance of your business more closely with less work, see the future more clearly, and plan more effectively.

- This book will take you through the entire process of determining your CRM needs, implementing and installing a CRM, getting your data into the CRM, rolling it out to your business and training staff, and customizing the CRM to maximize your business benefits.

- Throughout this book, we will follow the experiences of Doc Newhart, and his fictional business, RayDoc. The tales of his experiences here are taken from the real-life experiences of multiple CRM installations within smaller businesses.

In the next chapter, we will use the knowledge you have gained about CRM systems to begin to analyze your own business, identify its CRM needs, and understand what to look for in a CRM and its customization and configuration capabilities.

2
One Size Does Not Fit All— CRM Your Way

In the first chapter you learned about the history of how CRM software developed, how its affordability and accessibility for smaller businesses has been improving in recent years, and how important it is that a CRM is easily customized to suit your business.

You were also introduced to *RayDoc Carpets, Doors, and Windows*, and met Doc its proprietor. In this chapter, we will begin the process of analyzing the CRM needs of your specific business, and use our continuing RayDoc case study as an example of how to match CRM capabilities to the needs of a business.

Throughout this chapter, and indeed throughout this book to the extent possible, we shall focus primarily on the business objectives and benefits sought from the application of a CRM, not simply on the mechanics of installing and using the SugarCRM system specifically.

To that end, there are several extensive sections of this book devoted to the business analysis process you will need to go through in order to determine how a CRM can best benefit your business. This will enable you to identify the customizations you may need to make to an off-the-shelf CRM product in order to make it your tailored CRM solution. As the book progresses, the business analysis sections deal with successively more ambitious and advanced business functions, helping you identify your needs in these areas—as well as guiding you through the process of having those customizations implemented, and then introducing the CRM system into your business.

This chapter contains the first such business analysis section. The goal of this section is to provide a broad overview of the ways in which businesses differ, helping you to position and identify your own business within the multi-dimensional space of all smaller businesses. Do the CRM needs of a three-person firm in a single office that sells to other businesses via the Internet differ from those of a fifty-person firm with ten regional offices that sells to consumers by making house calls? They certainly do, and it is issues like these that we will be dealing with shortly.

The punch line of the old joke about how many psychiatrists it takes to change a light bulb is that it only takes one, but first the light bulb has to want to change. Similarly, it is not that hard to change your business using a CRM, but first you have to understand the CRM needs of your business, and who to involve in identifying them so that you make the right changes, and hence, ensure that the new system gains good acceptance when it is introduced.

Once we have studied the varying CRM needs of different businesses, we will see how Doc Newhart needs to apply CRM to improve the way RayDoc operates. We will also use a CRM Requirements Worksheet to identify the specific CRM needs of your business.

Lastly, we will address the practical issues of how to get your CRM customized, what sorts of partners to look for to help you in that process, how to document your customization requirements, and how to manage a customization contract.

Identifying the CRM Needs of Your Business

Some of the high-level characteristics of a business that cause one to have very different CRM requirements from another include:

- **The Business Model:** One location or many? Franchises? Regional Sales Offices? Products or services? High or low unit sales value?
- **The Customers:** Where are they? Who are they—businesses or individuals?
- **The Scale:** How many employees—2? 25? 50? 100?
- **The International Needs:** Multiple language support? Date format? Currency format?

Compensating and adjusting appropriately for these varying requirements will make the difference between a CRM that suits your needs, and is quickly embraced and adopted, and a CRM that never feels like a good fit, and quickly falls into disuse and is abandoned.

To genuinely understand why a CRM needs some measure of customization to become a truly effective tool within an organization, we need only examine what it is that a CRM is meant to accomplish:

- Sales force automation including lead capture, and the promotion of leads to Opportunities
- Opportunity tracking with sales stages and percentage likelihood
- Sales pipeline tracking, with graphical charts that offer a drill-down from the bar or segment of the chart to the data that underlies it
- Lead source analysis of sales and opportunities
- Service case tracking, and other service/support capabilities such as tracking software bugs, and managing support contract renewals
- Corporate calendar management for arranging meetings
- Corporate directory for contacting fellow employees
- Interface consolidation, bringing into the CRM environment, additional everyday needs in order to make a company website that employees can 'live in'—including news feeds, views of financial metrics, integration of external web links and applications, and integrated web-based email
- Document management and revision control, for managing and retaining reference copies of important corporate documents.

To be an effective tool, a CRM must perform all of these functions within an intuitive and easy-to-use graphical interface, be available at all times, and be accessible using a wide variety of devices.

Depending on the nature of your business, some other more advanced and useful capabilities to include within your CRM are:

- Project tracking and management
- Management of e-marketing campaigns
- Advanced report generation
- Definition of sales teams and territories
- Integrated views of financial metrics and performance
- Product catalog management, and tracking sales inventory, corporate assets, and client products covered by support contracts
- Creation of client quotations and/or invoices

Which Business Activities will be a Part of Your CRM?

As you approach the process of implementing a CRM within your business, one of the more important decisions you must make is the application scope of your CRM. You must make a high-level choice as to your philosophy about your CRM—are you using it uniquely to manage the sales process, or do you see it having a major role in your overall approach to business management?

You need to examine the lists of capabilities above, and decide which of these you will implement in the CRM for your business—at least for the initial implementation phase.

To help you sort through these topics, and help you make better-informed choices, they are explained here in greater detail with an emphasis on the kinds of choices, customizations, and variations commonly seen in smaller businesses.

Deciding which of the basic application areas to include in your CRM implementation is the first stage of identifying the set of customizations your CRM installation will require. Later on, in Chapter 6, we will discuss in detail how to actually perform some customizations to your SugarCRM installation, but for now our task is merely to identify the areas of the application that are most likely to require customization, based on the nature and needs of your business.

Beyond the basic CRM capabilities are the more advanced functions such as **project management**, **advanced report generation**, **e-marketing**, **managing product catalogs**, **asset registers**, and **quotes and invoice generation**. While we will examine this list of more advanced topics in later chapters (particularly Chapters 5 and 6), let us for now go over the initial list of standard capabilities.

Accounts and Contacts

Fundamentally, a CRM captures information about your accounts and the contacts you have at those accounts. By 'accounts', we mean the complete set of other firms you do business with— partners, suppliers, and customers. The CRM also keeps track of new business leads and once qualified, converts these leads into opportunities and relates these new opportunities to the accounts, contacts, and your own employees in charge of selling to those accounts.

This much is true of CRM use at most businesses, but even this basic capability needs modification at many firms. Some firms focus much more on contacts as they sell to individuals, while others focus almost uniquely on accounts as they sell only to businesses. Many firms go to the extreme of having a CRM that only shows either accounts or contacts in the navigation system.

To resolve these differences, it would clearly be useful for the CRM to have the ability to remove unwanted functions or data types from the user interface. The good news is that nowadays, most quality CRMs including SugarCRM provide this capability.

Tracking Leads and Opportunities

The next major differentiator between firms and their associated CRM implementations lies in the area of **leads** and **opportunities**. If you are a firm that generates, data mines, or purchases a lot of leads, then you are likely to want to distinguish between a lead and an opportunity—with an opportunity representing a lead that has been contacted and qualified as having some genuine sales potential.

If on the other hand you are a firm that does not have a lot of new leads, and what new leads you get tend to be genuine opportunities, then you will prefer to dispense altogether with the concept of a lead, and deal simply with opportunities.

Again, it would be useful to be able to customize the CRM user interface so as to remove any menus or navigation associated with leads for firms that don't need them. And again most good CRM solutions, including SugarCRM, provide this capability.

Note that one key consideration for leads is that the quality of data is typically not up to the level you will want for opportunities and contacts. Only when the accuracy of lead data has been established and verified should it be considered for inclusion in opportunity and contact data.

Different firms have many different ways of generating leads—from an Internet site, provided by a partner or a supplier, from advertising, by word of mouth referral, and so on. It is important to track what your most successful lead sources are, to gain the knowledge of where to focus your marketing efforts. So creating a list within the CRM software of the lead sources your firm uses is important. And then each new lead can be classified as to its source by simply choosing an option from a drop-down box on a screen form.

Populating drop-down boxes with options that are uniquely relevant to your business is a very common form of CRM customization, and one that is becoming widely supported as a 'do-it-yourself' feature by all mainstream CRM systems including SugarCRM.

Another option that commonly needs customizing is the *sales stage* of an opportunity. While there are relatively standard industry-accepted terms for the different stages of the sales process, they vary quite a bit by the nature of the business involved—its size, its customers, and the length of the typical sales cycle. The list of stages of the sales cycle you intend to track is a customization you will most likely want to make to your CRM.

Related to the sales stage is the percentage likelihood of a sale, ranging from 0% to 100%. Some organizations pay little attention to the percentage likelihood, and track opportunities based on sales stage. Other organizations do just the opposite and rank opportunities by percentage likelihood, paying little attention to the sales stage. And some track both. You need to decide which is important to you, and make sure that the list of opportunities and the charts of sales in the pipeline present that information, and give you the ability to filter and focus on opportunities based on that information.

Sales-Force Automation

One very important productivity tool that a CRM can provide is often referred to as **sales-force automation**. While this can include functions such as the Dashboard (dealt with in the next section on the sales pipeline), fundamentally, sales-force automation is an automated flow of sales leads into the CRM, their conversion into opportunities, and their tracking to a successful or unsuccessful conclusion. This includes features such as:

- Lead capture from a public website, or from partners
- Promotion of a lead to an opportunity when it has been qualified
- Automatic email notifications to sales people when a new lead or opportunity is assigned to them
- The tracking of current and historical account activities against both contact and account profiles
- The association of key documents to accounts and contacts, such as proposals, contracts and agreements, and marketing collateral

A key improvement in productivity comes from automated lead capture into your CRM from a lead form on your public website, or from leads sent to you from a supplier or other partner. If you have a current supply of sales leads, you should identify how to automate their entry into your CRM. Many CRMs, such as SugarCRM, have a **SOAP-based (Simple Object Access Protocol)** web service to which external systems can be linked in order to pass on lead data. If you do not have a current supply of sales leads, perhaps you should create a lead form on your public website, and devise a strategy for diverting traffic to your website.

Once a lead has been qualified as a genuine sales opportunity, it needs to be re-classified as an opportunity within the CRM system. Most CRMs have the ability to convert a lead into an opportunity. You need to decide if this is how you will use your CRM to manage the transition from leads to opportunities.

Your CRM server will be connected to the Internet, and will have an email system available to it. Because of this, it has the capability to automatically email salespeople when they are assigned a new lead or opportunity. Typically your CRM will let you enable or disable this automated notification system, and you will need to decide if your CRM will use it or not.

Tracking the Sales Pipeline

Each opportunity in a CRM system has an expected sales value, and an expected closing date. Adding up this information across all the opportunities in the system produces a prediction of the future sales of the business, known as the sales pipeline.

The sales pipeline is a key tool for anyone managing a smaller business. Usually a smaller business has more limited financial resources to buffer it from a downturn in business, making it that much more important to be able to detect a negative sales trend at the earliest possible moment.

Like most software designed to summarize financial activity for management personnel (known as **Executive Information Systems—EIS** or **Decision Support software**, or **Business Intelligence software—BI software**), most CRMs present the sales pipeline in a graphical chart form, frequently with the ability to highlight some portion of the chart and 'drill down' to the source data that underlies that portion of the chart.

A series of charts that support sales and business management functions is often called a **Dashboard** or a **Digital Dashboard** and can be a powerful tool for ensuring that sales are on track in the coming months and diagnosing and uncovering shortcomings in the sales process, product features, pricing, and personnel.

A fundamental choice that has to be made when presenting the sales pipeline is whether or not to discount the opportunities in the pipeline by the percentage likelihood of their closing. Should a 100,000 USD opportunity which is 25% likely to close be counted as 25,000 USD or as 100,000 USD? While the truth is that it will result in either no income, or 100,000 USD of income, the fact that the opportunity is considered only 25% likely to result in a sale may mean that you prefer to count this opportunity as only 25,000 USD in the pipeline. Both practices are very common, and only you can decide which behavior is correct for your business.

Tracking Service Cases and Support Contracts

Every CRM offers at least basic customer service and support features. Some of the capabilities typically offered are:

- **Case Management:** A service incident, trouble ticket, or case (different systems and industries use different terminology) can be created with a date stamp, contact information for the customer reporting the issue, and a description of the nature of the problem. If a potentially defective product is involved, the type or model of the product and the serial number of the unit may be tracked.

- **Software Bug Tracking**: If a service case involves a defect or issue in some customer software system then a Bug Report is created, and it will note the software involved, its revision, and the nature of the issue (bug or desired enhancement). It will also track the status of the issue, who is assigned its resolution, and will record the eventual disposition of the issue. This is, of course, applicable only for businesses involved in creating, or supporting computer programs.

- **Service Contract Management:** Service Contracts are typically tracked using the model of a master agreement for each account with any number of sub-contracts per master agreement. Each sub-contract may be related to any number of assets being supported. And each sub-contract and asset will have a service incident history associated with it to track the case history by item of equipment and by sub-contract. A mechanism usually exists to remind account managers when service contracts are nearing their renewal dates, so that a proposal for the renewal may be prepared and sent to the customer.

Not every business needs these service and support features. You will need to identify what your business requires in the service and support area, and decide if the standard features are a good fit for you, if some need to be hidden as they are not required, or if some extended capabilities need to be custom-built for you.

Corporate Calendar Management

A CRM is almost certainly the best place for you to enter all your appointments, meetings, scheduled calls, and planned tasks—in short, all the business activities that have a time and date associated with them. Not only does entering this information in the CRM help you to associate the activities with the related accounts and contacts, thereby helping to generate accurate account history, but it also provides a groupware environment for scheduling meetings that is aware of the all the scheduled activities for everyone in the company.

Prior to adopting a CRM, most small and medium businesses use Microsoft Outlook, Outlook Express, or Microsoft Exchange to fulfill their corporate calendaring needs. Other popular solutions include Lotus Notes and many other groupware products. While Outlook is a reasonable solution for calendaring for an individual, and Exchange helps to link together calendars across a business, this solution can never help you to position these activities within the larger CRM context, and automatically generate and track account history.

If all this talk of Outlook and Exchange, Lotus Notes, Outlook Express, and so on, is foreign to you—don't worry. They are simply other ways of addressing needs that your CRM will satisfy nicely and, in fact, more effectively from the perspective of managing relationships with your customers.

My recommendation to CRM users is to stop using Outlook for calendaring—just say no! And if your CRM has an effective solution for both incoming and outgoing email (as I write this SugarCRM has just introduced limited incoming email support), then I would recommend that you stop using Outlook for email as well, and that Exchange should also be shown the door. You will need to examine your organization's requirements and decide if you are in a position to act on these recommendations.

The counter argument to using a CRM for calendaring and email is that for many CRMs the synchronization options for linking the data in PDAs like Treo, BlackBerry, and PocketPC to your CRM data can be severely limited, full of software bugs, or non-existent. If mobile access to calendaring and email is important for your firm, check out your synchronization options before making the move to CRM-based email and calendaring. SugarCRM has the Sync4j option for mobile wireless synchronization, as you will see later on in Chapter 6.

Corporate Directory

If your business has only a handful of employees, then a corporate directory is likely unnecessary, and you may want to remove it from the user interface of your CRM system.

But as a company grows, and reaches 25, 50, even a hundred employees, it gets harder and harder to remember everyone's extension number, their email address, their position, even their face. Even a smaller business will make good use of a corporate directory if it is spread out across multiple regional offices.

A corporate directory is a very handy list of everyone's contact information, and often includes a thumbnail image of them for those situations where you just can't put a name to the face, or a face to the name.

Interface Consolidation

Interface consolidation refers to a series of tools and techniques used within a CRM to allow employees to spend much of their day logged in to the CRM, with few business activities not integrated in some way within the CRM.

Some of the activities and features commonly integrated into a CRM just to reduce the need to jump out of the browser interface to perform miscellaneous business tasks include:

- News feeds (RSS, Atom)
- Integrated web-based email
- Integration of external web links and applications
- Views of financial metrics

Clearly, by adding in news, email, commonly used external websites, and links to financial systems, the CRM becomes an environment that your employees can live in, one that they can log into in the morning, and leave up and running all day.

You should give some thought to what news headlines sources to include, and what external websites to link in, within your CRM implementation.

Document Management

A document that is only stored on the hard drive of the PC of one of your employees is not a company resource. A document that has a copy stored on every hard drive in the company is not standardized or revision-controlled. In between these two situations is the right answer—the document repository within your CRM system.

Typically, your CRM will let every employee store documents on the system, and give them a title, a description, a file type, a status, and a revision. Some keywords are also normally entered as they make it easier to find the document. Unlike your PC, a document repository usually allows the user to update a document with a later revision, while keeping each previous revision intact in case it is ever required. A document's status indicates if it is a draft document, an old archived document, or an approved current version.

Web-based document management provides key benefits for any business allowing all important business documents—medical claim forms, HR policies and guidelines, employee handbook, designs, specifications, sales collateral, contracts, and so on—to be accessed and downloaded remotely.

Document management is a vital capability for any business, and you need to decide which documents your business needs to store in your CRM, and how to organize them.

Business Models and Their Specific Requirements

In the previous section, we looked at the different components of the basic CRM applications, and identified a number of reasons why those applications might need to be customized for your business. In this section, we look at your business itself, and examine it for reasons why your CRM might need to be tuned to suit it perfectly.

Businesses vary widely in their fundamental nature. Who do they sell to, and how? What do they sell—a product or a service—and how expensive is it? Where is the business itself located, and does it have multiple locations? Let's look at some of these distinguishing characteristics of a business, and see how they affect the CRM needs of a business.

B2B or B2C?

One of the first differentiators in CRM needs is who your customers are. Are you a **B2B (Business to Business)** or **B2C (Business to Consumer)** business model? Meaning, do you sell to individuals or to businesses?

In a firm with a B2B business model, the typical CRM data model of accounts and contacts is usually a good fit. In extremes, some firms will prefer to remove menu access to contacts and focus on the accounts—leaving contacts only as names associated with accounts.

But in a B2C business model many firms prefer to remove the navigation access to accounts leaving a focus on the contacts—the individuals with whom the firm does business.

Products or Services?

What is the nature of your business? Do you make or re-sell products, anything ranging from ceramics to washing machines? Do you sell services, such as house painting, landscaping, or window cleaning? Or do you do both on a regular basis like the car mechanic who charges for his labor by the hour, but also sells the replacement parts he uses when making repairs?

If you only sell products, what about the product support or warranty services? Does the product regularly wear out or need service on a predictable time line giving you an automatic new sales opportunity, for instance, a car that needs regular oil changes?

If you have an element of product warranty or support in your business, you will want to be able to record which customer has what duration of support on what products. If your product needs regular service—such as a car dealership—you may want to record a good time to contact each of your customers for service.

In a CRM, products and services are dealt with rather differently. Products are usually listed in a catalog and are very standardized. When they are sold, they generate a one-time income event.

If your products have significant value, and have some support service sold with them (such as computer equipment—a PC or a printer) your CRM will need to capture the make and model (ideally, the serial number as well) of the product and link it to the customer record to track entitlement to contracted support services. Now your CRM will need to understand the concept of an asset in an asset register, and that of a service contract.

If your business delivers services to its customers, and those services are delivered over a significant period of time, your CRM will need to be able to model a sale that is not a one-time income event, but rather a stream of income (and potentially costs) over time. Kelly Girl, for example, delivers a service—the services of temporary office staff. If a Kelly Girl temporary worker were placed on an assignment for three months from June to August, then the sale should be modeled as an income stream of X USD in June, Y USD in July, and Z USD in August. There will also be a corresponding cost stream over the three months of the actual salary paid by Kelly Girl to the worker involved.

These sorts of sales are often modeled as a project that delivers over time, and if your business sells these kinds of services, your CRM will need to be able to track these 'income stream' opportunities, as well as the regular 'income event' opportunities.

Average Transaction Value, Sales Cycle, and the Recurring Business Model

If your business has a reasonably high average transaction value—say over 1000 USD—then it generally makes financial sense to track your customers, and your opportunities to sell to them— especially if you have a sales cycle of a couple of weeks or more in which to track the opportunity. This is the classic CRM application—tracking accounts and contacts and the sales opportunities associated with them and then rolling it all up into a sales pipeline that gives you a good feel for how sales will go over the next couple of months.

But what if your usual sales cycle is less than an hour? And your average transaction value is more like 20 USD than 1000 USD?

If you have a business like a CD music store, a video rental store, or a specialty frozen meats store, then you have lots of smaller transactions, each of them bordering on impulse purchases by the customer. In this case, your real reason for implementing a CRM is to enhance your recurring business model. If you typically get these same customers coming back again and again, you will get great benefit from tracking those customers in your CRM for marketing purposes. **Opt-in** email marketing campaigns, membership in a discount club as a loyalty mechanism—these are going to be some of your key activities. And you will need a CRM that can provide the kind of e-marketing and loyalty marketing capabilities that will propel your business to success.

In this case, you will still keep track of accounts and contacts, but leads and opportunities have much less significance. And your sales pipeline is also bordering on irrelevant. If yours is this type of business, recognize this fact, and understand the type of changes your CRM will need in order to help you and your staff focus on what is important for *your* business—not what would be important in another sort of business.

Location, Location, Location

Where do you sell? Do you sell from your shop? From your office? At your clients' premises? Over the Internet?

Where are your staff? Are they in the office? Out servicing and selling to customers? Do they work from a single central office or are they spread across multiple regional offices?

These are some of the most important variables in your CRM equation. After all, if we are trying to manage customer relationships, we need to know where those relationships are happening! And that means knowing where your customers are, and where your staff are.

If your business only generates sales within a single location—your store or office—then clearly your communications challenges are not as great as a business with a dozen outbound international sales representatives working out of their homes.

One of the key questions you need to answer is: *when you or anyone in your business with a customer-facing role is in contact with customers, are they sitting at their computer and online?* If not, you may need special CRM facilities so that they can access customer history when they need it, and so that they can enter updated information as it develops.

Let's study two of the more common scenarios:

- **Multiple regional offices:** If these are white-collar offices with primarily inbound staff, there is not necessarily any issue. The CRM server can be located anywhere in the world and staff in all the offices can access it via user name/password access— securely and with good performance—as long as they have a fast and reliable connection to the Internet. Smaller businesses with multiple regional offices are prime candidates for CRM installations, as they are likely to benefit greatly from the improved communications plus accurate and up-to-date account information provided by the CRM.

- **Outbound sales people:** No matter how many offices you have, these are the most difficult people to service well. Some of the ways in which they can use the CRM other than via the web browser on their home or office PC include:

  - Accessing their laptop on a hotel room's high speed Internet connection overnight to update the system with the day's activities and look up information in preparation for tomorrow's calls.
  - Connecting their laptop to the Internet at any time using high speed wireless data services like **EDGE (Enhanced Data rates for GSM Evolution)**, available from most wireless carriers.
  - Using a PDA browser for handheld access to a limited subset of the CRM capabilities.
  - Using a PDA that has the appointment and contact data within its native applications wirelessly synchronized with CRM data.
  - Using their notebook with a stand-alone 'offline' installation of the CRM. When they return to the office, their private CRM installation can be synchronized to the main installation, to update any new data from the trip.

If you recognize that your business has the need to service outbound sales people using one or more of the above techniques, you should take care to ensure that the CRM solution you plan to adopt can meet your requirements.

Size Does Matter: Two or Two Hundred?

The size of your business affects how you manage your CRM, the features you need from your CRM, and even the importance of the CRM to your organization.

In a smaller business, employees have broader responsibilities—and these narrow as the organization grows. The need for continuity of business process, communication, and documentation becomes greater as the responsibilities get narrower.

A business with fifty employees also has so many more employee-to-employee information pathways within it, compared to a business with five employees. Because of this, a CRM has even more to offer the larger firm.

Also, in a larger firm where not everyone knows everyone else's business, staff turnover can create a real risk that sales leads and opportunities created through work paid for by the business may be lost when an employee leaves. With a CRM there is an element of the **ISO (International Organization for Standardization)** principle that the process should transcend the individual. The employee may leave but their data lives on in the CRM, and another salesperson hired in his or her place will have all the account history to work on.

The larger firm also has other issues not likely found in the smaller firm. With a certain scale of organization, information privacy becomes important. Sales leads will not be entered into the system if sales people are concerned that another sales team or person may steal their leads. In a smaller firm, there is a tendency to have everyone know everything. If a lead is stolen, everyone will know who it really belonged to. But after a point, an organization becomes more compartmentalized and impersonal, and protecting leads and opportunity data becomes a real and valid concern.

All of this gives rise to a complex requirement for an **Access Control model**, or a **Permissions Management Infrastructure (PMI)**, as it is sometimes called. In this sort of system, roles are defined and the permission to view certain types of data and to perform certain actions is assigned to these roles. Then employees are assigned one or more roles, and the permissions from multiple roles just add to one another to give each employee their effective aggregate set of permissions.

In a North American sales organization, for example, accounts might be split into geographical areas such as the West Coast, East Coast, Central USA, and Canada. Most sales people would only see leads and opportunities within their region, but sales managers would want to see leads, opportunities, and sales pipelines for broader geographies.

Lastly, the size of a business determines what a realistic budget figure is for the acquisition and deployment of a CRM. In a firm of five people, a CRM implementation budget might be 3,000-5,000 USD. In a firm of fifty people, that budget would more likely be 25,000-50,000 USD. Also, the smaller firm is less likely to have any internal technical support capability—and running a CRM server in the office may be beyond its abilities.

You should give some thought to your firm's needs for data security and permission management, as well as setting an implementation budget for the CRM, and deciding if you have the internal capacity to manage a CRM server.

International Needs

If your employees live and work in multiple countries, the odds are that your CRM may need to support more than one language. Language support has many aspects to it, including the language used for any and all of the following:

- Information you enter into your CRM
- The user interface of the CRM application
- The online help system
- The written documentation for the CRM.

You will need to decide on the language to be used for data entry into your CRM, choosing one that you feel most users can understand, even if it is not their first language.

Many languages need to be able to use a set of characters and accents that do not exist in the English language, so your CRM will need to be able to enter, display, and print these different sets of characters if you need international support.

You should find out from your CRM vendor what languages are supported for the user interface of the application, as well as in what languages the online help system and printable documentation are published.

SugarCRM has support for nearly 20 different languages (although many languages are supported only via a non-validated user-created translation) at the user interface, but print-image documentation exists only in English, and no online help system is currently available.

Another aspect of international support is the format in which dates are displayed. Your CRM should store dates in its own internal format, but display them to users in whatever format each user has selected as their preference. Common formats include 12.23.2006, 23.12.2006, and 2006.12.23. SugarCRM handles all these formats just fine.

In addition to dates, different countries have differing formats in which numbers and currency are presented. The decimal separator in North America is . and the thousands separator is , —but in much of Europe (Germany, for example), the decimal separator is , and the thousands separator is .. Thus what in North America is 12,234,678.90 USD in Germany is 12.345.678,90 €. If your CRM needs to be able to present numbers and currency values to users in the format they are accustomed to use in their country, then check that your CRM is capable of supporting this feature. (At the time of writing, SugarCRM did not support the display of multiple international number and currency formats.)

How Do I Make Shrink-Wrapped Software Suit My Business?

As we saw in Chapter 1, CRM customizations fall into several classes:

- Minor cosmetics
- Minor user interface changes
- Major application changes
- Application integration

Minor cosmetic changes will need the skills of someone who knows how to use computer graphics software, and likely some simple **HTML (Hyper Text Markup Language**—the code used to describe the appearance of web pages). If none of your employees possess these skills, you will need the services of a local web development and graphical design company. If you already have a company logo and company colors, they should not charge you more than 300-500 USD to customize the look of your CRM to use them.

If your company has a logo and official color scheme, you are likely to have the logo in a high resolution electronic form somewhere, and also a technical description of what your company colors are—in terms of the Pantone color scheme, or something similar. Get this information ready for the web development firm before they quote you for the job, as it should lower the amount quoted.

Minor User Interface (UI) changes can often be accomplished by using tools within the CRM to make those changes. In SugarCRM for example, the Sugar Suite administrative functions allow system administrators to add new fields to screens, delete unwanted fields, rename fields, or just move fields around. Drop-down option lists may be customized, menu options may be renamed or suppressed, and external websites may be linked in to new menu items.

You can either learn to use these customization tools, and see if you can make all the minor UI changes you want that way, or you can hire a firm that specializes in customizing CRMs to do this work, as well as some of your more major customization work. There is some value in getting all the customizations done by one supplier, and this particular type of customization should take no more than a few days to do, and cost no more than 1000-2,000 USD.

Major application changes and application integration work will always need to be developed by professional CRM development and customization firms. Expect to pay 300-500 USD per day of work involved in your project. Only proceed on this type of customization work when you have checked off these issues:

- The original developer of your CRM recommends the services of the customization firm.
- You can see that the firm is not a general web development firm, but specializes in CRM implementation and customization—you want a partner with more CRM experience and knowledge than you have, not less.
- You have examined and approved sample work of similar complexity and size done by the customization firm.

- You have written up a requirements document with rough drawings of what new screens should look like including details such as the tab order, values that each drop-down box should have, the names and data types (text, number, date, or time) for each field, fields that are editable, fields that are shown as columns in the list view, and fields that may be used to filter the list

- You have a written quote from the proposed customization firm detailing how they will implement this requirement, how many days of effort they believe it will take, and quoting a fixed price for the work. The firm should also explicitly describe their warranty or acceptance period for the software developed and detail an acceptable schedule of payments that allows you to view the work as it progresses and see and test the final solution (possibly operating on one of their servers) before final installment payments are made

You may wish to make your customizations in a step-wise fashion, to ensure each step is affordable, and yields measurable real-world benefits, as well as to test the supplier. Take care not to get into a front-loaded agreement that has you shelling out most of your budget for customization before you see changes that give you some level of comfort with the supplier.

Customer-Centric Business Management

Most of this book deals with the issue of helping you identify and implement a CRM that is suitable for your business. However, neither SugarCRM nor indeed any truly effective CRM deals only with that narrowly defined set of topics that originally constituted a CRM system.

From product catalogs, quotes, and invoices to service contract management, and from email marketing campaigns to project management and resource tracking, extending your CRM into a customer-centric business management system is gaining increasing recognition as an appropriate and effective technique for small and medium businesses. (Note that a lot of what follows becomes less relevant for organizations whose size exceeds 200 employees. Larger organizations tend to need integrated solutions based around **Enterprise Resource Planning (ERP)** tools, which can resemble aspects of a CRM, but are significantly more detailed and simply more appropriate to larger scale organizations.)

At its heart, a CRM system is about consistently excellent communication—both inside and outside the business. In later chapters we will look at CRM extensions and integration, which bear on customer communications. For now, let's look inside the business.

On a sheet of paper, map out the various departments within your organization, and overlay on it the typical paths that information takes between those departments as customer transactions are processed. Think about pre-sales requests for information, quotations, order processing, customer queries about shipments they are waiting for, shipping, and after-sales support and service.

For each transaction think about where new information originates in your organization, and examine which other parts of the business need that information to perform their jobs properly. Jot down notes on what items of information in your industry are key to delivering an outstanding customer experience to your customers. Note where they enter your business or are created, and where they move within the business.

Now examine the CRM system, and check the various relevant modules to see if they keep track of all the information that you need to deliver excellence to your customers, and if they model all the transactions that are most important for your customers. Where they do not, you are identifying gaps in your CRM implementation. These gaps should be addressed by extending your CRM to cover them, managing the information for those transactions, and ensuring that all appropriate employees always have access to the latest information about those transactions.

When you have plugged all of the gaps with properly designed and integrated extensions to your CRM, you will have created what in essence is a customer-centric business management solution. And it will have eliminated the traditional islands-of-information problem that so many businesses (large and small) suffer from.

In case you are unfamiliar with this problem (or are lucky enough not to have lived it!) it is a term used to describe the situation where a business has an operations management system (such as manufacturing control, or job tracking for RayDoc's carpet cleaning business for example), an invoicing system, a customer service database application, accounting software to manage the ledgers, plus contact management or CRM software—all working on separate databases. Customer contact information gets out of date and out of synchronization between the systems. Data gets re-keyed two or three times—a technique not known for improving its accuracy. And the business' competitive advantage, **Sales General and Administration (SG&A)** expenses, and overall quality of service all go to blazes.

By doing your quotes and invoicing from within your CRM application and data framework, by managing customer support and operations from within the CRM, and by including your product and services catalog, marketing campaigns, and sales records within your CRM, you eliminate the re-keying of data, allowing each application native access to the same customer database. The result is also more than the sum of its parts, as now the customer service personnel can look at recent and projected sales history, marketing campaigns can target those customers who have ever had a certain product line quoted to them, and many other inter-departmental synergies will also develop as you go along.

It is possible, however, to have too much of a good thing. Some of the potential drawbacks of too much customization of your CRM include:

- You may spend more than is wise for your size of organization.

- You may create so much customized software that you over-extend your vendor's ability to port those customizations to later revisions of the base system.

- You may create a lot of software that is simply not applicable to other organizations, and so wind up being the only company running that software—never a good thing. Wherever possible, your goal should be to identify generic extensions to the CRM that your vendor will want to incorporate as standard—reducing your future porting costs, and improving the quality of the software, as more people will be running it and finding any bugs that may be present.

Requirement Analysis

In this section we analyze RayDoc's business and CRM requirements and use this knowledge to create your own CRM requirements worksheet. This will clarify all the theoretical and detailed information discussed till now and give you practical understanding and confidence when you decide the add-on components and customizations you will require.

RayDoc CRM Requirements

We begin with the analysis of the RayDoc business and its CRM requirements. To capture RayDoc's CRM needs, we will use a CRM worksheet:

RayDoc	Choices	Notes
Customer Model	**B2B** | **B2C**	RayDoc sells to both businesses and consumers, so it will want to track both accounts and contacts in its CRM.
Revenue Model	**Products** | **Services**	RayDoc sells both products (such as carpets, doors, and windows) and services (such as installation services, and general contracting services). For its bigger jobs, invoices will be issued to the customer over a period of several months, so RayDoc would benefit from being able to model an opportunity that generates income as a stream, not as a one-time event.
Support Services	Yes | **No**	RayDoc does not sell much in the way of support services. The few warranty claims it gets, it will handle by looking at the supplier invoices.
Transaction Value Sales Cycle Recurring Revenue	Smaller | **Larger** Shorter | **Longer** **Yes** | No	RayDoc does not have many transactions under 100 USD, and most are over 1,000 USD. Sales cycles are typically 2-4 weeks, and more than 60% of sales go to existing customers (hence, the recurring business model is quite healthy). RayDoc will model leads and opportunities, and measure the sales pipeline. It will also use its CRM to improve its recurring revenue model, by conducting e-marketing campaigns and managing a customer loyalty program.
Business Locations	**One or two** | Many **Outbound Sales**	While RayDoc has only the one location, both sales and service staff travel to customer sites and offices regularly. RayDoc would benefit from high speed wireless data services for laptops, PDA browser access to the CRM, or offline CRM support on staff laptops.
Business Size	2-20 | **20-100**	RayDoc has about 22 employees—pretty close to the dividing line between very small firms, and those beginning to gain critical mass. Its CRM implementation budget should be in the 10,000 USD - 25,000 USD range, including hardware (the server), software (the CRM), customization, and the first year's operating expenses. At its size, it may need some basic data security and permission management capabilities in the CRM.
Lead Tracking	Yes | **No**	Doc operates more on the basis of who he knows than what he knows. When he gets a lead, it is typically a real opportunity and needs no qualification. He intends to only track opportunities and remove lead tracking from the user interface.

RayDoc	Choices	Notes
Weighted Sales Pipeline	Yes | **No**	Doc runs RayDoc on a shoestring, and needs to be warned about any signs of a sales downturn. Never one to fool himself, Doc wants his CRM sales pipeline to weigh opportunities by their percentage likelihood, not just add in their gross amount.
Corporate Calendar	**Yes** | No	Doc and his junior partner Andrew disagreed on this one. Doc has never used Outlook or any other calendaring system. Andrew persuaded him to try out the CRM calendaring system, especially for managing the time of service personnel.
Corporate Directory	**Yes** | No	Doc chose to implement this feature, so he could keep the cell phone numbers for his service personnel close to hand.
Interface Consolidation	News Feeds Financial Views External Links Email	Doc wasn't used to much in the way of Information Management, and even a basic CRM would be a big step for him. He decided that at least for the first phase implementation, he would stick with just the basic sales aspects of his CRM.
Document Management	**Yes** | No	Integrated document management will let RayDoc keep quotes and contracts linked to accounts within the CRM—something both Ray and Andrew agree will be extremely useful. They will also keep product brochures, basic HR documents and medical claim forms in the CRM, for all employees to access.
International Users	Yes | **No**	RayDoc operates only in Canada, and has no need for most aspects of international support—but does need the application to work in both English and French.

When filling out the CRM requirements worksheet for your own business in the next section, you should expect to see some of the same principles at work as you see in the RayDoc worksheet above. Some choices are clear from the nature of your business, or some of the special requirements your business may have. Other choices are simply personal decisions based on your opinions and those of your advisors.

Your CRM Requirements Worksheet

In this section, you have an assignment. In the table below circle the choices that are appropriate for your business. This should give you some good indications of what components of a CRM are going to be most useful in your business, and what customizations you are likely to want to make.

Your Business	Choices	Notes
Customer Model	B2B | B2C	B2C Businesses may prefer to remove accounts and deal simply with contacts as customers.
Revenue Model	Products | Services	If you sell services, you may need to be able to model an opportunity that generates income as a stream, not a one-time event. Some CRMs model this sort of opportunity as a Project, delivered over time.

Your Business	Choices	Notes
Support Services	Yes | No	Businesses with support services will need CRM support for an asset register, and service contract management capability.
Transaction Value Sales Cycle Recurring Revenue	Smaller | Larger Shorter | Longer Yes | No	For businesses with transaction values of over 1000 USD, and sales cycles of two weeks or more, it makes sense to model leads and opportunities, and measure the sales pipeline. If you have a small transaction value and short sales cycle, you may use your CRM primarily to improve your recurring revenue model, by conducting e-marketing campaigns and managing a customer loyalty program.
Business Locations	One or two | Many Outbound Sales	Multiple office businesses will benefit greatly from a CRM. Outbound salespeople may require high speed wireless data services, PDA browser access to the CRM, or offline CRM support on their laptop.
Business Size	2-20 | 20-100	Your organization's size will determine your CRM implementation budget (think in terms of a maximum of 500 USD-1,000 USD per employee), and will influence your ability to manage an internal CRM server. Larger firms will benefit even more from a CRM than smaller firms, but need more sophisticated data security and permission management.
Lead Tracking	Yes | No	Businesses with little pro-active lead generation may wish to only track opportunities, and remove lead tracking from the user interface.
Weighted Sales Pipeline	Yes | No	Do you want your sales pipeline to weigh opportunities by their percentage likelihood, or just to add in their gross amount?
Corporate Calendar	Yes | No	There is huge value to breaking the Outlook habit—will you do it?
Corporate Directory	Yes | No	Only needed above perhaps 10 employees.
Interface Consolidation	News Feeds Financial Views External Links Email	Choose between a simple CRM, and one that integrates a wide range of other information—enhancing the CRM function, promoting CRM adoption, and providing many intranet capabilities as well.
Document Management	Yes | No	Integrated document management lets you associate documents to accounts and contacts, as well as keeping reference copies of important company resources under revision control.
International Users	Yes | No	If you have international users, you need foreign language support for your CRM application, plus multiple date and number format options selectable by each user

Summary

In this chapter we began the business analysis process required to maximize the benefit your business will gain from a CRM implementation. Some of the most important topics we discussed were:

- CRMs need more customization than most computer applications. Don't just focus on implementing a CRM—focus on implementing it in a way that suits your business.

- Some of the characteristics that will determine the CRM features and customizations your business really needs are its size, the number of locations at which you do business, whether or not you have outbound salespeople, if your customers are individual consumers or businesses, if you sell products or services, your average unit sales value, and whether or not you need support for international capabilities.

- You will need to decide if your CRM will only manage the sales pipeline, or if it will be a broader business management resource, used by everyone in the company.

- CRMs can integrate management of the corporate calendar for all employees, and link activities to their related contacts and accounts. Will your CRM take over your corporate calendaring?

- CRMs can integrate document management, keeping reference copies of important corporate documents under revision control, and linking documents to contacts and accounts with which they are involved.

- Making a list of requirements. You also filled out your own CRM requirements worksheet, after going through one for RayDoc in detail.

- You learned more about the capabilities of CRM systems in general, and especially what properties of your business will dictate just how your CRM is configured and customized.

In the next chapter we will have a change of pace. After reading a lot in the last two chapters about CRMs in general, and how the CRM needs of various businesses will differ, we will finally move on to the specifics of getting your CRM package—SugarCRM—up and running.

3

CRM Deployment Options: Which One Is Right for You?

In the first couple of chapters, we have had a somewhat theoretical introduction to using a CRM in a smaller business, and the special requirements you should expect to have depending on the nature of your organization and its business model and customers. Now finally, we get down to brass tacks—the practical reality of getting a CRM installed for your business.

In this chapter, we will take a systematic approach to making the right deployment choices for your business. First, we take a detailed look at the alternatives you have for a CRM deployment, including **On-Demand** (no installation at all for you), **Collocation** (someone else hosting an install on a server that belongs to you), a conventional **Self-Hosted** installation where you own and manage your own server, and a **Shared Server** hosting option for small organizations.

Having weighed the pros and cons of those deployment alternatives, if you decide that what suits you best is to deploy and manage your own server for SugarCRM, we then go on to detail how to do that.

Some of the issues involved in deploying your own server are:

- What server operating system should I install? What are the pros and cons between Windows Server and Linux? Between one Linux distribution and the next?
- What computer hardware will I need?
- Will some computer hardware I already have be usable for this purpose?
- What about backup? Security?
- How much Internet bandwidth will I need in each direction?
- What else do I need to install?

In this chapter we will deal with all of these issues in detail, making sure you know the pros and cons of the various choices available to you.

When it comes down to the gory details of actually installing the various software components you would require to run SugarCRM on your own server, this information is to be found in Appendices A and B (one each for installation on Linux or on Windows Server), so that it does not interrupt the flow of your investigations into running SugarCRM for your business. When you actually need to perform the installation—refer to those Appendices for step-by-step instructions.

Deployment Alternatives

Simply put, if you want to use SugarCRM as the CRM solution for your business, you will need to be able to connect to an Internet-accessible server that is running SugarCRM. You will then use it by typing the web address of that server into the address bar of the browser on your PC—no matter where your PC may be as long as it to is connected to the Internet.

So, we need to think about whose server that will be, where it will be, who will install SugarCRM initially and who will take care of that installation going forward.

You have four basic options:

- **On-Demand**: In this situation, you rent use of the SugarCRM application by the month, and by the user. You do not own the server it is operating on, nor do you have to take care of it at all. The supplier, often called an **ASP** (Application Service Provider) backs up the server, makes sure it is always available, and makes sure that adequate bandwidth is available to ensure good performance.

- **Server Collocation**: With this option, you buy your own server, or use one you already own. You load it up with exactly the software image you want, and then take it down to your local Internet Service Provider (ISP), who hosts it for a monthly charge. Again, the supplier backs up the server, makes sure it is always available, and makes sure that adequate bandwidth is available to ensure good performance.

- **Self-Hosted**: This option should be fairly self-explanatory—you buy your own server or use one you already have, load up the desired software on it, and then connect it to the Internet connection at your office, making it externally accessible for use by employees at home or on the road.

- **Shared Server**: The cheapest and lowest capacity option—you have your SugarCRM instance hosted on a server at an ISP, and that server is also used by the ISP to host the applications and websites of several more of their customers.

Let's look at a comparison chart of these options:

	On-Demand	Server Collocation	Self-Hosted	Shared Server
Initial Cost	Low	Medium	Medium	Low
Ongoing Cost	Medium/High	Medium	Low	Low
Initial Setup	Easy	Somewhat Complex	Complex	Medium
Your Ongoing Effort	Low	Medium	Medium	Low
Custom Fit	Often Poor	Excellent	Excellent	Often Poor
Data Security	Excellent	Excellent	Up to You	Excellent
Performance	Excellent	Excellent	Likely Excellent	Low Capacity

At the time you first set up your own server, or prepare it for delivery to an ISP for Collocation, your expenses will be higher than the On-Demand option. You have to buy a server, unless you already have a suitable server candidate available, and you may also need to buy a server operating system (if you choose to use Windows instead of Linux). You may also have some costs associated with developing a backup solution. And you need someone with at least a bit of a technical bent working for you to perform the software installation.

Once you get going, however, the On-Demand service may prove to be quite expensive—often as much as 40 USD per user per month for SugarCRM (that is for Sugar Pro, and higher for most alternative commercial CRMs). Depending on your business, that may seem a good deal for relieving yourself of the need to buy and maintain a server, or it may not.

The Shared-Server approach is the easiest way to get a taste of what it is like to use SugarCRM, and is cheap to run and fairly easy to set up, but has limitations in how much customization you can do, and the size of organization you can expect to run on it. As well, these installations are typically very light on disk space, so if you are using a lot of documents, or generating a lot of PDF files, or other binary attachments to notes or emails, this can make this option less viable. As well, these shared server offerings often have tight limits on bandwidth you may use—which will likely be exceeded greatly if you are uploading and downloading a lot of documents and email attachments. This option is typically only applicable to businesses with at most 10 employees.

For most businesses with more than 10 employees, as should be clear from the table above, the choice between the deployment options is a tradeoff of cost versus complexity and effort.

- Except when you write the check once a month, going with an On-Demand service is easy.

- Hosting the system yourself will take some effort to set it up, require some funds for a server, and take some ongoing effort to make sure the system runs reliably and your data is safe and secure. But it is the cheapest option by far—at least in terms of direct costs.

- Somewhere in between is the Collocation option, which takes a little effort to set up, none or very little to manage month to month, all at a price somewhere between the On-Demand and self-hosted models.

One important point to note is that when you go with an On-Demand service, there is usually little accommodation for substantial customizations to the CRM software to suit your business. The hosted application tends to be very standardized—that is how the ISP/ASP controls the costs of managing multiple servers for multiple clients. In the Collocation option, you get to load the software on your own server, and then deliver it to the ISP—so a fully customized software image is no problem. It is also usually easy to update later on, without removing it from the ISP. In the self-hosted model, of course, your solution can be as customized as you like, and it may also be easier to link the CRM server to your other business systems (accounts, intranet, customer portal), which may reside securely behind your company's firewall.

If you decide to go with the self-hosted option, or the Collocation option, you will need to know about computer server hardware, server operating systems, and the choice of the LAMP stack versus WAMP or WIMP. These topics are covered in the following sections.

Even if you go with the On-Demand option, it is still useful to gain an overview level of understanding of these topics, as this information will make you an informed consumer of the product offered to you by On-Demand vendors. Will that bandwidth be enough for me? Will that server offer good performance and scalability? What about your backup procedures?

Server Issues for Self-Hosted and Collocated Deployments

Both the Self-Hosted and the Collocated deployment options need the user to buy a server and set it up. There are various parameters that need to be looked into when you are in the process of setting up your own server. This section is devoted to these issues and is focused on dealing with them.

Choosing a Server Operating System

Just as a server may physically resemble a PC while differing from it greatly, a server operating system may look a lot like a desktop operating system while being in actuality very different. A desktop operating system, like a PC, is optimized to give good service to the user to whom is it dedicated. A server operating system has to be talented at getting work done for many people at once, while keeping them all happy. It also typically has less need for a rich, powerful graphical user interface, as it is frequently used and managed remotely.

Server and network operating systems have been around for a long time. While many years ago Novell Netware and Banyan Vines, plus many variants of UNIX (including notably Solaris from Sun Microsystems) were major players in this marketplace, today the largest players in network/server operating systems for small to medium applications are Windows Server, and Linux. While UNIX still has a very large share, it is growing slowly, and relates much more to the high end of the market.

While Windows Server comes only from Microsoft, Linux exists in many versions, from many sources. Red Hat is perhaps the best known product (or **distribution**, as different versions of Linux are called), with SUSE (originally a German Linux vendor, now owned by Novell) a close second. SUSE tends to be the preferred vendor in Europe, and Red Hat in the USA. Major commercial Linux distributions, while still mostly open source, are far from free, as they command substantial annual support contracts, and initial licensing costs.

At the time of writing, Windows Server 2003 Enterprise Edition for 25 Users costs 3,999 USD. Support costs extra. Enterprise Linux ES from Red Hat costs 349 USD per server with one year of a basic level of support, or 799 USD including a year of higher level support. Somewhat similarly, SUSE Linux Enterprise Server 9 costs 349 USD per server (with up to 2 CPUs) per year, including support. Personally, I prefer SUSE Linux to Red Hat, as I find it has a more approachable user interface for the average human being who knows Windows XP and little else. For this reason, Appendix A, which describes installing SugarCRM on Linux, uses SUSE Linux Enterprise Server 9 as the worked example.

The costs involved in purchasing a server operating system are as detailed above, and the choice is yours. Clearly, Linux is cheaper to buy. My experience has been that both are very reliable in use. The choice to me comes down to spending more to get the familiar Microsoft user interface, or paying less, and dealing with the less familiar Linux user interface.

The level and type of technical resources you have access to will no doubt have some influence on your choice as well. You will need someone local at the very least to be on call in case of emergencies, perhaps to come in and set things up for you in the beginning, and possibly to perform backups each week. There are many independent network and server support people who make their living working as the outsourced computer support technician for perhaps ten small businesses. Working with one of these people might cost you 5,000-10,000 USD per year, and depending on your circumstances, could well be right for you. Or is the 40 USD per user per month at the On-Demand supplier starting to look better now?

Web-Based Application Platforms

In today's computing world, there are three major web-based application development and delivery platforms:

- Microsoft's proprietary .NET platform
- Sun Microsystems's partially open Java platform
- The Open Source LAMP (Linux-Apache-MySQL-PHP) platform

Each of these environments provides a comprehensive set of tools for developers to build and test new web-based applications, and for users of the applications to run them.

Microsoft's .NET platform has very good cross-language development capabilities, but is tied to Microsoft-proprietary products, including its operating system and other server products.

Sun's Java platform is widely popular across many vendors (Sun, HP, IBM, and so on) as a scalable platform that is largely hardware and operating system independent, and non-proprietary.

While the Java platform has world-class scalability, and an excellent security model, it has been recognized that it is not the most productive environment for leveraging reliable business applications from expensive development resources.

Accordingly, while .NET will likely remain the platform of choice for Microsoft's partners and users who don't mind being irretrievably tied to Microsoft products, there has been a big need in the market for a non-proprietary platform with Open Source components and the practical ability to build applications in a particularly cost-effective manner. That platform is the LAMP stack.

LAMP stands for Linux, Apache, MySQL, and PHP (plus Perl and Python—two other popular Open Source scripting languages we will not discuss further here). The LAMP stack looks like this:

PHP Hypertext Preprocessor Scripting Language
MySQL Database
Apache Web Server
Linux Operating System

The LAMP Stack

As you can see, Linux and Apache are the base on which the LAMP stack is built. And what a solid base—between them they are the two most successful Open Source initiatives in the world.

MySQL, a popular Open Source database was developed and released into Open Source by MySQL AB of Sweden and is known for speed, scalability, and reliability. It would be fair to say it is also known as a less sophisticated database, lacking some advanced capabilities such as stored procedures and triggers—features that were finally delivered in the 5.0 release of MySQL. If MySQL is a Ford Mustang—simple, fast, and reliable, then Oracle, the leading commercial database, would have to be characterized as a Bentley—smooth, slick, fast, and expensive. We know which one suits the smaller business.

While the four elements of LAMP work very well together, they can be used in different combinations. Other than the use of alternative scripting languages, the most common change to LAMP is to make it WAMP, by using Windows Server underneath it, rather than Linux. Another possible change is to make it WIMP, by using Windows Server and Microsoft Internet Information Server (the Microsoft web server) underneath MySQL and PHP.

Generally speaking, Windows Server has a much greater footprint than Linux—so WAMP will require the server it is installed on to have more memory than if LAMP were utilized. For an average 25-person business, your CRM server can get away with 2 GB of memory if you use the LAMP stack, but 2.5-3 GB is a safer bet if you want to use WAMP. Otherwise, there are no other drawbacks to running WAMP—and potential advantages as Windows Server presents a user interface that many more people are familiar with.

As for WIMP, I believe the bottom line should be to just say no. To run PHP with complete stability on IIS requires that it be done in a way that badly limits system performance. You would be better off following the masses, and going with LAMP or WAMP.

Specifying Your Server Hardware

At home, most of us use our PCs as isolated workstations for work or play. A few may connect several PCs at home into a network, in much the same way they are connected at the office. When several PCs are connected in a network, there is often value in attaching one or more special computers to the network, designed to act as a shared resource for all users. These special—typically more powerful—computers are called servers.

Most of us are familiar enough with a home or office Personal Computer or PC. The usual product is a so-called three-box configuration—the system unit, the display, and the keyboard. While a computer server can look quite similar to a PC, it has a number of quite fundamental differences, as summarized in the table below:

	PC	Server
Form Factor	Desktop, Tower	Tower, Rack mount
Memory Type	Non-parity	ECC (Error Checking and Correcting)
Memory Size	512 MB-1 GB	1-4 GB
Hard Disk Technology	IDE / SATA	SCSI
Hard Disk Speed	5,400-10,000 RPM	10,000-15,000 RPM
LAN Interface	Ethernet 10/100, Wireless	One or more Gig-Ethernet

	PC	Server
Power Supply	Single 250-400W	Redundant 400W
Processor (CPU)	Single Pentium 4 / Athlon	One or more Xeon / Opteron
Video	Often High Performance for Gaming	Low Performance
Users	One—Local	Many—Remote

Note that there are plenty of low-end servers from the likes of HP and Dell that use non-parity memory, IDE or SATA disk drives, and a single power supply. They can be used for small (up to say a dozen users) SugarCRM installations fairly effectively. But my personal recommendations would always be for a higher capacity, and better level of reliability, using what I might like to call a proper server. Most of the differences in a proper server are there to make the server more reliable than a PC, and to make it better suited to handling the needs of many users at once. Going to a lower specification is to me a false economy; but not everyone would agree.

ECC memory for example, has the ability to detect and correct the most common forms of errors that could be made by semi-conductor memory when it starts to fail. Typical PC memory, by contrast, will have no idea if it is starting to fail and make errors (due to the lack of a feature called parity), and certainly has no ability to correct those errors. The only time a PC checks to see if its memory actually works is at system boot time, when you turn it on. As you intend to leave your server on all the time, that approach clearly will not work.

Similarly, a server power supply often has two actual power supplies connected in a redundant manner, so that when one fails, it is reported, but the system carries on running on the one power supply that remains, giving you a chance to buy a replacement power supply, and schedule down time to replace it.

The SCSI (Small Computer System Interface) hard drive in a server is designed to service multiple requests from unrelated user activity in the most efficient way possible. Elevator seeking is just one feature that illustrates this point. If a SCSI drive receives multiple requests for information from different sources, it will service those requests as the internal drive head passes by the information, regardless of who made their request first. An IDE (Internal Drive Electronics) or SATA (Serial Advanced Technology Attachment) hard drive will service requests in the order they arrived, even if this means that the drive head will be scooting back and forth over the same area many times. Since the mechanical movement of the drive head is the main activity that makes a hard drive so much slower than system memory, this means that an IDE or SATA drive will perform worse in a server application than a SCSI drive—especially in a situation where the server is heavily loaded with many simultaneous users.

The Central Processing Unit (CPU) or processor used in a server is typically an Intel Xeon or AMD Opteron (again—low end servers for small installations may use Intel Pentium 4 or AMD Athlon processors). These processors have a larger and more sophisticated on-chip cache design, that lets multiple users keep processing quickly, by staying mostly in the cache memory on the processor itself, and going out to normal system memory as seldom as possible. By contrast, an Intel Pentium 4, the leading desktop processor, has a caching system that when dealing with multiple users will more often go out to system memory, slowing down the system throughput.

System memory size is perhaps the biggest difference between a server and a PC. Most PC users (other than those doing graphics design and other demanding tasks) work happily with 512 MB of memory in their PC—or at most 1 GB. By contrast, few servers use less than 1 GB of memory, and most use 2 to 4 GB—or more. With more memory, the work being done for many users can stay in memory simultaneously as it is performed, rather than being sent temporarily out to the hard disk if memory gets too full. As system memory is at least 100 times faster than the hard disk, anything that involves the hard disk will slow down the system substantially.

Servers are used for many tasks. A network may have a specific server to act as a database server, for example. That type of server would be optimized for fast and reliable disk storage and high memory capacity. Another server might be an application server—one on which applications are run, with the results being communicated to the users on the PCs using those applications. An application server is typically optimized with lots of memory and CPU power—to get through all that application processing quickly. An example of an application server is a SugarCRM server— the SugarCRM application is actually running on the server—and multiple user PCs are just running web browsers that display web pages that communicate to the users what is going on in their particular session.

For a business with 10 users or less, my personal recommendation for the configuration of a SugarCRM server to be used as a combined database and application server would be along these lines:

- 80-100 GB of IDE or SCSI storage
- 1 GB of ECC memory (or 1.5 GB if you are using Windows Server)
- A single Athlon, Pentium 4, Xeon or Opteron processor running at 2 GHz or faster
- A single Gig-Ethernet connection to the network
- An Uninterruptible Power Supply (UPS)
- SUSE Enterprise Linux or Windows Server

For a business with perhaps 25 users, I would recommend a server configured along these lines:

- 150 GB of SCSI storage
- 2-3 GB of ECC memory (depending on the operating system used)
- A single Xeon or Opteron processor running at 2 GHz or faster
- A single Gig-Ethernet connection to the network
- An Uninterruptible Power Supply (UPS)
- SUSE Enterprise Linux or Windows Server

For a business with 100 users, my recommendation would move up to something more like:

- 300 GB of SCSI disk storage
- Dual Xeon or Opteron processors of 2 GHz speed or faster
- 4-8 GB of ECC memory, depending on the operating system selected
- Dual Gig-Ethernet connections to the network
- An Uninterruptible Power Supply (UPS)
- SUSE Enterprise Linux or Windows Server

Most ISPs and ASPs use fairly low-end hardware for their servers, and seem to charge a lot of money for them each month when offered as dedicated servers. If you use SugarCRM as an On-Demand service, you will in all likelihood not have a whole server dedicated to running SugarCRM for your business. Instead, your ISP/ASP will likely be using a shared server facility—a controlled portion of the resources of a physical server—to support your business's CRM.

If you are planning to use your CRM to house a lot of shared documents for your business, you should check with your On-Demand service provider what your disk space limitations are—they are often surprisingly low.

Clearly if you collocate your own server at an ISP, or use it at your own premises, you will likely have a better hardware platform to run on, and it will offer some room for expansion, compared to the On-Demand situation. But Collocation can be expensive too, and managing your own server is not for everyone.

In the end, you will need to make a choice balancing several factors—your access to technical staff (and the cost of it), how difficult it is for you to invest in a server, what price you can find for an On-Demand service of good quality, and how much customization you feel your installation of the software will require.

One last word of warning: Most businesses have an old PC or two lying around relatively unused. There is a great temptation to use one of these as your SugarCRM server. This may be a fine idea for an initial trial installation of SugarCRM for evaluation purposes. But when you make the decision to put SugarCRM into production in your business, you should consider the performance, future expansion, and reliability factors of such a PC as compared to a modern server (see the comparison table above)—and unless cash is very, very tight, you should just say no.

Backup and Security Considerations

Backup and security are the two things that are most likely to suffer if you host your server yourself, compared to housing it at a professional hosting centre. If you are going to be hosting your own server, and have little experience with servers, backup, and network security issues, this is an important section for you.

Clearly, when you have got your dream CRM up and running, you will want everyone in the organization to be using it, and the business to be largely run from it. With such a vital role in the organization, and all your business's vital data on it, you will not be able to afford to have the system fail and lose your data, or produce prolonged down time.

Accordingly, you will need to devise a data backup strategy. One solution is to buy a data backup device—which typically will be tape-based, but could also involve network-attached disk storage. Most backup solutions are not cheap, but unfortunately, adopting a reliable backup plan is completely mandatory.

Some inexpensive backup solutions do exist, such as connecting an external USB hard drive to your server, and backing up the server hard drive to the external hard drive. You can also buy a second drive within your server, and backup the drive that way. But files open at backup time will likely not be backed up by a simple operating-system level file or drive copy—so be *very* careful.

Whatever solution you adopt, the most likely cause of failure will be because you did not use it regularly, or properly—or did not test that the backups it made could be successfully restored. So pay more attention to the policies and procedures for backup, and testing restores, than you ever do to your choice of backup technology. Personally I recommend the internal tape backup unit with proper tape backup software, a daily incremental backup, and weekly full backup. Rotate the tape used in the tape drive each week, and keep 5 tapes in the rotation. And once a month, test your backups by identifying a document that has been recently created and checking it can be successfully restored from the backup.

Server Security

Your CRM server will be permanently accessible via the Internet, and will house your most vital and sensitive business information. Right away, bells should be going off in your head, warning you to make sure that the server is properly secure. Malicious attacks, or the attempted theft of your competitive information, are two among many very real threats you must plan for.

For a start, security specialists will always tell you that nothing is completely secure. There are simply levels of security—each more cumbersome and expensive than the last, and you need to implement a level of security that is sensible and appropriate in your business context.

Some minimal security measures you should consider include:

- A UPS (Uninterruptible Power Supply) to save your server from crashing when there is a power outage. Windows and Linux both have utilities that can receive a message from the UPS notifying the server when the UPS has gone over to battery backup, so that the server can be shut down in a controlled manner if the power remains out for too long.
- A locked server room, so only authorized employees can access the server, reducing its chances of being stolen, being damaged, or having its data compromised or stolen.
- A firewall between the server and the Internet connection, with only limited and specific access to the web server being permitted from the Internet.

If you are installing the SugarCRM server at your own office, you will typically position the server behind your firewall to the outside world, but allow external access by opening ports on the firewall to the web server on your SugarCRM server. From a security point of view, it would be even better to actually have separate web and application servers, with security rules between them—but this is likely not a necessary security measure for smaller firms.

If your SugarCRM server will be collocated at an ISP, a similar networking configuration should be used—talk to your ISP.

If you are using an On-Demand service—none of this will be vital to you, except insofar as you may wish to ask your ASP what security architecture is in place, and how it handles the web server and application server issues.

Bandwidth Capacity and Reliability Considerations

We have all been on Internet sites where we liked the information provided, but were frustrated by the slowness of the site. We need to make sure no one using your CRM ever feels that way about it!

Bandwidth, or connection speed, is an important link in the chain of good performance for a web-based CRM.

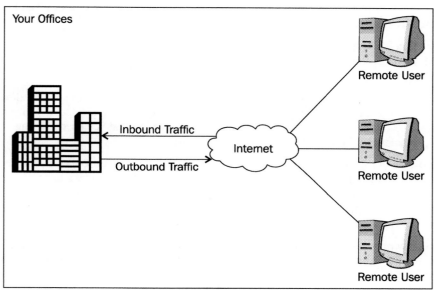

SugarCRM Internet Connection

In the diagram above, the Outbound Traffic leaves Your Offices for the Internet at a speed called the uplink, or upload speed. Inbound Traffic arrives at your building at the downlink, or download speed. Notice that with the server at your office, for a Remote User it is important that the uplink speed be good, for data to get from the office to the remote user quickly.

Usually, your employees will complain if the office download speed is slow as web browsing, or retrieving email from an external email service, will be slow if the office has a poor Internet download speed (traffic moving in the direction of the Inbound Traffic in the diagram above).

Now we see that employees will also complain (at least the ones who access your CRM while away from the office) if the office's Internet connection has a slow uplink speed (traffic moving in the direction of the Outbound Traffic in the diagram above).

So the conclusion we must draw is that if we intend to house our CRM server at the office, we need to make sure the office now has not just a good download speed on its Internet connection, but a good upload speed as well.

What is a good speed? Well, that depends on how much each employee has to use the Internet to do their work. In a software development company, the Internet bandwidth required per employee will likely be much greater than in a T-shirt printing firm, or for that matter, at RayDoc Carpets.

For the average white collar business (if there is such a thing), for each 25 people in the company, in my personal experience I find you need something like two megabits of download bandwidth. With a CRM server at the office being accessed by remote employees during the day, or at night from home, you will likely need something like one megabit of upload or uplink speed for each ten concurrent remote users.

Personally I find it's best to avoid an uplink speed lower than 768 kilobits for remote access to SugarCRM. It will still work on slower connections of course, but you may find the response becomes sluggish—and there's really no room for that in business these days!

Many Internet connections tend to be faster in the download direction than the upload direction. These connections are referred to as *Asymmetric*. If your CRM server is located at your offices, your business becomes a candidate to have an Internet connection that is closer to being *Symmetric*, or balanced, in its upload and download speeds.

When you use an On-Demand service for your CRM, or have your server collocated at an ISP, your server benefits from the fact that the Internet connection at the provider's location is much faster in both directions than it is at your offices, and as well it is more reliable. Typically, an ISP or ASP has multiple suppliers of its Internet connection *pipes,* so that if the connection provided by one supplier fails, those from another suppliers will automatically carry on moving traffic.

This redundancy of an Internet connection is something that is hard to afford for the smallest businesses—and so you may have to accept that your level of service (reliability) for a self-hosted CRM won't be quite as good as if your server were professionally hosted and managed. Check out pricing for redundant connections in your area, and as well, check out the level of guaranteed availability offered by the ISPs in your area, and their reputations amongst your business associates.

Lastly, if you choose the On-Demand or collocated server options, be sure to check out how much bandwidth you are allowed to consume (per user, or for your whole server) before bandwidth surcharges come into effect. With many suppliers the standard bandwidth allowance is very small, to help generate another couple of hundred dollars of income for the supplier each month from charges for excessive bandwidth use.

Performing the Installation

In order not to interrupt our CRM business analysis context with a lot of procedural instructions, the actual details of installing SugarCRM may be found in Appendices A and B, which cover the complete process of installing SugarCRM on top of SUSE Linux and Windows Server.

Summary

In this chapter, we covered the practical considerations of installing and running SugarCRM in your business. The key points included:

- Comparing the advantages of an On-Demand service versus a Collocated, Self-Hosted, or Shared Server, we saw the up front costs of your own server were the alternative to paying substantial fees every month to an On-Demand service. As well, we explained the minimal support for customizations available with an On-Demand service or Shared Server.

- If you choose to deploy SugarCRM on your own server, you will need to select the operating system and hardware configuration for your server, and also make decisions regarding server security and Internet connection bandwidth.

- You can use Windows or Linux as the server operating system on your SugarCRM server. If Linux, then with the Apache Web Server, the MySQL database, and the PHP scripting language, the whole combination is known as the LAMP stack. With Windows, the combination with Apache, MySQL, and PHP is known as WAMP.

- For security, you should consider a UPS (battery backup), a locked server closet, and a firewall to protect your server from Internet intruders.

- Your offices should have an Internet connection of at least 768 Kbit for both download and upload speeds, and you will need about 2 Mbits of download speed for every 25 employees, and about 1 Mbit of upload speed for every 10 concurrent remote CRM users.

- Appendices A and B include the procedural details of the actual installation of SugarCRM within the Linux and Windows Server environments respectively.

In the next chapter, we assume you have now deployed SugarCRM, and go on to start using your new CRM in earnest, explaining a lot of the basic CRM terminology and concepts as we go along. Why is a CRM so much better than a contact manager? What are the normal navigation techniques for operating a CRM? How do I get my data into a CRM? All these topics and more are coming up next.

4
CRM Basics

Now that we have covered some of the essentials of what a CRM offers, itemized the value to a smaller business of a web-based CRM such as SugarCRM, and studied the theoretical aspects of how CRMs need customizing to properly fit each business that uses them, it is time we made use of the SugarCRM server we deployed in the last chapter.

In this chapter, we will take a guided tour of SugarCRM. Our task-oriented, systematic treatment will also relate the specifics of the SugarCRM system and its user interface with the general principles of CRM systems.

This chapter will cover the basic CRM functions and show how they are interpreted and performed within SugarCRM. These basic CRM concepts include:

- Common CRM processes and terminology
- Creating accounts and contacts, and relating multiple contacts to a single account
- Following links between related data to answer questions as quickly as your mind can raise them
- Creating and tracking the Sales Pipeline from leads to opportunities to contacts and accounts
- Creating and monitoring sales activities and accumulating activity history
- Scheduling activities with colleagues by referring to their calendars

In the next chapter, we will complete the exploration of how SugarCRM delivers on comprehensive CRM functionality by dealing with the more advanced CRM topics such as Interface Consolidation, Project Management, Document Management, and Customer Service Management.

CRM Processes and Terminology

At its fundamentals, a CRM is a system that first needs to be taught all there is to know in terms of the static information about your accounts and the contacts you have at those accounts. Once the CRM gains that knowledge, it leverages that knowledge by using it to organize and retain information about all your daily business activities as they relate to those accounts and contacts.

After just a few weeks of regular use, a quick look at the CRM can remind you about the history of successful and unsuccessful sales opportunities in your accounts, what each account's service history has been like, and what new sales opportunities are coming up in each account.

Let us take a quick look at SugarCRM to get an initial feel of the powerful organizational and managerial boost it will give your business.

Accessing the SugarCRM System

Before you begin using the system, ensure that you have the appropriate software installed and configured on your system. All you will need is:

- **A current web browser running on your computer**: SugarCRM has been tested with and supports a variety of browsers. The following browsers are known to work with SugarCRM:
    - Mozilla version 1.7 and higher: www.mozilla.org/mozilla1.x
    - Firefox version 1.0 and higher: www.mozilla.org/firefox
    - Konqueror version 3.2 and higher: www.konqueror.org
    - Microsoft Internet Explorer version 5 and higher: www.microsoft.com/ie

  You may encounter problems if you try to access SugarCRM using older web browsers like Internet Explorer 4 or Netscape 4.x. If you are unsure about which web browser version you are using, click Help | About... or similar options on the menu bar in your browser. The version number will be displayed.

- **JavaScript and cookies support enabled in your web browser**: Both JavaScript and cookies support must be enabled in the security settings of your browser and are usually turned on by default.

  If you encounter problems accessing the system, check your browser configuration to ensure both JavaScript support and cookies support are enabled. (See Tools | Internet Options | Privacy and Security tabs in Internet Explorer, or Tools | Options | Privacy and Web Features tabs in Firefox.)

- **Network access to a server that is running the SugarCRM software**: Your system or network administrator will be able to provide you with an Internet address (URL) at which the system can be accessed.

Next, we need to log in to the system, and choose a language, and a theme (which determines how the application will look). If you do not provide the correct user name and password, SugarCRM will not allow you access to the system.

Using the admin area within the system, your system administrator assigns log in information—a user name and password—to every system user. This admin area is only accessible to users with administrator privileges. If you haven't got your user name and password combination, contact your system administrator.

To access SugarCRM, type the URL into your web browser's address bar. You should see a screen similar to the one below. This is the SugarCRM log in screen. If you do not see a log in screen, verify that you have entered the URL correctly. If you did not make a typing mistake, contact your system administrator to verify that you have the correct URL.

If you click on Options, you may also choose the Language you want to use with the system (US English, Franco Canadien, Espanola or others that may be available on your particular system) and the Theme or visual appearance you want the system to have. The theme illustrated throughout this guide is High Contrast—a theme something like the default Sugar theme, but developed at **The Long Reach Corporation** specifically for this book so that the screen images in the book look good in print. Other themes include *Links* (golf theme), *Shred* (winter sports), *Pipeline* (surfing theme), and many more.

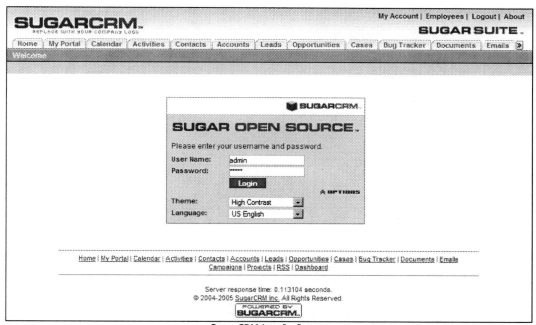

SugarCRM Log In Screen

Once the SugarCRM *log in* screen (shown above) appears, follow the following steps to log in:

1. Type your user name in the User Name box. (Use admin for now—the examples in this chapter assume that you log in as admin).

2. Type your password in the Password box. (Again—use admin for now. Note that system passwords are case-sensitive).

3. Select the Language and Theme that you want to use (if applicable).

4. Click the Login button.

A Quick Tour of SugarCRM

When you log into the system, the Home tab is displayed, as shown below. Various key elements of the screen layout are highlighted, as follows:

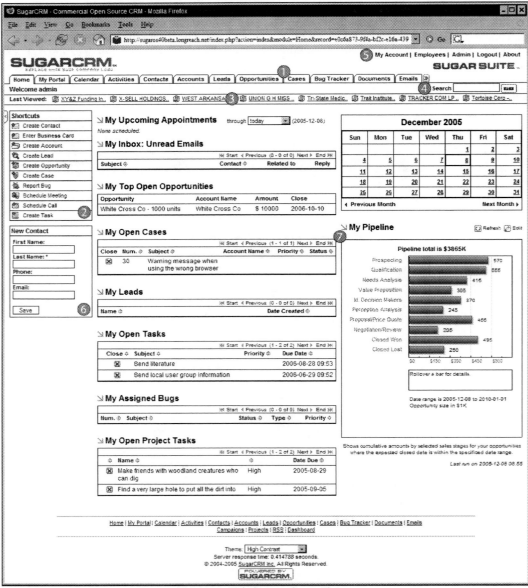

The Home Tab Screen: Sugar Theme

1. **Navigation Tabs**: Click to choose a module to display. A drop-down menu lets you select other modules if you have more than 12 tabs.

2. **Navigation Shortcuts Box**: Specific shortcuts that are useful within each module.

3. **Last Viewed**: A useful trail of recent records you have viewed.

4. **Search Box**: Search for a text string within key data held by SugarCRM.

5. **System Links**: My Account, Employees, Logout, and About. The Admin link is only available to users defined as system administrators.

6. **Quick New Item Box**: Quick data-entry box to create a new item for the current module.

7. **Main Screen Body**: On the Home tab, this includes Cases, Opportunities, Appointments, Leads, Tasks, a monthly calendar, and the sales pipeline graph.

The screen layout in the Home tab uses the same layout as all of the other tabs. As you move between the tabs, the shortcuts available in the shortcuts list change according to the specific tab, and the main screen body displays the information indicated by the tab name. The Quick New Item box changes to offer quick access for creating new items based on the tab, for example, New Contact, New Account, New Opportunity, and so on.

Themes

When you were logging in, we mentioned that you could choose an alternative theme if you wanted to. Let us take a quick look at that before we carry on. In the System Links area of the screen (top right), click on the Logout link. (Note that when you are finished working with the system, you should always log out of the system rather than just closing your web browser. When you log out, the system performs several *clean-up* procedures, and then automatically returns the web browser window to the log in screen.)

This time on the log in screen use the Options link to choose the Links theme, and then log in.

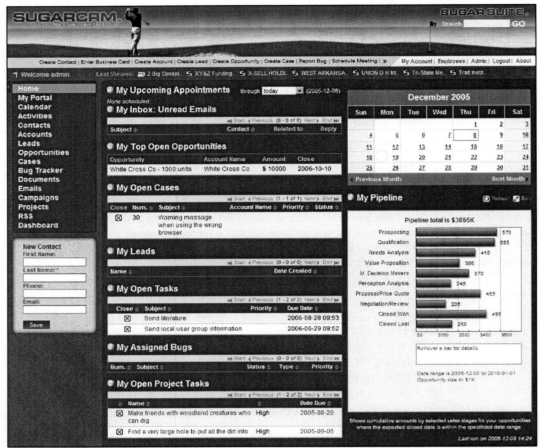

The Home Tab Screen: Links Theme

Notice how many aspects of the SugarCRM screen can be varied by changing the theme. The navigation tabs are no longer tabs, but a side menu system. Essentially, the shortcuts have switched positions with the tabs. In addition, the color scheme and graphics are very different.

No matter what theme you use, the same CRM information is displayed. It is just laid out differently. Pick the theme that you prefer, or change it now and then to keep some fun in your use of the CRM.

For the rest of this chapter, we will assume that when you installed SugarCRM, you also opted to install the sample data. (See the Populate database with demo data? checkbox on the screen entitled Step 3: Database Configuration within the appendices on installing SugarCRM.) Later on, we will quickly re-do the installation to remove the demo data, and then import your own organization's data, as you get closer to your live implementation.

CRM Navigation Basics: Accounts and Contacts

So—here we are—SugarCRM!

Let's get a little more familiar with using the system. First, (and I will assume you have switched back to the normal Sugar Theme from now on) try clicking on a few of the module tabs—such as Accounts and Contacts. Different sets of information are organized within different modules, and each module has a tab you click on to use it. The module screens are displayed within your browser very promptly after you click on them—SugarCRM is nice and fast! In addition, your browser caches certain graphical portions of the screen displays for each module, so each screen gets even faster after the first time you access it.

Notice the arrow after the last tab on the right. This leads to a list of modules there was not enough room to display. If you have cause to use any one of those modules, it becomes sticky, and replaces the last module tab shown before the arrow. Sugar Open Source 4.0 contains the following 16 user modules:

- Home
- My Portal
- Calendar
- Activities (Meetings, Calls, Tasks, and Notes)
- Contacts
- Accounts
- Leads
- Opportunities
- Cases
- Bug Tracker
- Documents
- Emails
- Campaigns (and Prospects, Prospect Lists)
- Projects (and Project Tasks)
- RSS
- Dashboard

Sugar Pro 4.0 adds modules for products, quotes, forecasts and reports, as well as team sales and workflow features.

The system administrator can control which users will be able to see and use which modules, so for many users there will be no need for the arrow to link to extra modules, as they will often have no more than will fit comfortably on the screen. In addition, if a theme is used that lists the modules on the left side like a menu system (such as Links or Pipeline), all the modules to which a user has access are always displayed.

List and Detail View Screens

Now click on the Accounts tab. This shows you a list of all accounts in the system. Screens that show a list in SugarCRM are called **list views**. This screen is the Accounts List view. If you have the demo data installed, your screen should look something like this:

The Accounts Module: List View

Let's imagine that what we are looking at is a list of RayDoc's accounts—a sample set of accounts, contacts, leads, opportunities, and so on for the RayDoc organization. Clearly, the names of the companies are made up as we cannot expose information about real companies here, but the sample data here has been created to demonstrate all the key capabilities of the system needed to make your CRM deployment a success.

At the top right of the list of accounts, you can see some controls and information that indicate that there are actually 97 accounts in the system, and that you are currently looking at accounts 1 through 20. Next and Previous controls are provided to step through sections of the full list of accounts, as well as controls to go to the overall start or end of the list.

You can also see an Account Search panel at the top of the screen, which is useful for finding a specific account by the name of the account, or by other fields such as the city or phone number. It is important to understand that this search panel is really a filter panel—only accounts that match the filter criteria will be listed. More than one limiting criterion may be applied—you could look for all accounts that start with a, and which are in New York City, and all accounts that satisfy these constraints (filter conditions) will be listed. To go back to seeing the entire list of accounts, simply click on the Clear control in the search panel to remove all filter conditions.

To access a more comprehensive set of filter conditions, click on the Advanced control in the Account Search panel.

It is important to understand that the Accounts List shown to you by default is the entire set of accounts in the system. Sales people using the system may wish to focus exclusively on their own accounts, which they may do by selecting the Only My Items checkbox in the search panel.

As you move your mouse pointer around within your browser window, you can see that each account name has a link on it. If you click on the name of an account, you will go to the detail view for that account. Let's do that now, and click on 2 Big Consolidation Corp. You should see something like this:

The Accounts Module: Detail View

Main Panel and Sub-Panels

Examining the Accounts Detail screen, we see a block of general information about the account at the top, and a series of blocks of information below that with related information, such as Activities, History, Contacts, Opportunities, Leads, Cases, and so on.

The block of general information at the top is referred to as the main panel. The blocks of related information below are called sub-panels—so we see a sub-panel for Activities, one for History, another for Contacts, and so on.

We also see a few buttons just above the main panel—Edit, Duplicate, and Delete. These buttons act on this specific account record, allowing us to edit, duplicate, or delete it.

Just above each sub-panel, we also see a number of buttons. Let's take a look at the Activities sub-panel as a specific example. This sub-panel offers buttons for Create Tasks, Schedule Meeting, Schedule Call, and Compose Email. While we will discuss these different activities in more detail shortly, for now it is enough to understand that these buttons allow you to add new activities into this detail view screen, which are automatically linked to or associated with this particular account.

Within the Activities sub-panel, notice that there are links on the Subject, Contact, and Related to fields within each open activity. Clicking on these links will take us to the detail view of the activity, the related contact, or the related account. This is your first glimpse of the enormous power of the links within a CRM that speed up the navigation between related items of information.

Still within the Activities sub-panel, to the right of each activity listed, notice the links edit and rem. These are provided to allow you to quickly edit or delete the activities.

For each of the other sub-panels, similar principals apply—buttons and links are provided to create new items of information related to the current account, to edit or remove those items of information, or to go to the full detail view of those related items of information.

The detail view screen layout also includes the following additional handy controls:

1. **Hide Controls for each sub-panel**: Enabling the user to limit vertical screen scrolling to focus on the data that is important to them specifically, and to reduce the bandwidth requirements of each screen, which will increase system performance. Each hidden sub-panel may be restored by clicking on the Show link, which appears on collapsed or hidden sub-panels. Hiding a sub-panel is a sticky action—the sub-panel will stay hidden indefinitely until you click on the Show link.

2. **VCR Controls**: On each detail screen, there are Next and Previous links at the top (also known as nudge controls), which enable the user to step through records in a module at the detail view level, without having to return to the list view between each record. Start and End Controls are provided to go directly to the first and last records in a module.

3. **Return to List:** This link at the top of each detail view may be used to return to the list view for that module.

4. **View Change Log**: Each module's change log tracks certain key field values on every record. A change log is automatically created each time any of these fields is changed, noting the field changed, the old and new values, the user that made the change, and the date of the change.

Edit View Screens

If you look on the left-hand side of your screen, you will see the navigation shortcuts box. From this menu (assuming again that you are using the standard Sugar theme), click on the Create Account shortcut. You will see the Account Edit view screen:

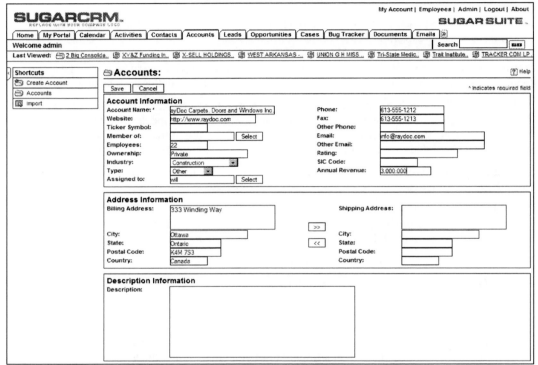

The Accounts Module: Edit View

To gain some first-hand experience we are going to create an account for RayDoc—even though we are imagining that this CRM contains the database for RayDoc and it is perhaps a little odd to have RayDoc as an account in its own CRM.

Enter the data for the RayDoc business, as shown in the screenshot above, and then click on the Save button. You will be directed to the Account Detail view screen for the RayDoc account.

One important note at this point is that you have now saved some data within SugarCRM for the first time. In a browser-based system like SugarCRM, this data has not been saved on the PC or notebook you are using, but on the SugarCRM server instead, from which anyone in your company can retrieve it (if they are permitted). The beauty of this is that no matter where you are, if you can get access to an Internet-connected PC with a browser on it, you can access your SugarCRM system, and all the CRM data your company possesses. The PC you use to access the system does not have to have anything special installed on it—just a browser. Nor does the use of the system save any data on the PC used, other than a few user preferences as browser cookies.

Now—click on the Create button in the Contacts sub-panel—we are going to add a new contact at RayDoc.

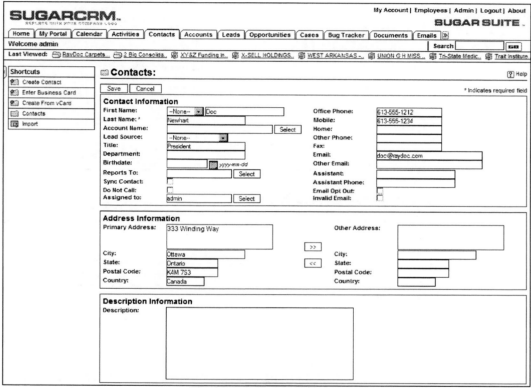

The Contacts Module: Edit View

Of course, that new contact can only be Doc himself! Enter his data as shown above. Note, as you do, that even though you started in the Accounts module, the Contacts tab is now highlighted and you are in that module as you enter the details of the new contact at RayDoc.

Now click on the Save button to save Doc's contact record. Notice that in the Last Viewed area of the screen (above the shortcuts box) you are beginning to accumulate a list of the items of information you have been working with within the system. These are available as links, to take you back to any item of information you have been working with recently.

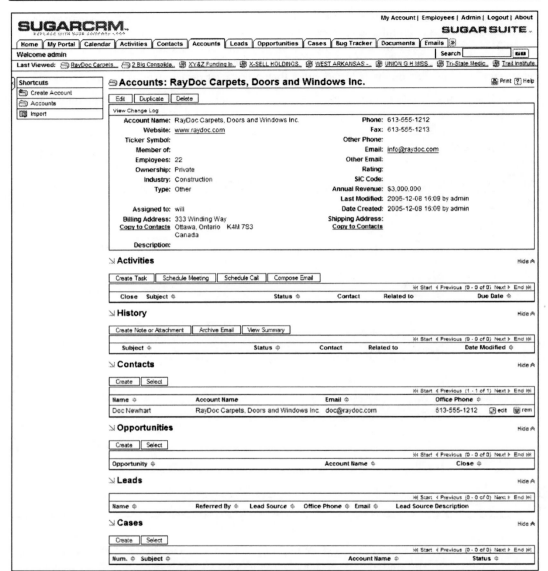

Contact Linked to Account

You should now see a screen like the one opposite—showing the Account Detail view for the RayDoc account, with Doc Newhart as a contact at that account. To reinforce the ability to link back and forth, up and down, and sideways within SugarCRM (and any good CRM)—click on the contact name of Doc Newhart to link to his Contact Detail view screen. From that screen, click on the account name link, to come right back to the Account Detail view screen for RayDoc.

Now—add yourself as another contact at RayDoc, repeating the process described above. You should now see two contacts listed in the Contacts sub-panel of the Raydoc Account Detail view screen. This is another important point. We have re-used all the basic account information in the main panel of the RayDoc account for a second contact. We did not have to type it in again. In addition, if any of the RayDoc account information changes, we will only have to edit the RayDoc account record, not the information we have about our contacts there. This is one of the key advantages of a CRM over a contact manager like Microsoft Outlook 2003—it understands that accounts and contacts are two separate types of information that are linked together, not crammed together into one unsatisfactory amalgam.

Linking and Searching

Again, to reinforce the speed and power of navigation in SugarCRM, browse to your own contact information. Then back to the Account Detail view. Then on to Doc's contact record. A contact can lead to an account, which can lead to other contacts at that account—all extremely quickly. Moreover, very relevant to your everyday work needs.

Go ahead now and explore by yourself the Contact List view. Notice that you can search for a specific contact in the Contact Search panel above the list of contacts. Click on the small highlighted Advanced link (under the Clear button) to get a more comprehensive search capability.

Contact List View with Advanced Search

After his installation had been completed, and he had been using the system for a few months, I asked Doc what he liked most about using his SugarCRM system, and his favorite feature was "*I can search contacts for the name of someone I've only met once or twice. I only know his or her first name, but that is OK—it can show me everyone with the same first name in the system right away. I pick the one I want from the list and link to his or her detail view, from which I can call him or her. If he or she is out, I link to his or her account detail view, and it shows me whom else we know in that company and I link to one of them and call them. I do this maybe fifty times a day, and so it makes a huge difference to me that I can do it so quickly and so naturally. I swear this system thinks the same way I do!*"

Now I know Doc fairly well, and this last point may not be the best recommendation for SugarCRM—but I know what he means!

The Sales Pipeline: Leads and Opportunities

Now that you have practiced putting accounts and contacts into the system, and linking contacts to accounts, let's go on to learn about a few more key types of information your CRM can organize for you.

Within just about all CRM systems, there exist the dual concepts of **Leads** and **Opportunities**. They are kept as separate items of information, even though they may sound very similar to each other. The generally accepted distinction between them is that a lead is a person's name, and company name, which have come to you in a way such that you cannot be certain they are interested in your products and services. An opportunity is what a lead becomes once you have been in touch with the person and confirmed that they do have a genuine and qualified interest in what your company has to offer (they have a real business problem, and the money to fix it, and you're talking to someone who has the power to do so).

In CRM terms, the process of selling goods and services to your customers comes down to a series of steps that look something like this:

1. Acquiring and tracking leads
2. Qualifying them as real opportunities
3. Quantifying these opportunities, and setting an expected closing date for them
4. Aggregating all opportunities together into a sales pipeline to see the big picture
5. Closing the opportunities as sales

By having an automated system that remembers all your leads, can convert them into opportunities once qualified, can add them all up to show a sales pipeline, and can accumulate a history of account activities, your business gains three big improvements.

1. You can now see how business is shaping up over the next couple of months in a more tangible and quantifiable way than ever before. The sales pipeline is your distant early warning system—it shows you when business levels are falling off, or growing faster than anticipated. In a smaller business, it is your best friend when it comes to business planning, giving you a more detailed and distant view into the future, helping you to make appropriate staffing and expenditure decisions.

2. All your sales leads, opportunities, and account history are now formally recorded in a central system that the business owns. Your vulnerability to threats and blackmail from sales personnel, or to the sudden defection of sales personnel, is much reduced. If a sales person leaves the organization, you still have all the leads and opportunities the business paid to develop, and the account history needed to help a new sales person take over the account quickly and effectively.

3. The sales person on an account is not the only person in the organization with access to details of activity history. Accounting and service personnel who have direct customer contact can now base their decisions about grey-area judgment calls in the account on hard information from the account history.

How did all of this work for Doc when he first came to grips with his new system? Our initial task was to find all his leads. Most of them were fairly dormant in the inboxes of the sales staff—something to do on a slow day if they felt like it.

So Doc had to round up all the sales people and *harvest* all these leads. On an ongoing basis, most leads came to the company (generally from suppliers that RayDoc partners with) and not the individual sales people, and so could be entered in the system by Kay, the receptionist, in her spare time and then assigned to a sales person, ensuring they would be tracked. Leads that came directly to a sales person would have to be entered by that sales person—and this would be a matter for training in the near future.

Once all the historical leads were gathered together, Kay typed them in for us. Now, let's type in one ourselves to get familiar with the process. Click on the **Leads** tab, and then on the **Create New Lead** shortcut on the left-hand side of the screen. Notice that there are shortcuts for importing leads in bulk, and for creating a lead from a **vCard** (an electronic business card, such as you may save from Outlook, or get beamed to you from a Palm organizer).

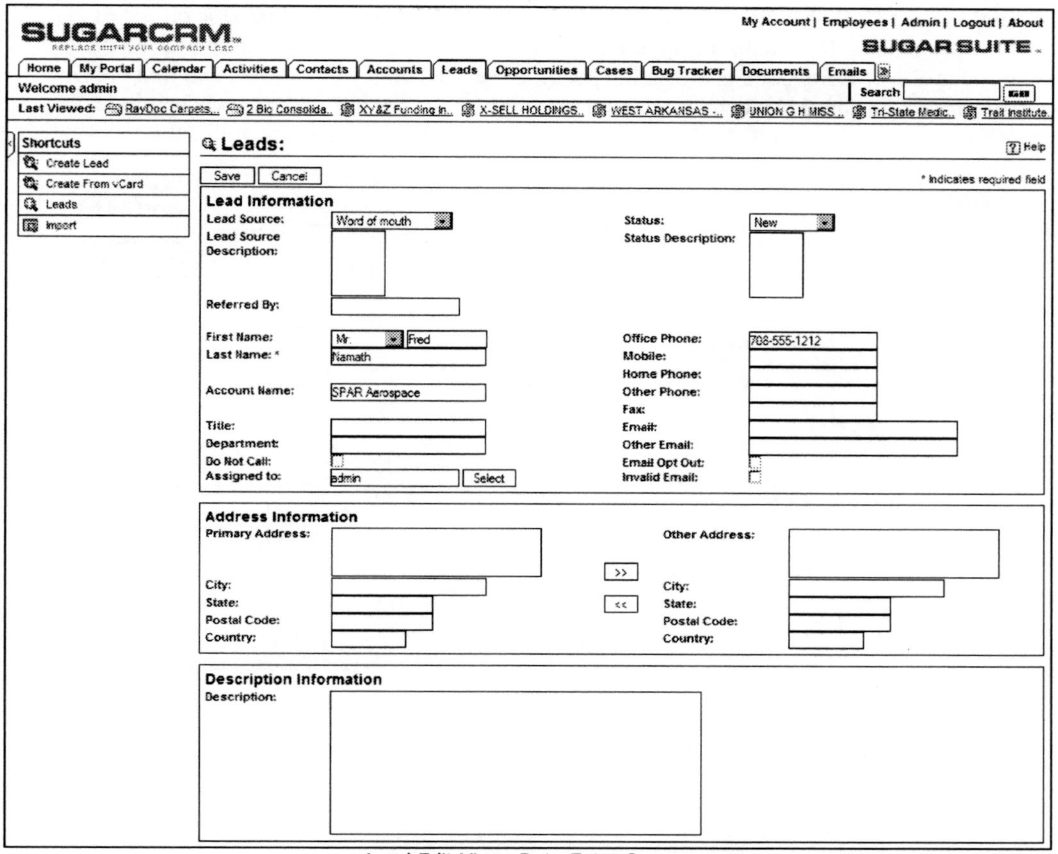

Lead Edit View: Data Entry Screen

Using the screen pictured above, enter the data for our new lead, and click on the Save button. You now see the Lead Detail view screen, with its main panel, and sub-panels for Open Activities and History. These sub-panels will let you track what your sales people are doing with the leads you pass on to them.

One key field on each lead is the status field. It is set to New when a lead is first entered, and then to Assigned when the lead is assigned to a particular sales person. It becomes Converted if the lead is converted into an opportunity. Another key field is the Lead Source. Between these two fields you can track what proportion of leads that you get are converted into opportunities (and/or sales) and how that proportion varies according to the source of the lead. Gaining empirical knowledge that identifies your most effective and successful lead sources is a key business enabler.

To continue our worked example of the lifecycle of a lead, let's imagine that Doc or one of his sales people calls up Mr. Namath from the lead overleaf, and after talking with him for a bit, decides that SPAR Aerospace is a genuine potential new account for RayDoc, and that the lead with Fred Namath should be converted to an opportunity. At the top of the Lead Detail view screen is a Convert Lead button. Click on it now, and you should see a screen like this:

Lead Conversion Screen

As you can see, converting the lead basically turns the lead into a contact, and optionally will also create an account, an opportunity, and even an appointment. In the Related Records sub-panel, check **Create Account** (it is checked by default), **Create Opportunity**, and **Create Appointment** if you want to generate those items of information as well. You can even create a note or attachment (an uploaded file, such as a Microsoft Word or Excel file) to be linked to the Account record.

Based on Doc's conversation with Fred, we have chosen to click on the Create Opportunity box, and enter data for an opportunity to sell some replacement windows. Note that you must put in an amount for the opportunity, and an expected close date. When you are done, click on the Save button to save all the new information records at once. You see a screen like this, which confirms the successful lead conversion:

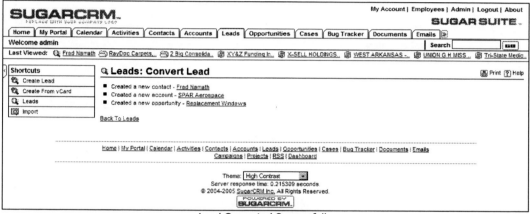

Lead Converted Successfully

Now click on the Accounts tab, and use the search panel to find the account record for SPAR Aerospace. Click on that record to view the detail screen, which should look like this (Note that we have collapsed a few sub-panels to shorten the image):

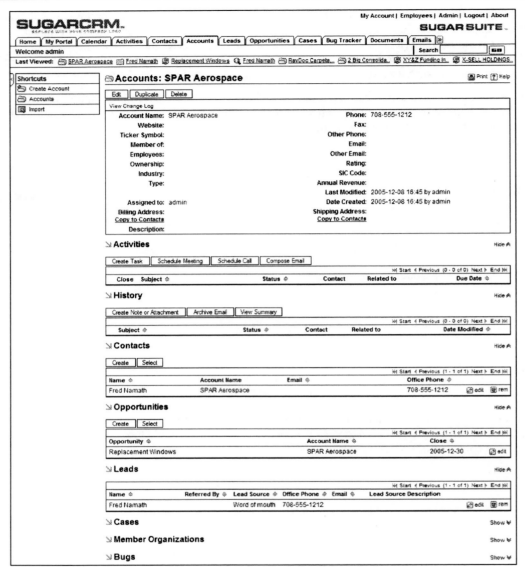

New Account, with Linked Contact and Opportunity

Notice that in addition to the original lead, we now have an account, plus a contact and an opportunity linked to that account. Again, just practice navigation a little. Click on the opportunity. The resulting screen shows the contact. Click on the contact. That screen shows the account. Click on the account. We are back where we started. This is the joy of CRM—everything is connected, and from one small item of information, you can link to volumes of account history, contact history, related contacts, and related opportunities or leads.

Aggregating Opportunities: The Sales Pipeline

Now that we have looked at creating accounts, contacts, and leads, and converting leads into contacts and opportunities and accounts, we have all of the capabilities we need to start assembling a sales pipeline. Now click on the Opportunities tab to see a list of all the opportunities in our demonstration RayDoc set of data. You should see a screen like this:

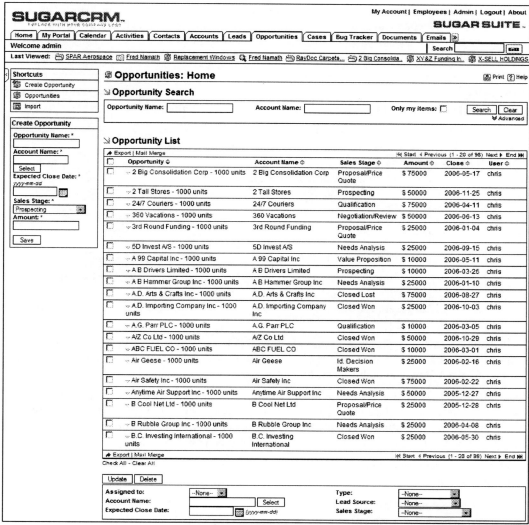

Opportunities List View

Clearly, being able to see all the opportunities we have identified for future business is very useful. But there are drawbacks. We can't see all of the opportunities on this screen—only 20 of the 98 in the system. We have to page back and forth to see them all. We also see an estimated value for each opportunity, an estimated close date for the business, and the sales stage to indicate where we are in the sales process for each opportunity, but we see no percentage probability of closing the sale, and no automatic totaling of the opportunities. We might also like to see a total of the opportunities weighted by the percentage probability of closing them—to gain a more realistic expectation of future sales.

First let's take a detailed look at an opportunity to understand what information is kept for an opportunity. We generated an opportunity in the last section, but without actually using the Opportunity Edit view screen. Click on the first opportunity listed to see an Opportunity Detail view screen, and then click on the Edit button to go to the Edit view. You should see a screen like this:

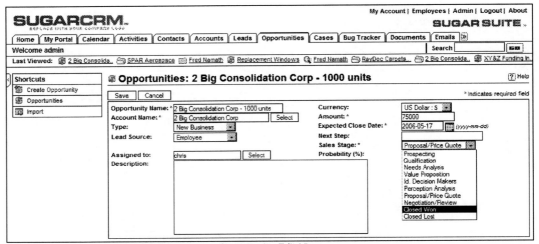

Opportunity Edit View

One key attribute of an opportunity is the sales stage. In the screen above you can see the drop-down box for sales stage with all the options visible. (These options can be customized if they do not match how you do business, of course.)

Other important information contained in an opportunity is the estimated close date for the business, the next step to close the business, the percentage probability of closing the business, the lead source for this opportunity, and the type of business (new or existing business). We are done with this Opportunity Edit view. Click on the Cancel button to exit the screen.

As useful as the Opportunities List view screen is, there are clearly a number of views and what-if questions not addressed by the list view screen that we would love to apply to our opportunity data:

- What is our best lead source?
- What is our total sales pipeline?
- How does it break down by month for estimated close dates?
- At which stage of the selling process do most of our opportunities come in?
- Who are the most successful sales people at the moment?

The Dashboard

To address the need to answer questions like this, high quality CRMs have a graphical dashboard that shows visual breakdowns of opportunity data, totaling them overall and sub-totaling by key indicators such as sales stage, lead source, and account representative.

You may have already seen one such graphical chart on the Home tab screen, but to see the complete set of charts, click on the Dashboard tab. You will see a screen like this:

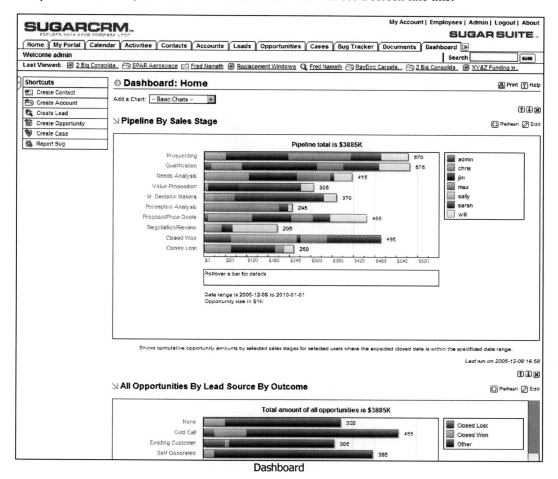

Dashboard

The four charts displayed are:

- **The Pipeline by Sales Stage chart**: This chart is the one repeated on the Home tab except that the one on your Home tab shows only your own opportunity data, not the entire organization's data. This chart is usually used by the owner of a small business, or the sales manager to gain an overall sense of the maturity of the sales pipeline. He or she can answer the question—"Is there enough future business to meet sales targets?" In addition, the stacked bar chart presentation gives a visual indication of which sales people have the greatest dollar value of opportunities, and if some of them have an undue proportion of their opportunities in the early stages. In Doc's case, he uses this chart to watch out for any sales person who may be bluffing about how much business he or she has coming in—as this normally shows up by a lot of opportunities, most of which are in the early sales stages.

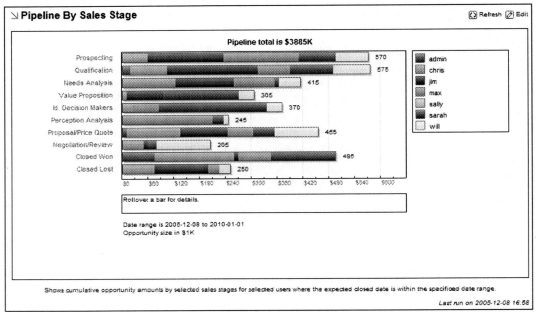

The Pipeline by Sales Stage chart

- **The Opportunities by Lead Source by Outcome chart**: This chart is handy for giving you a quick visual indicator of which lead sources are producing the greatest value of opportunities, and the color-coded stacked bars show you if some lead sources are especially good or bad at being converted into sales. It shows Doc if his money is better spent advertising replacement doors and windows in a home improvement magazine, or on the TV Guide channel in his local market.

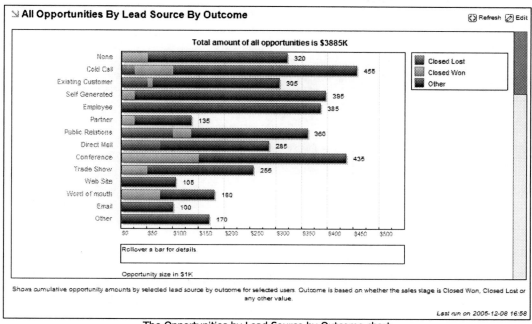

The Opportunities by Lead Source by Outcome chart

- **The Pipeline by Month by Outcome chart**: This chart shows how your next few months of sales are shaping up. The stacked bars break down the opportunities according to whether their sales stage is closed won, closed lost, or anything else (meaning the opportunity has its expected close date in the month shown, but it has still yet to close in favor of our business, or a competitor).

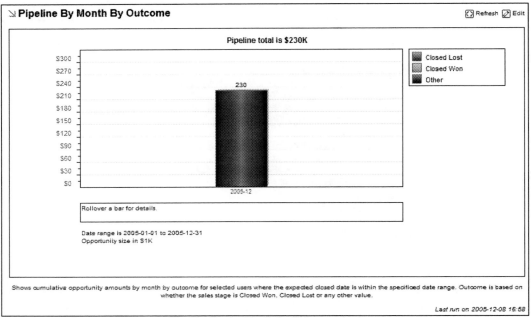

The Pipeline by Month by Outcome chart

- **The All Opportunities by Lead Source chart:** This chart provides a useful pie-chart visualization of all opportunities, breaking them down by lead source.

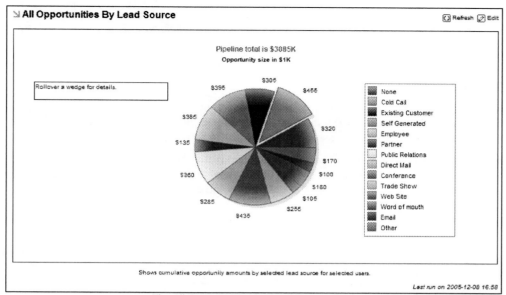

The All Opportunities by Lead Source chart

Each of these charts has an edit control at the top right that allows you to set a few filters on the data driving the chart. Opportunities shown on the charts can be limited to those from specific sales people, to opportunities due to close in specific time frames, or to those opportunities with specific sales stages, or from specific lead sources.

Each chart also provides you with the ability to mouse over areas of interest, to see more information. If on the first chart you roll your cursor over those leads in the prospecting stage, the area under the chart will show how many opportunities there are in this stage, and their total value.

Lastly, and most usefully, each chart offers a facility known as **drilldown**. If you roll your mouse cursor over the opportunities at the prospecting stage in the first chart again, and this time click on the bar in the chart that represents those opportunities, the system will bring up the Opportunities List screen, automatically filtered to show exactly those opportunities that are behind the chart's graphical representation of the data. While some people understand information more easily from a graphic, and some from numbers and text, this drilldown system would appear to represent the best of both worlds.

Taken together, these capabilities of the dashboard should significantly improve your ability to know what to expect in sales for the next few months, to understand what lead generation strategies are working most effectively for you, and to root out problems with sales people who may habitually overstate the value or probability of their sales pipeline or repeatedly fail to close business by forecast dates.

For the sales people themselves, this tool can act as a motivator to generate new opportunities, or to close business that is visibly lagging against its forecast dates, as well as a handy way to organize the information on their opportunities.

Calendaring

Being in business is a large series of small events—meetings, telephone calls, notes, emails, or reminders to revisit an issue in a few months. A very important aspect of any CRM is the ability to schedule these activities, and to associate them with the accounts and contacts they involve.

In SugarCRM, there is a full group calendaring system that is capable of scheduling all these activities and helping staff schedule meetings or telephone calls at times when people are free to attend them. It will also make a note of these meetings and calls in the calendars of all those invited to take part in them.

Click on the Calendar tab now, and you should see a screen like this:

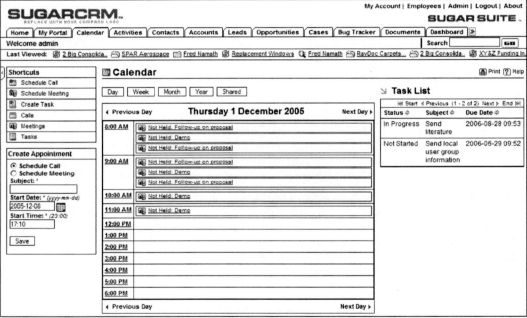

Calendar: Day View

This is the default view for the Calendar tab—the day view for today's date. As you can see, there are buttons to see views for the current week, month, or even year. In addition, within each of these views, there are nudge controls to go to the previous or next day, week, month, or year.

Take a moment right now to click on the week, month, and year buttons, to get familiar with the display layouts and the navigation buttons offered by the application. Notice that on each of these views, you can click on the number of any day to *zoom* to the day view for that date.

The day view, unlike the week, month, or year views, also shows a list of current tasks down the right-hand side of the screen. These tasks are specific to the user currently logged in, as are the activities shown on the calendar.

To see how the calendar works, let us make ourselves an appointment for tomorrow at 11AM with Rachel Barnes of 360 Vacations to discuss their plans for renovations. From the current screen, click on the Next Day link. When you see the activities for that date, click on the 11:00 AM link on the left-hand side of the calendar display, and you will see a little pop-up box that lets you quickly schedule a call or meeting. Choose the radio button for Meeting, enter a subject for the meeting, and click on Save.

You now can see the detail screen for the meeting, which should look something like this:

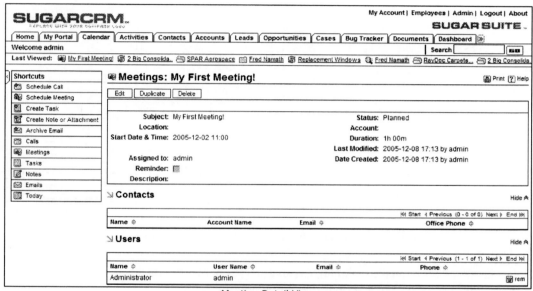

Meeting Detail View

To invite more attendees—either employees from your company (defined as *users* within the CRM system) or customers (from contact data within the CRM)—click on the Edit button, and go down to the Add Invitees area at the bottom of the screen. In this case, type Rachel into the first name box, and click on the Search button. Your screen should look like:

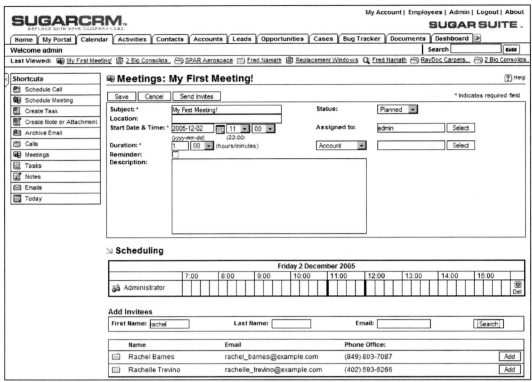

Adding Invitees

Now just click on the Add button to the right of Rachel Barnes' name to add her to the list of invitees for the meeting.

Note that the small icon to the left of both Rachel and Rachelle tells you that they are contacts. Users would have the type of icon shown for the administrator.

While in the Edit view for the meeting, you can also add more details to the record of the meeting that were not available on the little pop-up box when you created the meeting. You can specify an account related to the meeting, tune the duration of the meeting (it is set by default to an hour), enter a location for the meeting, and add people to or delete people from the list of invitees.

To illustrate some of these capabilities, let us set the meeting duration to 90 minutes, and let's invite Selena Gould from 360 Vacations, while noting that this meeting concerns the 360 Vacations account. When you are done, your Meeting Detail view should look like this:

Meeting with New Invitees, Duration, and Account

Again, the power of the CRM to connect all your customer information together comes into play here. Click on the link 360 Vacations. You see the detail screen for that account, with a number of open activities, including the meeting you have just added. On that activity, it shows Rachel Barnes as a contact. Click on the link to her detail view, and you will see the new meeting also listed among her open activities. Now click on the subject of that meeting, and you return to the detail view for the meeting.

This gives you an initial overview of the calendaring capabilities within SugarCRM. In the next section we will learn more about the various activities that users of the system can create and track—and we will learn more about the calendar then as well.

Sales Activities

While we learned about the calendar in the previous section, we also learned something about the activities that may be defined and tracked within SugarCRM. The five different types of activities are **Meetings**, **Calls**, **Tasks**, **Notes**, and **Emails**. Let us now look at these activities in more detail.

All five kinds of activities may be created and viewed within the Activities tab of the SugarCRM system. Click on the Activities tab now, and have a close look at the list of shortcuts available within this module. There are shortcuts to go to the list view for each of the five kinds of activities, or to create an activity of any kind except an email (for which you must go to the Emails tab). The Calls List view is the default screen you see when entering the Activities tab—and that is an example of something you might do differently for your business. Perhaps most of your employees would prefer to see a list of meetings or tasks as the initial screen.

The email activities are something of a special case within SugarCRM, as they have their own tab in addition to their presence within the activities tab. You will notice that when you click on any of the email-related shortcuts, the Emails tab lights up to show that you are in the emails module.

In a somewhat similar fashion, you will notice that if you click on any of the call-related or meeting-related shortcuts, the Calendar tab lights up to indicate that you are now within the Calendar module. So in effect, only tasks and notes are contained completely within the activities module.

Activities are important within a CRM for two different reasons. Firstly, they are important to help everyone schedule their activities, and remind them of when they are coming up. The Home tab makes a point of highlighting My Upcoming Appointments, and My Open Tasks, to remind users when they log in of impending activities. Secondly, it is very important that each user's activities be scheduled within the CRM (as opposed to Outlook or the like), as when the activities have been completed, they still perform a very useful function by adding to the activity history for contacts and accounts. This activity history is vital to assist sales managers and general managers, as well as any sales personnel who inherit accounts from a previous sales person, in gaining a quick and comprehensive understanding of the status of an account.

Let us look at the activities for 360 Vacations in a little more detail. Click on the last viewed entry for this account to get you there quickly—or click on the Account tab and then look them up. The top part of the screen should resemble this:

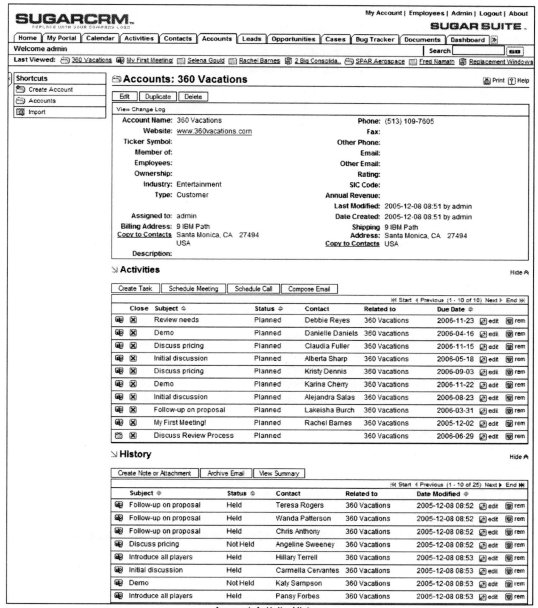

Account Activity History

Each activity has a small icon to the left showing whether it is a meeting, call, note, email, or task. In the Activities sub-panel, you will only see meetings, calls, and tasks. Emails and notes, as well as closed meetings, calls, and tasks, are all listed under the History sub-panel.

We see our upcoming meeting listed in open activities, with Rachel Barnes linked to it, and a status showing Planned. To illustrate how account history works, let us pretend we have held that meeting, and click on the close box for that meeting—shown as an X. You get a chance to add any notes you might like to the record of the meeting, and then click on Save. Now the meeting is shown under the History sub-panel, with a Held Status.

Once your CRM has been in operation for a few months, with everyone in the company scheduling their activities in the system and gradually accumulating activity history for all accounts, your business will have acquired a remarkably valuable resource it has never had. Namely, a history for every account and contact that is searchable at any time of the day from any PC in the world, and will not go away when the sales person concerned leaves the firm.

Creating a Note

Let us explore some more types of activities, starting with notes.

Imagine that when we met with 360 Vacations they discussed a significant renovation of their premises—including new doors, windows, and carpets. Rachel Barnes actually went through a PowerPoint slide show of the renovations that had artists' drawings of the resulting building, and a breakdown of the numbers and sizes of new doors and windows, and square footage of the new carpets needed.

To make sure that anyone who is in contact with this account has access to this detailed information, let us make a note on the detail view of this account, and attach the PowerPoint slide show. In the History sub-panel, click on the Create Note or Attachment button. The Account Name is pre-filled. Select the contact, enter a subject for the note, and some documentation in the Note field for people reading the note, and then click on the Browse button to select a file to upload as an attachment to the note. Once you have selected a file, click on the Save button. The file will be uploaded, and the note will be saved, producing a screen that resembles this one:

Note with Attachment

Using the Last Viewed link, go back to the history sub-panel of the 360 Vacations detail view, and you can see the new note now included as part of the account history. Notice the little paperclip that indicates an attached file.

Creating a Task

Now that we have had a meeting, and added notes to the account history, we really need to assign ourselves a task to prepare a quotation for Rachel at 360 Vacations. From the Account Detail screen, go to the Activities sub-panel and click on the Create Task button. You will see the Task Edit view, which looks like this:

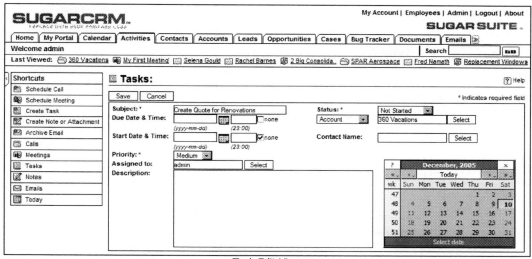

Task Edit View

As shown above, type in a Subject, then select a Due Date & Time by clicking off the None checkbox at the end of the due date, and then selecting a date using the calendar pop-up. Within the calendar pop-up, you can move forward or backward through the calendar by month or year with the controls provided, and then click on the day you want, in order to select it.

You can also set the Priority of the task, assign it a Status (Not Started, In Progress, Completed, Pending Input, or Deferred), and enter a Description for the task.

Press the Save button once you are done and, you are back on the Account Detail view for 360 Vacations, with a new task in the Activities sub-panel. Now click on the Home tab, and you should see this task listed in your My Open Tasks area. As well, if you go to the Activities tab, and click on Tasks in the shortcut bar, you should see all your tasks listed out, including this one.

Scheduling a Call or Meeting

A few days pass, and Doc completes his proposal for Rachel before the due date he set himself. He then marks the task as completed, and wants to email the proposal to Rachel, and then call Rachel to talk about it. He emails the proposal to Rachel (see the section on managing emails coming up next), asking her when would be a good time for a call. She mails back with a time and date, and Ray needs to book that call into his calendar. He clicks on the Activities tab, and then on the Schedule Call shortcut. He is presented with a screen like this:

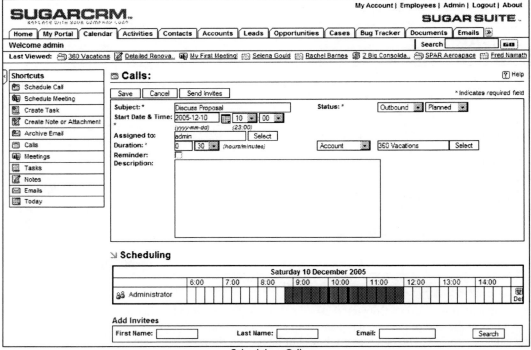

Schedule a Call

He starts entering the call by typing in a Subject, and then setting a Date (using the calendar pop-up) and Time, and selecting an Account. Then he looks lower down on the screen, and realizes he has a problem. The start and stop time for his phone call are marked on the timeline of his day with a dark colored block. Unfortunately, there is a blue segment of his day marking a pre-existing commitment, and this call is on top of it. In this case, he emails Rachel and asks her if a little later at 13:00 the same day would work for her.

Your CRM lets you book calls and meetings that involve multiple employees and customer contacts by adding their names as Invitees at the bottom of the screen. Enter their first or last name, look them up, and add them to the call or meeting. To avoid scheduling conflicts, all employees have their free/busy status displayed in the same way Doc's was displayed.

What is the point of adding customers as invitees, if you cannot see their calendar of commitments? Because the Send Invites button at the top of the screen lets you automatically email all attendees (employees or external contacts) so they know about the meeting and can accept it or reject it. As well, any employee invited to calls or meetings will see these activities scheduled on their home tab, where they have controls to accept them, accept them tentatively, or decline them.

The following information is included in the email an invitee receives when the Send Invites button is used:

- Who has issued the invite?
- Is it for a meeting or a call?
- What is the subject of the meeting or call? (In this case it would show as SugarCRM Call—Discuss Proposal)
- What is the status of the meeting or call?
- When does it start, and what is the duration?

Three links are provided, to enable the recipient of the email to accept, tentatively accept, or decline the invitation.

Note that at the time of writing the mechanism of accepting (or not) an invitation is not functional. SugarCRM intends to correct this shortcoming in a future release.

Managing Emails

In the last section, when Doc needed to email Rachel with the proposal, he was able to do the whole thing within SugarCRM. This is because SugarCRM includes its own ability to send outgoing emails, and then automatically link those emails to the account and contact records they involve.

Let us go over how Doc would have sent his email. If it is still visible, click on the Last Viewed link to the 360 Vacations Account Detail view, or look up the account from within the Accounts tab.

Within the Activities sub-panel for that account, locate the Compose Email button, and click on it. You will see the Compose Email screen, which, when completed by Doc would have looked much like this:

Compose Email

Notice that Doc has used the Browse button to attach the proposal to the email. When he clicked on the Select button to choose whom to send it to, a short list of contacts at 360 Vacations popped up for Doc to choose.

When Doc clicks on the Send button to send this email to Rachel, he will get a confirmation that the message has been sent. He can then link back to the 360 Vacations Account Detail record, and see that the email is now included in the History sub-panel for the account for the reference of anyone else at RayDoc who comes into contact with people from that account.

As ever, the email activity is listed in the History sub-panel along with its related contact and account—making it easy to quickly navigate between the email, the related account and contact, and any other items of information that are in turn related to that contact or account.

Let us learn a little more about the email capabilities of SugarCRM. Click on the Emails tab, and then the All Emails shortcut within that module and you will see the list view screen for emails as shown below:

Emails List View

In the list of emails, observe that each email is assigned a type—Draft, Archived, or Sent. Examine the shortcuts list closely—notice that you can compose an email, use All Drafts to see a list of only draft emails, choose All Emails to see the full Email List view, choose Email Templates to see a list of available email templates, create a new email template, or create an archived email.

Within the Compose Email screen, as you can see a couple of pages back, you can compose an email and save it for now, without sending it. You use the Save Draft button at the top of the Compose Email screen to do that. Once you have saved a draft email, it can be displayed with all other draft emails by clicking on the My Drafts shortcut. To send the draft email, click on its subject from the list view screen, and when on the detail view screen, click on the Send button at the top of the screen.

It is now clear what the Draft and Sent types of email are, but what is an Archived email? This is an email that you have received in your regular email reader, and want to file in the CRM system as part of account or contact history.

To file an archived email, copy the text of the email from your email reader, and then click on Create Archived Email. You then select the To: and CC: recipients, type in the subject, paste in the main body of the email that you had copied, choose what Account, Bug, Opportunity, Case, Lead, Project, or Project Task to relate to the email, and click on the Save button.

With the introduction of Sugar Open Source 4.0, a group of shortcuts was added that deals with your personal SugarCRM email inbox, your sent email, your draft emails, and your group inbox. Your **Group Inbox** allows you to belong to a group of users (such as a technical support group, a sales territory group, or an inside sales group) that jointly subscribe to a company email box (such as info@company.com, or support@company.com) and can move email between the group box and their personal email box, as well as other useful workflow functions. The system administrator creates and defines subscription to group email inboxes.

Email Templates

Email templates are referenced when composing an email (notice the Use Templates field on the Compose Email screen above). When you create an email template, you can insert variable placeholders for information such as first Name, Last Name, Address, or Email. The saved template can then be applied, and the variable placeholders filled with real data, when composing an email for one or more individuals, or in an emailing campaign for bulk marketing (dealt with later in this book).

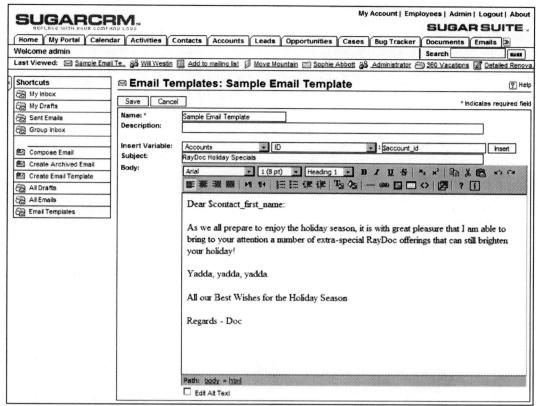

Email Template

Advanced User Interface Features

Before we leave this introductory chapter, we need to address some important SugarCRM user-interface features.

Printing Information

Most of the list view and detail view screens in the CRM have a print icon in the top right of the main body of the screen. Click on this icon to change the screen content to a more printer-friendly version of the same information, and then use the browser print button. The following image shows an Account List view screen transformed for printing:

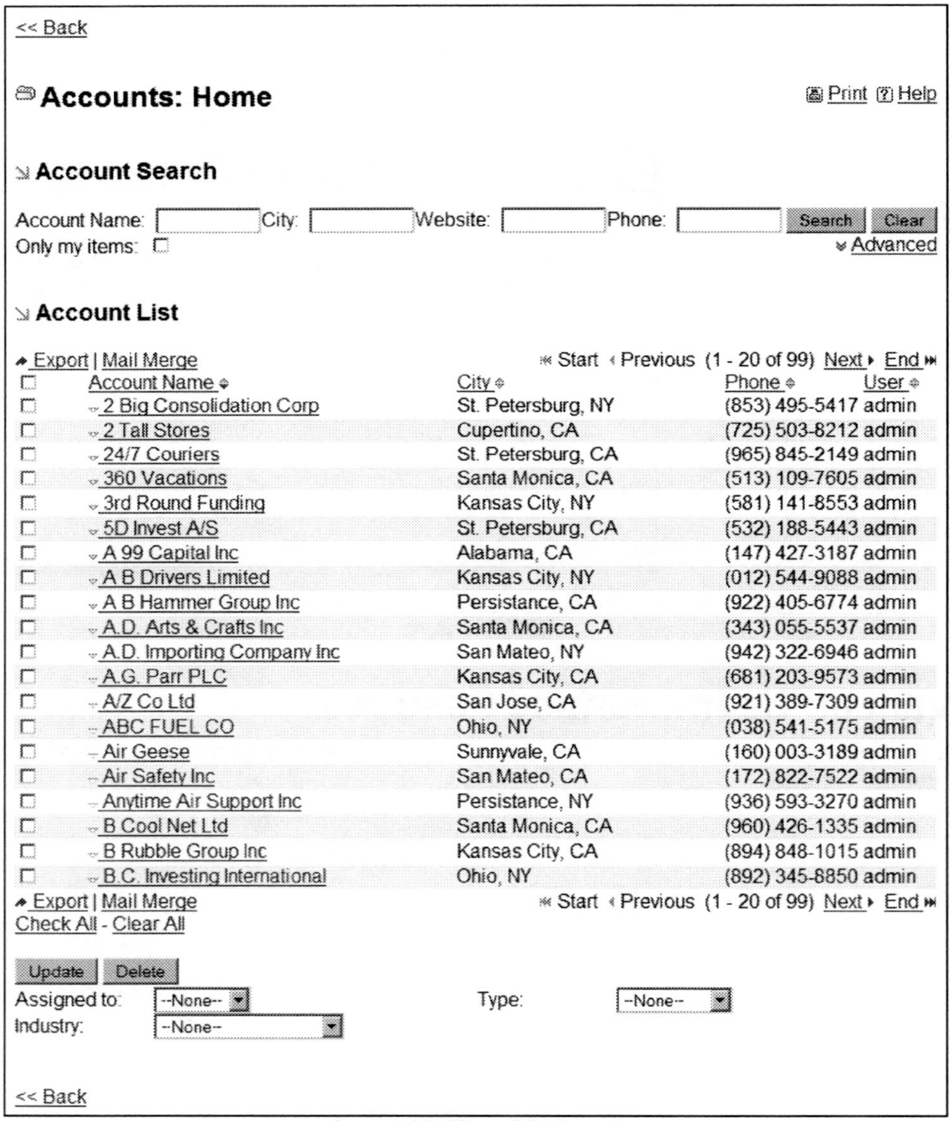

Account List View: Print Layout

Getting Help

As with the Print icon, most SugarCRM list and detail view screens contain a Help icon in the top right of the main screen body. Click on the help icon to see this screen:

 Documentation

All you need to know about configuring and using Sugar Open Source.

Sugar Open Source v3.5 User Guide (2.65 MB PDF)
Sugar Open Source v3.5 User Guide (4.57 MB DOC)
Previous Versions >>

Sugar Open Source Installation Guide (67 KB DOC)
Sugar Open Source Installation Guide (71 KB PDF)

 Sugar Plug-in for Outlook

Download the demo version of the Sugar Plug-In for Outlook to learn how Microsoft Outlook integrates with Sugar Open Source. Click here for configuration instructions.

Sugar Plug-in for Outlook Demo (701 KB ZIP)

 Free Themes

Personalize SugarCRM based on taste, mood or whim. Change themes when you please.

Fudge Theme (Posted: 10/27/2005)
Sugar Golden Gate Theme (Posted: 09/15/2005)
Sunset Theme (Posted: 06/16/2005)
CallRooM: Clean, Business Themes (Posted: 05/28/2005)
Sugar Pipeline Themes (Posted: 05/27/2005)
TrueBlue Skin (Posted: 04/20/2005)

Help Screen

It is not really a normal help screen, but from this screen, you can link to many different documentation resources that can help resolve your questions or concerns.

Exporting Information

Essentially all list view screens within SugarCRM have a highlighted Export link at the top left and bottom left corners of the list of entries. (Note that not only the displayed items, but also the currently selected list are exported. You might have 200 accounts, with 35 selected because they are in the same state and with only 20 of those 35 shown on the current screen. Export will export 35 account records in this case.)

Use the Export link to export your account information to a **Comma Separated Values (CSV)** format file (which may be easily read by Microsoft Excel). Try it—and open the exported file from your desktop using Excel to see what is in it. Here is a sample:

id	date entered	date modified	mod	as	name	par	account_type	industry	amp	pho	billing_address_street	billing_address_city	billing_address_state
874fd	01/12/2004 20:00	01/12/2004 20:00		1	Otc Bb		Customer	Government			9 IBM Path	St. Petersburg	CA
89ee4	01/12/2004 20:00	01/12/2004 20:00		1	2M Invest A/S		Customer	Not For Profit			777 West Filmore	Santa Monica	NY
8ba6f	01/12/2004 20:00	01/12/2004 20:00		1	A 77 Capital Inc		Customer	Education			345 Sugar Blvd.	Santa Monica	CA
8d5ef	01/12/2004 20:00	01/12/2004 20:00		1	Absa Group Limited		Customer	Education			999 Baker Way	Los Angeles	CA
8f274	01/12/2004 20:00	01/12/2004 20:00		1	Ab Watley Group Inc		Customer	Telecommunications			111 Silicon Valley Road	San Francisco	NY
90e1f	01/12/2004 20:00	01/12/2004 20:00		1	Ag Media Group Inc		Customer	Engineering			123 Anywhere Street	Cupertino	CA
92c5	01/12/2004 20:00	01/12/2004 20:00		1	Aits Inc		Customer	Manufacturing			9 IBM Path	Salt Lake City	CA
9a78	01/12/2004 20:00	01/12/2004 20:00		1	Ail Intech		Customer	Banking			123 Anywhere Street	Persistance	NY
9626	01/12/2004 20:00	01/12/2004 20:00		1	Ami Resources Inc		Customer	Energy			345 Sugar Blvd.	Alabama	CA
97ed	01/12/2004 20:00	01/12/2004 20:00		1	Ams Marketing		Customer	Shipping			48920 San Carlos	Alabama	NY
999e-	01/12/2004 20:00	01/12/2004 20:00		1	A Novo Broadband Inc		Customer	Chemicals			48920 San Carlos	Cupertino	NY
9b4a	01/12/2004 20:00	01/12/2004 20:00		1	Aoi Coal Co		Customer	Machinery			9 IBM Path	Cupertino	CA
9cf6	01/12/2004 20:00	01/12/2004 20:00		1	Art International Inc		Customer	Shipping			321 University Ave.	Sunnyvale	CA
9aa5f	01/12/2004 20:00	01/12/2004 20:00		1	A&D Co Ltd		Customer	Media			48920 San Carlos	Sunnyvale	NY
a055	01/12/2004 20:00	01/12/2004 20:00		1	A&E Capital Funding Inc		Customer	Not For Profit			48920 San Carlos	San Mateo	CA
a204	01/12/2004 20:00	01/12/2004 20:00		1	A-Com Ab		Customer	Telecommunications			67321 West Siam St	Ohio	CA
a3ce	01/12/2004 20:00	01/12/2004 20:00		1	A-Fern Medical Corp		Customer	Hospitality			345 Sugar Blvd	Santa Monica	NY
a67f3	01/12/2004 20:00	01/12/2004 20:00		1	A-Max Holdings Ltd		Customer	Shipping			1715 Scott Dr	Santa Monica	CA
a73b	01/12/2004 20:00	01/12/2004 20:00		1	A-S China Plumbing Products		Customer	Shipping			777 West Filmore	San Mateo	CA
a8f28	01/12/2004 20:00	01/12/2004 20:00		1	A. Schulman Inc		Customer	Utilities			111 Silicon Valley Road	San Jose	NY
aa9e	01/12/2004 20:00	01/12/2004 20:00		1	A.A Importing Company Inc		Customer	Machinery			48920 San Carlos	Sunnyvale	CA
ac55	01/12/2004 20:00	01/12/2004 20:00		1	A.C. Moore Arts & Crafts Inc		Customer	Utilities			123 Anywhere Street	San Mateo	CA
ae03	01/12/2004 20:00	01/12/2004 20:00		1	A.C.L.N Ltd		Customer	Government			321 University Ave.	Santa Fe	NY
afcbc	01/12/2004 20:00	01/12/2004 20:00		1	A.D.A.M Inc		Customer	Utilities			777 West Filmore	St Petersburg	CA
b177	01/12/2004 20:00	01/12/2004 20:00		1	A.G. Barr Plc		Customer	Chemicals			345 Sugar Blvd	Denver	CA
b349	01/12/2004 20:00	01/12/2004 20:00		1	A.G. Edwards Inc		Customer				123 Anywhere Street	Ohio	NY
b4f8c	01/12/2004 20:00	01/12/2004 20:00		1	A.G.D. Mining Ltd		Customer	Communications			123 Anywhere Street	San Francisco	CA
b6ed	01/12/2004 20:00	01/12/2004 20:00		1	A.J. Ross Logistics Inc		Customer	Food & Beverage			999 Baker Way	Los Angeles	CA
b89a	01/12/2004 20:00	01/12/2004 20:00		1	A.M. Castle & Co		Customer				1715 Scott Dr	San Francisco	NY
ba4b	01/12/2004 20:00	01/12/2004 20:00		1	A.O. Smith Corp		Customer	Entertainment			67321 West Siam St.	St Petersburg	CA
bc17	01/12/2004 20:00	01/12/2004 20:00		1	A.O.G. Air Support Inc		Customer	Biotechnology			9 IBM Path	St Petersburg	CA
bdcf5	01/12/2004 20:00	01/12/2004 20:00		1	A.T. Cross Co		Customer	Communications			123 Anywhere Street	San Mateo	NY
bf95	01/12/2004 20:00	01/12/2004 20:00		1	A.T.&E Corp		Customer	Utilities			9 IBM Path	Los Angeles	CA
c159	01/12/2004 20:00	01/12/2004 20:00		1	Abitibi-Consolidated Inc		Customer	Shipping			777 West Filmore	Cupertino	CA
c32b	01/12/2004 20:00	01/12/2004 20:00		1	Aes Gener S A		Customer	Apparel			345 Sugar Blvd.	San Jose	NY

Exported account data in Excel

Updating Several Records at Once

Each list view screen in SugarCRM has a feature that involves a checkbox at the left of each item in the list, and Update and Delete buttons (often accompanied by several fields) below the list.

- The checkboxes are used to select entries in the list, and the buttons and fields at the bottom of the screen (often referred to as the **Mass Update** panel) are to enable you to either delete multiple entries at once, or to update multiple entries at once.

- If we use the Account List view screen as an example, multiple accounts could be reassigned to another user, or assigned a new industry classification or type. Simply select a new account type, such as Customer, select several accounts via their checkboxes, and then click on the Update button.

- Note that if the list has multiple pages of entries, only entries from the current page may be checked—once you navigate to the next page of entries, any checks on the previous page are forgotten.

Input Business Card

One of the best-kept secrets in SugarCRM is the Enter Business Card shortcut. It is available on the Home tab, and on the Contacts tab. This feature allows users to enter a new contact, but as seen below, also provides the option to create a new account, opportunity, and follow-up meeting, all in the same screen.

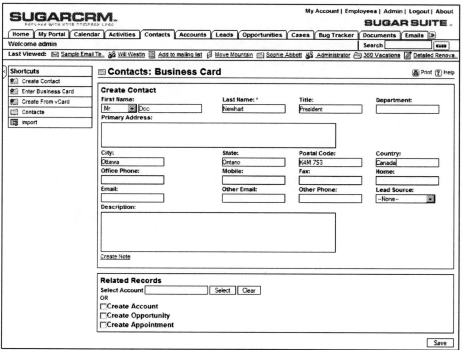

Enter Business Card

Create from vCard

On the Contacts tab is a shortcut called Create from vCard. This feature lets you create a contact very quickly if you already have a vCard from your contact. Many people these days have taken to attaching a vCard with their emails, so this can be a really quick and handy form of data entry for new contacts.

If you have the vCard for a new contact on your desktop, for example, just click on the Create from vCard shortcut, and you will see the screen shown below. Then click on the Browse button, and from the pop-up file finder dialog box that comes up, find the vCard you want and select it. Then you arrive back at the SugarCRM screen—click on the Import vCard button, and voilà! You are done.

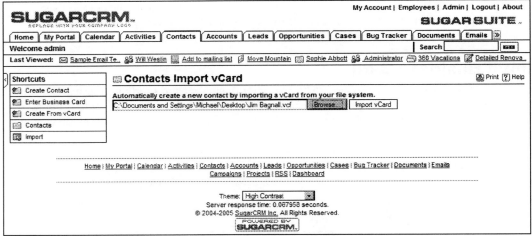

Import Contact from vCard

Quick New Item

Just about every tab in SugarCRM has a Quick New Item box on the lower left side. This box will vary according to the module or tab you are in, in order to create a new item of the type appropriate to the tab, for instance, New Contact, New Account, New Opportunity, and so on.

It does not have all the fields possible to include in the new item, but all the mandatory fields are there, allowing you to quickly add a new item of information. A bit like a handy sticky note—it is there when you need it, and it keeps track of the new information so you don't lose it.

Summary

In this chapter, we covered the basics of using a CRM—entering information into the system, and navigating quickly through the linkages between related items of information. Some of the key topics dealt with included:

- How to access the CRM. How to use different themes to brighten up the user interface, and the major components of the screen layout.
- How to navigate the CRM, use the different module tabs, and the list, detail, and edit view screens for each module.
- How to enter accounts and contacts, and the linkages between them.
- What the structure of a main panel and related sub-panels of information on each detail view screen looks like.
- How Leads become Opportunities, and Opportunities are aggregated to form the sales pipeline.
- How Dashboard helps you visually interpret your sales pipeline, breaks it down by month and by sales person, and provides a distant early warning system for business upturns and downturns.
- How to use the SugarCRM calendar to plan your business days, check for schedule conflicts, and consult your colleagues' calendars.
- How to enter business activities within SugarCRM, and the value of accumulating activity history for all your accounts and contacts.
- A number of special user-interface features designed to speed data entry and ease the execution of several common tasks.

In the next chapter, we will erase the sample data in the CRM, import your own data, and then explore a number of the more advanced ways in which CRMs can assume a broader role within your business.

5
Extending Your CRM's Business Role

In the last chapter, we introduced the CRM basics of accounts, contacts, leads, opportunities, and the sales pipeline—as well as group calendaring of activities including meetings, calls, and tasks.

In this chapter, we deal with the expansion of the role of your CRM system within your business beyond that of basic CRM functions. We will cover a number of other related applications that are commonly found in better CRM systems. These applications are frequently added to a CRM system to take advantage of the fact that the CRM system is in use by most people at a company and already contains all the information there is to know about the business's customers, partners, and suppliers.

These advanced CRM topics include:

- **Marketing campaigns**: Creating and running email marketing campaigns.
- **Document management**: Filing version-controlled documents in a repository of operational, sales, and administrative reference material.
- **Project management**: Tracking what projects are active, who is working on them, what tasks they involve, and how they are performing.
- **Customer service management**: Tracking services cases and software bugs by account, creating an account service history.
- **Email reminders**: As a part of the overall system workflow and function, automated email reminders may be sent to users when tasks are assigned to them.
- **Employee directory**: A handy list of all employees, with their contact information, job title, department, etc.
- **Interface consolidation**: Adding commonly needed but potentially unrelated capabilities into the CRM to create a single system that employees will want to remain connected to all day—a virtual focal point for your business. Capabilities such as an RSS News Reader and My Portal (Linking to External Sites) are discussed in this chapter.
- **Assessing Changes**: Assessing the changes you need to make to your CRM to make it a better fit for your business.
- **Tuning your current CRM implementation**: Using the Sugar Studio to define new fields, alter screen layouts, define new options on drop-down lists (and indeed, whole new drop-down lists), and altering what tabs within the system are seen by each user.

We will also go through the process of removing the sample data from your CRM installation, and importing your own account and contact data.

In Chapter 6, we will complete our exploration of the capabilities of the SugarCRM software family by working through a number of business scenarios using the extended features provided by Sugar Pro (the commercial version of SugarCRM) as well as features of other SugarCRM commercial and open-source add-on modules.

Importing your Data

To start off this chapter, let's first get rid of the sample data in your SugarCRM installation. Throughout this chapter, we will be showing a number of worked examples of entering data into the system, and using data already in the system. However, it is time you start working with your own data in the CRM. So, while we will show examples of Doc working with his data in the system, you should be working with your own data so that activities meaningful to your own business are taking shape in the system.

The first step is to re-install SugarCRM without the sample data. Then you will need to import your own data into the system.

Depending on which operating system you have chosen for your SugarCRM server—Windows or Linux—refer now to Appendix A or Appendix B, which deal with the mechanics of installing SugarCRM.

In Appendix A, for Linux, refer to the *Install SugarCRM* section and start at step 6, where you run `install.php`. You will have to refer to the section entitled *Re-running the Installation* to re-enable the ability to run the installer.

For Windows Server installations, refer to Appendix B. You will need to re-enable the ability to run the installer. Refer to the section on Re-running the Installation.

In either case, once the installer has been re-enabled, rerun the installation, but this time in the database configuration step do not check Create Database or Create User, do check Drop and Re-create Existing SugarCRM Tables, and do not check Populate Database with Demo Data. The fields for Database Name, User Name for SugarCRM, and Password for SugarCRM should all fill in automatically. Then just carry on with the installation until you complete all the steps. Then you can proceed to log back into SugarCRM—this time with no data.

Now read through Appendix C, and import your account data, and then your contact data, into the SugarCRM system. The appendix also gives you instructions for exporting your account and contact data from your current contact manager (using Microsoft Outlook as an example), to feed the process of importing that data into SugarCRM.

If you like, you can also import leads and opportunities into SugarCRM from Salesforce.com, or from a custom comma- or tab-delimited file.

Once you have imported your own account and contact data, feel free to start adding in opportunities as well, so that the dashboard begins to reflect the true state of your business.

Marketing Campaigns

So far, we have seen how a CRM like SugarCRM can be useful at managing customer-related information and history, as well as tracking opportunities and a sales pipeline. Now, let's begin to explore how effective it can be to broaden the scope of a CRM—applying the detailed customer knowledge to tasks other than those within a narrowly defined CRM, and integrating other high-traffic applications to create an organizational nexus. Let's start with email marketing.

A particularly powerful and potentially very profitable aspect of a CRM is the ability to conduct email marketing campaigns. At first sight, I suppose we should not be at all surprised at the idea of an email marketing campaign being developed in a CRM. After all, the CRM keeps track of leads and contacts, and has access to sending email. Let's study an email marketing campaign in detail, and see if it really is such a natural fit for a CRM.

To illustrate how a marketing campaign is developed, managed, performed, and then tracked for success, we will develop a sample marketing campaign for RayDoc. While you follow the example in this book, you may wish to develop one for your own business in parallel.

Targets versus Leads and Contacts

To start, we need to understand a little new terminology. A new type of information is involved in creating a marketing campaign—the **Target**. Here's a quick overview of targets, and how they relate to leads and contacts.

- Targets feed into a marketing campaign. Targets can come from rented lists, web registration forms, trade shows, your leads, or your contacts. You may or may not have an existing business relationship with the person. Let's say you create a campaign called *My July Email Campaign* and email a newsletter to a list of 12,000 targets—comprising 10,000 email addresses you purchase as well as 2,000 existing customers who meet your target criteria.

- Leads are the result of a campaign. They are people who respond to a campaign, but are not necessarily somebody you are selling to yet. A campaign can be an *on-going* inbound campaign like your standard website registration form. Alternatively, the campaign could be an outbound email campaign. Let's say you get 200 people who follow the link to the special website registration form for your *My July Email Campaign*, and complete and submit the form. These 200 people who just registered are now leads inside of Sugar with a lead source of the *My July Email Campaign* you initiated out of Sugar.

- Now you start a lead qualification process by analyzing the information you collected about these leads. You find that 50 of these leads fit your target qualification criteria. You now assign these 50 leads to the appropriate sales people.

- The sales people attempt to contact the leads and initiate a selling process. Let's say Doc speaks to one of these leads and the lead expresses an interest in learning more about the product. Doc will now convert this lead into a contact and create an opportunity.

To summarize, targets feed into campaigns, leads are the results of campaigns, and contacts are qualified leads that are interested in buying or have bought. Then leads, contacts, or any other list of names become the input material for you to assemble the target list for your next campaign.

Now that you understand the theory, let's get some practice. Click on the Campaigns tab—you should see something like this:

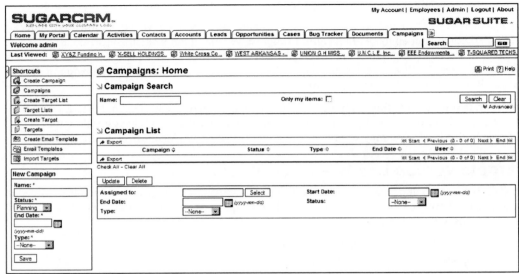

The Campaigns Screen

In SugarCRM, you create a marketing campaign to manage an outbound email campaign, and the targets that you create and assign to that campaign. You can add targets to the target list for a campaign either by selecting them from contacts or leads, or by importing them in bulk from either Comma Separated Values (CSV) or Tab Separated Values (TSV) files.

Let's start by creating a campaign for RayDoc.

Doc has just started to get supply of a new type of laminate wood flooring called Superflor that he is excited about. It has an excellent look and manufacturing quality to it, comes from one of his key suppliers, and he gets it at a very competitive price. He wants to get word out on it, and get some early sales to show to his supplier.

To create a Superflor campaign, we click on the Create Campaign shortcut, and fill in the basic details for the campaign, like this:

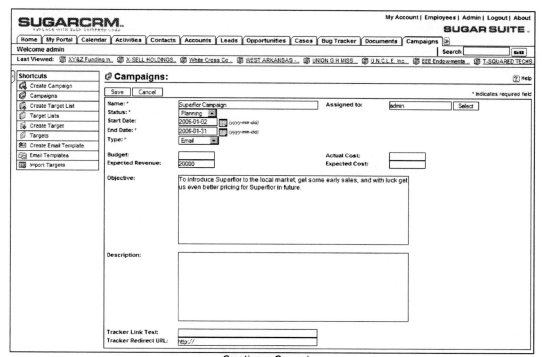

Creating a Campaign

When you are done, click on the Save button. You should see the Campaign details, which should resemble the following:

Campaign Detail View

Creating an Email Template

There are many types of marketing campaigns. These include Telesales, Mail, Print, Web, Radio, and Television. For this campaign, we have chosen an Email campaign.

To execute an email marketing campaign, Doc will need an email template. To create one, go to the Emails tab, and click on the Create Email Template shortcut. Fill it in like this:

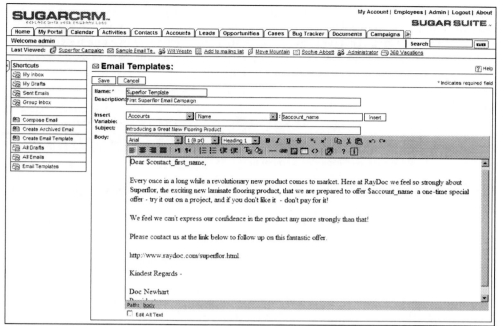

Superflor Email Template

Notice how variable fields were inserted in the text, using the controls to select fields from accounts or contacts, and the Insert button. This lets you customize the email for each target automatically.

Creating an Email Marketing Program

Next, go back to the Campaigns tab, and click on the Superflor Campaign. Although we have already indicated this is an email marketing campaign, we must click on the Create button in the Email Marketing subpanel, and fill in more details about the specific email marketing program within this overall campaign, like this:

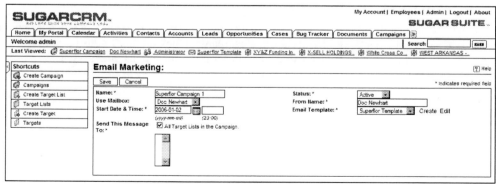

Create Email Campaign Details

Notice that you have to reference an email template, which is why it is easier to create it first—although there is an option to create the template from inside this screen. You will also have to reference a User Mailbox. This will have to be configured beforehand by your system administrator as a mailbox with *Bounce Handling* as a permitted action. Now click on **Save**, and you should see the beginnings of your email campaign:

Superflor Email Campaign Taking Shape

Adding Targets to the Campaign

Now we need to see some targets for this email marketing campaign. First, let's create a target list to hold all the target prospects we identify for this campaign. Click on the **Create Target List** shortcut, and fill in the name **Superflor Targets** and description for the list, and save it.

Next, you need to import, or type in, the data for some target prospects using the Import shortcut, or the Create Target shortcut. Here is the list view screen for targets, with the first target added in:

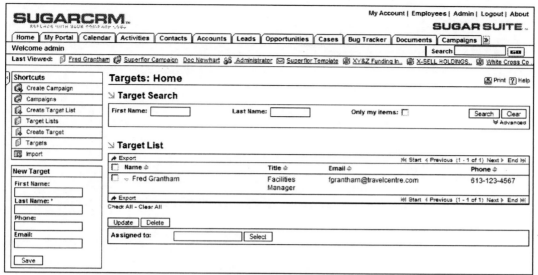

Targets List View

Next, you need to select some targets from the general list of targets above, as well as any leads and contacts that you would like to include in the campaign, and add all of these people to the Superflor Targets list. You do that by opening up the detail view of the Superflor Targets list, and in turn, clicking on the Select button for each of Targets, Contacts, Leads, and even Users—and selecting whomever you wish from those lists. This will produce a detail view for the Superflor Targets list that resembles this:

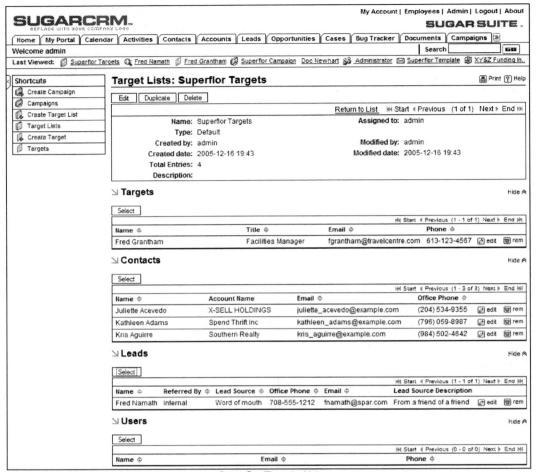

Superflor Targets List

Now that we have selected some targets (in practice, of course, you would select many more) we need to add them into the Superflor marketing campaign. So click on the Campaigns tab, choose this particular campaign, and then in the Targets List subpanel, click on the Select button to select the list we just prepared. Note that you can add more than one target list here—so if you have them separated out by geography or some other criterion, you can include several lists here to make up the full campaign.

Here is the Superflor campaign with its email marketing programs subpanel, and its reference to the Superflor email template, and the Target List subpanel filled out as well.

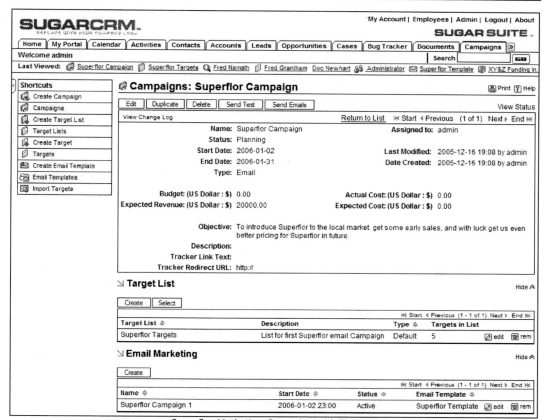

Superflor Marketing Campaign with Targets

The Mass Emailing Queue

Now that we have edited the email template to be used, created the overall marketing campaign, and attached the email marketing program information and a targets list, how do we send the actual emails? On the Campaign Detail view screen, click on the Schedule button. This will place all the emails from this campaign into the **Mass Email Queue**. When the day and time comes that is specified in the email-marketing subpanel, the status of the email-marketing program will automatically become In Progress (it is initially set to In Queue). It will be changed to Sent once all the emails have been sent. If you have administrative access for the system, look in the Mass Email Manager section within Admin and you will see something like this showing the mass email queue:

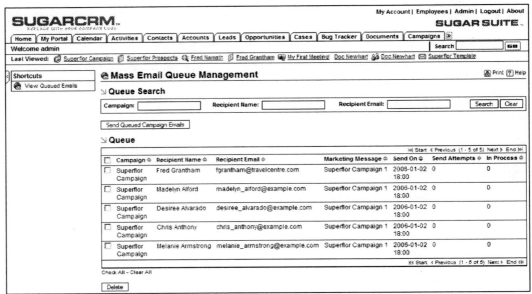

Mass Email Marketing within Administration

On this screen the administrator can observe the action of the mass email queue mechanism, and also delete any emails as desired.

Tracking a Campaign

You will have noticed, at the bottom of the main panel for a marketing campaign, these two fields:

- Tracker Link Text: This is the text to be displayed for the hyperlink to that page on his public website—something that is more presentable than the actual address itself.

- Tracker Re-Direct URL: This contains a hyperlink to which the SugarCRM campaign tracker software will redirect the user, once it has counted his or her click for the purposes of campaign tracking. In our example, if Doc wants his targets to click on a link in the email and wind up at a page on his public website, then the address of that page on his public website should be entered into the Tracker Re-Direct URL field.

Document Management

I think we can all remember promises of the paperless office—always just a few years around the corner. By now, most of us have come to accept that in reality, one thing any business simply cannot do without is paper, whether it is for hard copies of presentations, for business proposals and quotations, or for financial transactions. However, we can still try to cut down on it.

SugarCRM has the ability to manage and maintain a repository of revision-controlled documents within it. This ensures that anyone in the business with system access, no matter where they are or what time of the day it is, can instantly access electronic copies of the business's important documents and know that they are getting the correct version of these documents as well.

Just knowing that everyone in the company is looking at the most recent employee handbook, has all the latest medical insurance claim forms, and has access to all the latest sales collateral, is a huge step for the typical small business. Knowing that they can access these documents anytime, anywhere—Priceless!

Knowing that your sales people can remotely pick up brochures and presentations they did not think they would need for a customer they are out visiting—just this one thing—how much could it make your company this year?

With luck, you now agree that there is significant business value in being able to access key business documents via the CRM. Now the question is how do we do it? To begin, let's click on the Documents tab, and put one of Doc's new Superflor brochures into the CRM.

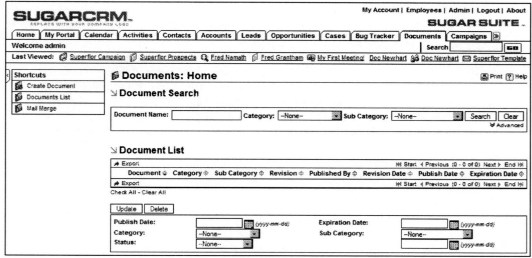

Document List View

This is what the document list view looks like. Notice the shortcuts to Create a Document, or to see the Documents List, as well as to Mail Merge. Let's add a new document by clicking on the Create Document shortcut.

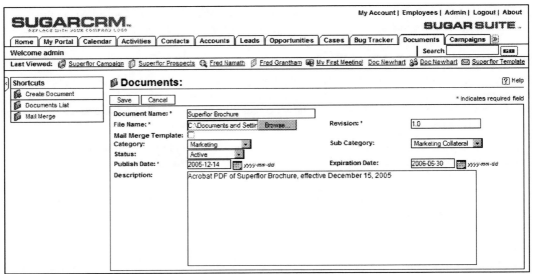

Creating a New Document

In the above screen, simply type in the Document Name and Revision, select the Category, Subcategory, and Status, set a publish date (defaults to today anyway), and then click on the Browse button to find the file you want to upload to the SugarCRM server. Once you find the file you want, and the rest of the fields on the screen above have been filled in, click on the Save button. The document will be uploaded (there may be a lengthy pause, depending on the size of the document and the speed of your Internet connection) and you will see the document details:

Document Detail View

Notice in the figure above that by adding in one document, the system has created a main panel for that document, as well as a subpanel containing a list of revisions for it—with the initial revision at the top.

In a few months' time, if Superflor comes out with a few new colors and styles, and Doc needs to put a newer version of this brochure up into his CRM, he can simply click on the Create button in the Document Revisions subpanel, and add in a revision, calling it presumably something like 2.0. He will simply have to browse to the newer file, enter a new revision, and optionally add in a descriptive phrase for the Change Log—what is new or different in this revision? Here is what the document details look like when a second revision has been uploaded to the SugarCRM server:

Document Revision

Notice that the Download File link at the bottom of the main panel always offers the most recent revision of the document for download. If for some special reason the user needs an older revision of the document, clicking on the miniature icon at the left of each revision (showing the file type of the document) will give access to those older revisions.

Now—go back to the document list. Click on the Advanced link in the Search panel to see the expanded search capabilities.

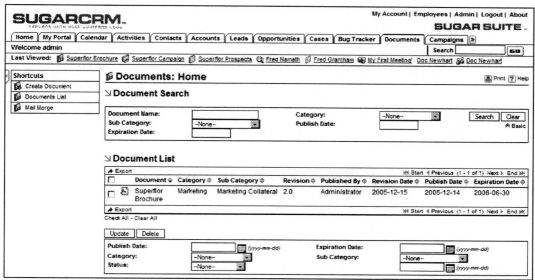

Document List View with Advanced Search

As you see in the figure above, the publishing date of our new document as well as the date and time on which it was revised are now shown in the list. Again, you have the miniature icon with which to download the document.

Looking at the Document Search panel, you can see the importance of the category and subcategory fields. Without having them filter your view of the list of documents, it might take longer finding a document in here than it would in the office! The document name is useful as well, as you can match a document with just the first few letters of the document name.

However, there are limitations to the document searching capabilities you should be aware of. You can't find a document using a word or text, say flor, in the middle of the document name unless you use the % character in front of the search text. Therefore, %flor in the Document Name field of the search panel will successfully find the document in the example above.

Neither can you search for a document by filtering to just the right type of document—such as a Microsoft Word file, or an Acrobat PDF file.

Nor can you search for a document based on certain keywords associated with the file as metadata (data about data). In the case of this document, keywords might have included *laminate, flooring, superflor, durable*. Then a search for all documents concerning *durable flooring* or *laminate flooring* would have brought up this document and others like it.

The biggest limitations in SugarCRM's document capabilities however, are:

- You can't associate a document with an account, contact, lead, opportunity, project, or case.
- You can't attach a document to an outgoing email without downloading it first.

As with all things, however, SugarCRM is making quick progress, and there is good reason to hope that these issues will be addressed in new releases of SugarCRM coming out shortly.

Project Management

If we look at the way a sales opportunity is modeled within SugarCRM (and most other CRMs), we see an assumption of a one-time event. While in a product sales model that is typically correct—when the sale comes, the product is shipped, an invoice is produced, and the opportunity has been fulfilled—that is not true of a services sales model.

While later in this chapter we look at service and support issues (which also have income streams, not blips), right now, let's deal with the management of a project. A project can be an internal project or one being delivered for a customer.

First, click on the Projects tab. You will see a screen layout that resembles the following screenshot. (Note that I have shown the sample data here, even though you will have erased it by the time you get here. Not to worry—you will soon have created plenty of your own project data.)

Project List View

Notice that there are shortcuts to create a new project, to list all projects (the default view), to create a new project task, and to list all project tasks. We see in the list view that each project has a name, and keeps track of estimated and actual hours of effort expended on the project.

Now, click on the Setup Booth at Tradeshow project, and let's examine the makeup of a project.

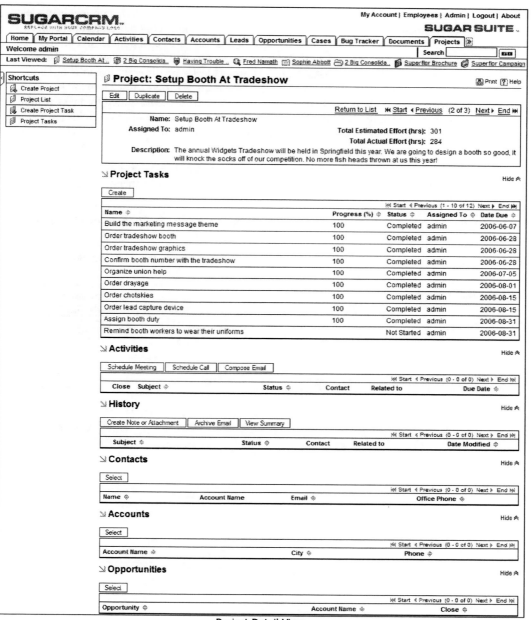

Project Detail View

In the figure overleaf, we can see that like most other items within SugarCRM, a project is modeled with a main panel containing basic descriptive overview information about the project, as well as a number of subpanels linking in related information. In this case, we see a number of common subpanels—such as Open Activities, History, Contacts, Accounts, and Opportunities—but also a brand-new subpanel entitled Project Tasks. Note that project tasks are different from the tasks we have seen previously, as they include fields of information such as Progress %, Order, Milestones, Depends On, Utilization%, Estimated Effort, and Actual Effort that are better suited for tasks within a project. A very handy feature is that the total estimated and actual hours of effort fields (which are read-only) within the main panel auto-total the relevant fields from all the project tasks within the project.

Now that we have had a quick look at how projects are organized and what information they keep track of, let's work through an exercise in building a project for Doc's forthcoming remodeling of the offices at 360 Vacations.

First, click on the shortcut to create a new project. Type in a name (Remodeling of 360 Vacations) and description for the project and then click on Save.

Next click on the Create button in the Project Tasks subpanel, to add the first new project task.

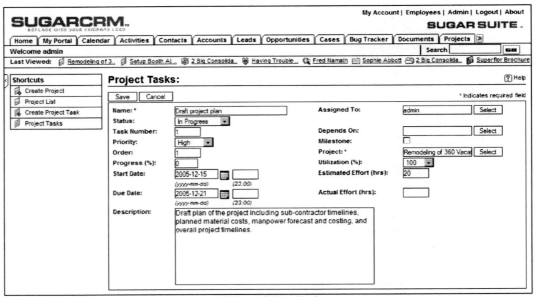

Adding a Project Task

As you can see in the figure opposite, most of the fields are optional, and are simply text fields—just type in the information you would like to keep track of. Click on the Save button to save this project task and you will see it listed in the subpanel for project tasks within the remodeling Project Detail view.

We can go on adding the various tasks involved in this project until we feel that we have the work well represented, so that it can be tracked to ensure a timely and organized completion, while monitoring cost variance via ongoing level-of-effort totals.

As this stage, one would begin to add the smaller tactical activities to the project—the calls, meetings, and regular tasks, that would be part of the Open Activities subpanel, and which when completed would join the History subpanel. You should also be aware that even when a project task is completed, it does not become part of the project's activity history, but stays within the Project Task subpanel.

Then add in the contacts you will be dealing with on the project—this makes for a very handy list of just the people you will be working with on the project.

Once complete, our project will look something like this:

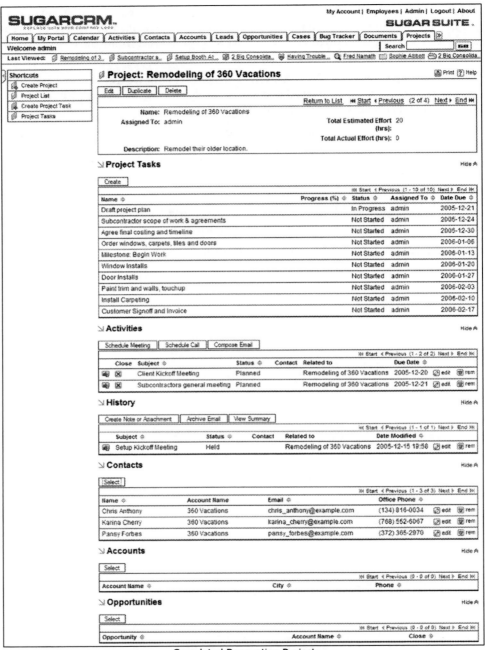

Completed Renovation Project

Now, Doc can keep track of all the projects, including this one, that are going on at RayDoc, quickly and efficiently, at any time of day, from anywhere including his home or a hotel room. He can watch the actual versus estimated level of effort as an indicator of how the project is going, and plan his billing accordingly. It doesn't quite model and forecast income and costs for the project neither does it integrate that information with the conventional product sales income on the dashboard, but it is a very good start.

Customer Service Management

Anyone running a smaller business knows very well that customer interactions are not limited to the sales activities. In fact, there is a good reason for maintaining that you only really get to know a supplier, partner, or customer well, when the chips are down and there is an issue to be dealt with. I know in my own experience that many customers make a point of sticking with the suppliers who have proven that they are caring and efficient when there is a problem to overcome. They are sophisticated enough to understand that there will inevitably be some problems, and that the real issue is how they are handled.

Within SugarCRM, the Cases module keeps track of customer issues. Let's click on that tab now to see what the system offers:

Cases List View

You can see some of the basics in this view—each case has a case Number, a Subject, an associated Account Name, a Priority, a Status, and a User to which it is assigned.

Now, click on the Create Case shortcut. In our example, let us imagine that RayDoc is working on the renovations at 360 Vacations and someone in the office at 360 Vacations phones in with a problem with one of the newly installed windows. The figure overleaf shows an example of entering the data for this case.

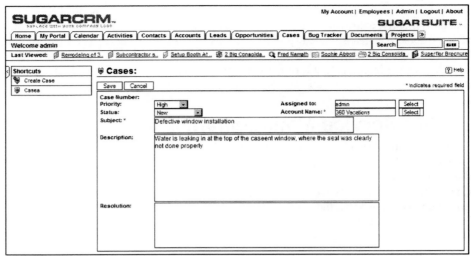

Creating a New Case

Once the data has been entered, clicking on the Save button will result in the detail view.

Case Detail View

As you can see opposite, each case can have related Contacts, Activities, and History, as well as associated software Bugs (if relevant to the business you are in).

During the lifecycle of a case, its status can be edited to reflect progress—standard values are New, Assigned, Closed, Pending Input, Rejected, and Duplicate.

Ideally, one would analyze case data to understand the effectiveness of your service organization—looking for metrics such as on average, how long a case remains open, how many open cases there are, and how many cases are reported per month. Unfortunately, SugarCRM Open Source edition has no reporting capabilities, and there are no dashboard charts available to show this sort of derived information.

While one can reasonably expect these sorts of developments in the not too distant future, for now, the best practice is simply to open the Case List view screen, and filter it by status or priority to gain a feel of the quality of your customer service.

Software Bug Tracking

One aspect of customer service management within SugarCRM Open Source is the software bug tracker. While this is clearly not relevant to many smaller businesses, for those businesses that create, resell, or support software products, it can be an excellent tool.

Click on the Bug Tracker tab for a quick look at this module:

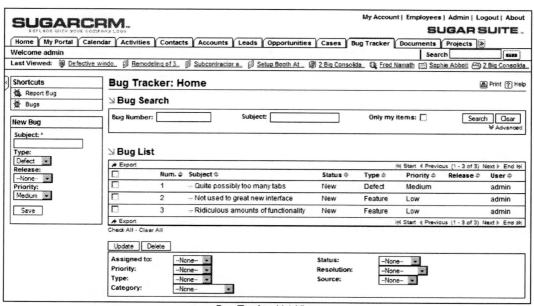

Bug Tracker List View

A few sample bugs have been entered for the figure overleaf to give you some idea of the information this module keeps track of. As with cases, there are no metrics on bugs available to you yet within SugarCRM, but using filters on the Bug Tracker List view screen can tell you a great deal about what is going on with your various major software products.

Each bug report can have associated activities and history, contacts, accounts, and cases. The edit view of a bug report looks like this:

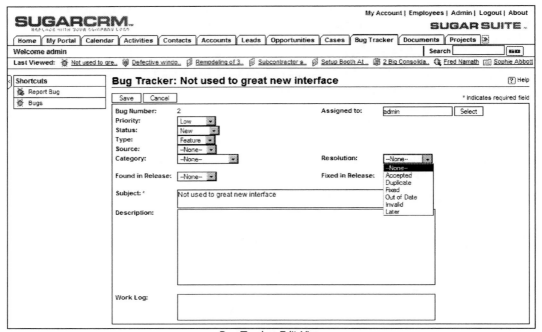

Bug Tracker Edit View

One key element of bug reports is typically the release or version of software in which they are found. Within the administration area of the system there is a function to maintain a list of release numbers, which may be referenced within a bug report.

Email Notifications

Something that SugarCRM does really very well is to take advantage of its ability to send email. Aside from the marketing email campaign capability, SugarCRM can also send notification emails to users (and in some instances, contacts outside the business) when they are assigned new tasks, when they are invited to meetings, when they get new leads, and so on. Note that these notification emails are not sent when a user enters the data themself—only when a user creates the information, and assigns it to someone else.

When these notification emails arrive, they usually have a form similar to this lead notification:

```
From: SugarCRM
To: kay@raydoc.com
Subject: SugarCRM: Lead-Bruce Levis
doc has assigned a Lead to Kay Holland.

Name: Bruce Levis
Lead Source:
Status: New
Description:

You may review this Lead at:
<http://www.raydoc.net/index.php?module=Leads&action=DetailView&record=b197529
5-223a-5f58-3ef1-42e8ca818273>
```

There are several administrative settings that must all be set correctly for the email notification features to work correctly, including:

- The notifications must be enabled throughout the system.
- Each user's notification can be enabled or disabled individually, and a default can be set to determine if new users are set on or off by default.
- The information must be entered to specify how the SugarCRM server should access email, using what standards, and using what name and address to say whom the email is from.

Email notifications are sent when another user assigns any of the following types of data to you:

- Task
- Lead
- Contact
- Opportunity
- Project
- Case
- Bug report

Clearly, there are some very useful workflow advantages to having an email sent proactively to you to notify you of new information, rather than having the system wait for you to log in and find the information yourself. Especially for things like leads, bugs, and cases where there may be a real sense of urgency about the information, this is an extremely valuable business tool. When combined with the use of a *push email* device such as a BlackBerry, these emails can improve customer response times remarkably, improving both customer satisfaction and the bottom line.

Interface Consolidation

To understand the value of interface consolidation, let's picture Kay—Doc's receptionist—as she goes through a typical business day. Sometime in the morning, she has her first occasion to refer to the CRM, and she fires up a browser session, and logs in to the CRM. She then tends to try to keep that window open for the rest of the day—although sometimes she closes it by mistake, and sometimes the active browser session is used when she clicks on a link emailed to her, and the browser goes to some unrelated page.

Meanwhile—what else is she doing on her PC? She has Microsoft Outlook 2003 running as a local application. A sociable girl—she is logged on to MSN messenger to keep in touch with her friends, family, and a few favorite customers and coworkers. She also has a few other browser windows open—reading the news of the day, visiting some supplier sites for contact and product information, and checking on local weather and weekend entertainment options.

While Kay has good mental agility, even she has some difficulty managing the PC with all these windows open. Sometimes she closes the SugarCRM window by mistake, sometimes she has trouble finding it, and other times it just seems to disappear all by itself.

To cut down on all this desktop juggling, and to help ensure that a CRM session stays open on the desktop of most employees all day long, many CRMs integrate the ability to access other websites from within them, as well as RSS news feeds. While the information access this integrates has little or nothing to do with the subject of CRM, it has everything to do with simplifying the desktop for employees like Kay, as well as improving their efficiency, and encouraging them to always keep a browser window open to the CRM.

RSS News Feeds

Let's look at RSS news feeds first.

Click on the SugarCRM tab for RSS. You should see something like this:

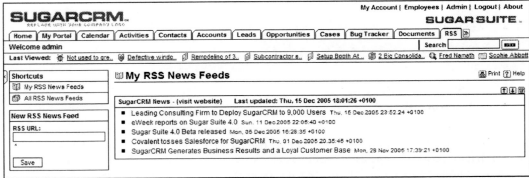

Initial RSS Screen

By default when you enter it, this module shows the user **My RSS News Feeds**—information feeds that have been selected by the user. Each user of the system has a different set of feeds stored in their user profile. By default, each user is started off with one entry in their **My RSS News Feeds** profile—a feed giving information on the SugarCRM open-source project. Let us assume this is not a feed you wish to keep, and delete it.

Do this now, by clicking on the miniature icon on the far right of the news feed—right after the up and down arrows.

Now let's add some feeds of particular personal interest. As I can't ask you for yours, I will use a few of mine as an example here—but why don't you pick a number of your own favorite news sources as we go through the example?

To do this, click on the shortcut for All RSS News Feeds. You should see a screen like this:

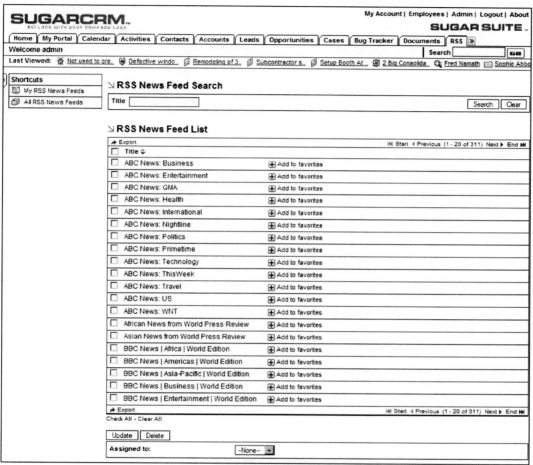

All RSS News Feeds

SugarCRM ships with hundreds of popular news feeds pre-programmed into it. Scroll through the entire list, clicking on the + sign to the right of each feed that you wish to include on your custom news page. When you are done, simply click on the shortcut to My RSS News Feeds, and you should see a page like this:

Customized MY RSS News Feeds

You can reorder the feeds however you like, by using the up and down arrows at the top right of each feed. Each feed typically has the five latest headlines for that feed displayed. For each feed, you can click on the title of the feed at the top to visit the related website or on one of the headlines to bring up the full related story in a new browser window.

If there is an RSS news feed available that you want to include, but it is not in the SugarCRM preprogrammed list of feeds, you can add it manually by using the New RSS News Feed box.

By now you can see that the RSS News Feeds page is a very handy way to focus the latest news from all your favorite sites onto one list of headlines on a single web page. Visiting here once a day should get you up to date on all your personal and professional interests, as well as national and international events quickly and effectively, without leaving the friendly confines of the CRM.

Linking in External Websites

The My Portal module is used to link pages from external websites into the CRM so that they can be referenced without the user leaving the CRM.

Click on the My Portal tab now—you should see a screen like this:

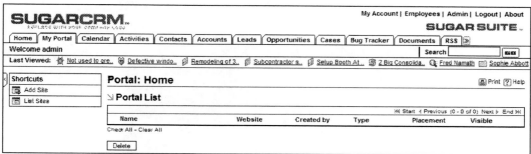

My Portal: Initial View

Let's add a few links to sites that would be of interest to Doc, and the employees at RayDoc Carpets. Click on the Add Site shortcut.

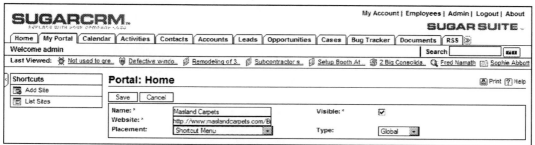

Add New Site Screen

You will see a screen like the figure above, prompting you for a site name and the website URL. You can click to select if you want the site to be currently visible or not—as you might want to hide some shortcuts without deleting them from the list. You can also select whether the shortcut displays in the shortcut list on the My Portal screen, as a tab on the tab menu, or both. Administrators can select whether the site is Personal (for the current user), or Global (for all users).

The example data in the screen above will be used to add a new site for Masland Carpets—one of Doc's carpet suppliers, which has a site showing all the colors available for its broadloom carpets. The site will be visible, and available to all users via the shortcut list in the My Portal tab. Once we click on Save, the site is added to the shortcut list. We can click on the site name in the shortcut list to see the site—like this:

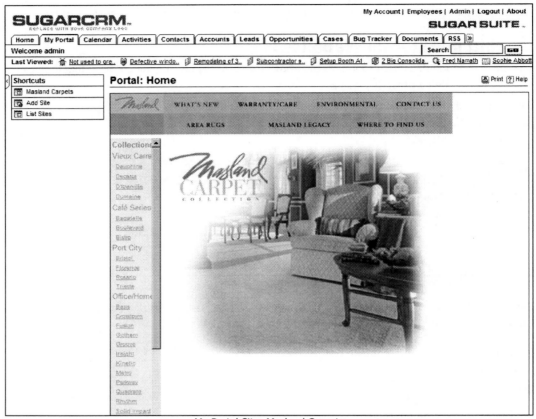

My Portal Site: Masland Carpets

Notice the shortcut for the site in the list to the left.

Linking in a Security Camera

After adding a few more sites of global use to all RayDoc employees, Doc goes on to add a special site to his own shortcut list—a link to a web-based surveillance camera. In this example, we set up a LinkSys WVC-54G wireless Internet video camera as a site.

LinkSys Wireless Internet Video Camera

Retailing for about 250 USD, this wireless video camera is quite sophisticated, and contains its own web server, and its own 802.11g (the high-speed 54-megabit wireless standard) network interface. Simply plug it in to a power outlet, configure it briefly, and then see what it sees by viewing a particular web address. In this case, defining a new site called Security Camera, with a website of `http://192.168.1.115/img/image.cgi?next_file=main_fs.htm` will do the trick. Note that you must currently use Internet Explorer as your browser to do this, as viewing the video feed requires the installation of an ActiveX control—only supported by Internet Explorer.

Here is a sample of the browser screen viewing My Portal with Security Camera selected as the current site:

Viewing Security Camera via My Portal

As you can see above—hardly an application you might anticipate as part of a CRM application, but a very handy feature for owners of smaller businesses—and somehow all a part of keeping an eye on your business! Doc finds it a good way to relax at home, knowing that all is in order at the office. He has a visual check of the premises from home when the alarm system goes off. He can even use multiple cameras to get comprehensive coverage of the offices as well as the warehouse area.

Assessing your CRM Customization Needs

As we saw in Chapters 1 and 2, CRM customizations tend to fall into the categories of cosmetics, minor user interface changes, major application changes and additions, and application integration. While we are looking at ways to extend your CRM's business role, it makes sense to look at the modifications you can make yourself to better adapt your CRM to the precise way that you do business.

In terms of user interface changes some common changes are:

- Changing the names of modules to better match the terminology used in your business (such as changing Contact to Customer, Tenant, or Investor)
- Changing the values used in a drop-down list, such as for Account Type, or Lead Source
- Adding or removing fields on a Detail or Edit screen
- Rearranging the layout of Detail and Edit screens to group fields differently
- Renaming fields on Detail and Edit screens

Early in your CRM adoption process, you should methodically go through all the modules of your CRM system and examine all the terminology, and all the field names and sets of drop-down values, to identify all the tasks of this sort that would make your CRM a better fit for your business. Write down the full set of tasks you identify, and keep good track of them until they have all been addressed. Consult with your peers on the CRM implementation team to make sure everyone agrees.

Making Changes to your Existing CRM Modules

Once you have identified the user interface changes you would like to make, you will want to have a look at the tools that Sugar makes available for you to be able to address a number of them yourself.

This section describes the various Sugar Studio functions, which collectively enable administrative users to perform a broad range of user interface customization tasks, significantly reducing the need for custom software development. To access it, you need to go to the Administrator area of your SugarCRM installation and look under Sugar Studio.

Field Layout Editor

The Layout Editor lets you rearrange the fields and panels on most of the screens available within Sugar Open Source, to customize them to fit your needs.

Begin by selecting the name of the file (actually a specific view from one of the system's modules, either the list view, detail view, or edit view) that you want to customize. Choose the file name from the drop-down box provided, and then click on the Select File button. If you're not sure what file to edit you can select the Edit in Place checkbox; this will add an edit icon 📝 to all the editable screens throughout Sugar Open Source. Now go to the screen you want to edit, click on the 📝 icon, and you will enter the screen layout editor to customize that screen layout.

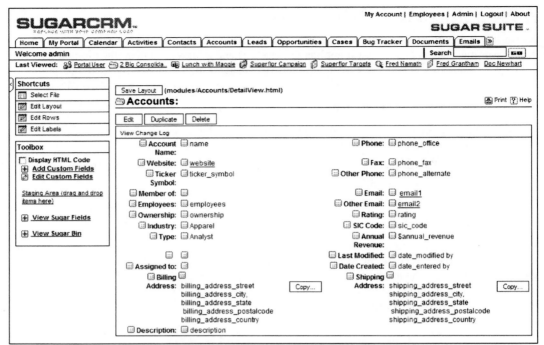

Using the Screen Layout Editor to Edit Account Detail Screen

Within the field layout function, there are three very special shortcuts available in the Shortcuts Box (not all are available at all times):

- **Select File**: Sends you to the screen first seen when entering the field layout function, to select a file to edit. If you select this shortcut when you are in the middle of editing a screen, edits on that screen are lost if not already saved.

- **Edit Layout**: Within the Layout Editor, Edit Layout is a mode that lets you drag and rearrange individual fields or their labels within the details panel. Select the item handle (the little square grey box) next to the field or label you want to move, and then click on the item handle where you want the field or label located. This will move the item from its previous location to its new location. If there was already a field or label at the destination the two items will swap positions. Edit Layout also lets you move sub-panels. Moving sub-panels is the same as moving fields; select the source sub-panel handle and then click on the destination sub-panel handle, and the two will switch locations.

- **Edit Rows**: Within the Layout Editor, Edit Rows is a mode that allows the addition and removal of rows in the details panel. Pressing the ⊞ adds a row below the one currently selected, and pressing the ⊟ removes the row currently selected.

- **Edit Labels:** Within the Layout Editor, the Edit Labels mode displays in the toolbox area all the field labels on the page. Displayed in edit boxes, you may edit one or more labels, and then Save.

The Toolbox provides a workspace to add new fields and labels to a screen, to temporarily hold items that have been removed from a screen, and to discard items that are not needed. Its functions include:

- **Add Custom Field**: Opens a dialog box, which lets you specify the type of field you want to add and its name label. Click on the Add button to put your new field and its label in the Toolbox workspace, and close the dialog box. Next, to move your new field from the Toolbox to the screen select its item handle and then click on the item handle where you want the field located.

- **Display HTML Code**: To test this feature, select this checkbox and then move your cursor around the screen being edited. As the cursor passes over each field or label in the screen you will see the HTML that creates it displayed as 'Alt' text in a floating box below the cursor. Note that while this function can be informative it is very CPU intensive, and should only be used when necessary.

- Removing an item is accomplished by selecting its handle and dragging it to the Staging Area (drag and drop items here) area within the Toolbox. This will deposit the selected item in the Toolbox workspace.

Use the Save Layout button to save changes while in the Layout Editor. To discard changes simply choose the Select File shortcut to work on another file, or exit the Layout Editor entirely. Remember to un-check the Edit in Place checkbox before you leave the field layout function, or all your screens will still have the ✎ icon on them.

Dropdown Editor

The Dropdown Editor is a very valuable tool for the Administrator. It permits the values in all of the drop-down boxes in the system to be edited. The options presented to the user may be edited, existing options may be eliminated, and new options may be added. For example, when defining a new Account, in the Account Type field, the user must normally choose from a set of drop-down options, including Analyst, Competitor, Customer, Integrator, Investor, Partner, Press, Prospect, Reseller, and Other. By using the Dropdown Editor, this option set may be altered, with more or less options, and different option values.

To use the Dropdown Editor, select a name of a drop-down list, from the drop-down list of their names (if that is not too confusing a statement!). For example, account_type_dom is the second option on this list. If you select that option, and then choose the language US English (only those language packs that have been installed on your system will be available as choices), and click on the Select button, you will see a list of the Account Type options.

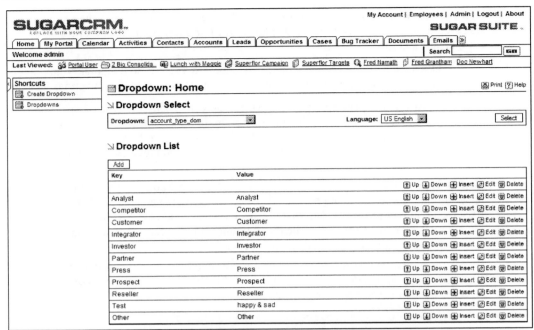

Using the Dropdown Editor to Edit Account Type Option List

On each line of the list, you will see a number of controls on the right hand side. The up and down arrows controls allow you to promote or demote an option, to a higher or lower position on the list. The Edit and Del controls allow you to edit or delete the drop-down options, respectively. The Ins control will add a new drop-down option into the list above the item on the line you click on.

Edit Custom Fields

You can add custom fields to any module in Sugar Open Source. First, select the module in which you want to add or edit custom fields. Then you can define the field using Field Name, Field Label (the label displayed on the screen within the module), Data Type, Max Size, Required Field (indicated by asterisks for users), and Default Value. After saving a new field, you can view and edit information about the field in the Custom Fields list for the module. In Field Layout, you can place the custom field on the module page by dragging it to the new location, just like any other field.

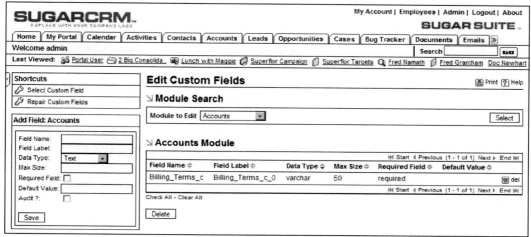

Editing Custom Fields in the Accounts Module

A good exercise for you right now would be to work through an example of making changes to the Accounts Detail and Edit screens, with new drop-down fields, making some changes to the layout, adding some new fields, and dropping some existing fields. Do it on a trial installation of Sugar Open Source that you can remove or over-install it afterwards.

Summary

In this chapter, we covered a number of more advanced CRM capabilities—ones that extend the role of your CRM system beyond the narrow confines of pure CRM functions into a somewhat broader business management role. Some of the key topics discussed in this chapter included:

- The business analysis required to identify pinch-points in your system, which will yield the best return on investment for customization efforts

- Getting rid of the sample data we experimented with at first, and importing your live data

- Marketing Campaigns: how to create email templates that enable each target to get a personalized email, how to assemble lists of targets for email marketing programs, how to control the mass email queue within SugarCRM, and how to automatically track the *click-through* rate of success of an email campaign

- Integrating a revision-controlled document repository to contain the latest versions of key company documents such as sales and marketing materials, HR policies and employee handbooks, and so on

- Managing a project within SugarCRM—including tracking planned and actual hours of effort, monitoring status of all project tasks, and keeping all project contacts and activity history conveniently in one place

- Managing customer service cases and software bugs, and tracking their status and severity

- Automated email notifications when new opportunities, tasks, projects, contacts, cases, or bugs are assigned to you

- Integrating an RSS news headline page—customized for each user—into the CRM system, to keep users inside the CRM system for more of their day

- Integrating external websites into the CRM system—and even how to link live video surveillance into your system for building security

- The use of Sugar Studio to make minor changes to your CRM installation

In the following chapter, we will see even more examples of advanced CRM system capabilities, features that are not included currently in the standard SugarCRM Open Source product. Exploring the additional CRM modules available in the commercial Sugar Pro product or elsewhere, you can get a good sense that there are few limits to the business management abilities that can be or have been integrated into the SugarCRM framework.

6

Commercial and Open Source Add-Ons for SugarCRM

In the last two chapters you have read about the basic CRM functions provided by the SugarCRM system. We have also seen a number of extended capabilities the standard system can perform, which take it beyond pure CRM into a broader business management role.

In this chapter we will explore a number of commercial and open-source add-ons to Sugar Open Source that can extend it even further in myriad directions.

These add-ons can be categorized as shown below:

- Free Add-Ons
    - **Role management extension**: Access control within Sugar Open Source 4.0 is a welcome addition, but limited in scope. This long-standing weakness of SugarCRM (the fact that all users can see and change all data in the system, if they are to share data with others) has spawned a series of open-source add-ons that address the need very well. Here, we examine one free patch that allows you to create teams that can share data, super users who can see all data, and even users with read-only access. You can control access rights down to every sub-panel of every module in the system, and you can prevent the unauthorized importing and exporting of data.
    - **Photographic company directory**: This free patch for Sugar Open Source (version 3.5 or later) provides a photographic company directory, complete with thumbnail and business card views, a red/green online indicator for each user, and links to send users email or text messages.
    - **Wireless synchronization**: For many businesses, their CRM needs to be a constant traveling companion. The Sync4j open-source project lets you synchronize SugarCRM with your PocketPC, Palm or BlackBerry mobile device.

- Commercial Open Source Add-Ons
  - **Human Resources management**: This commercial add-on module (for Sugar Open Source version 3.5 or later) provides a human resources management system. It includes the ability to track an employee's vacation and sick days, links to HR documents such as résumés, performance evaluations, and warnings, and keeps additional HR information such as emergency contact number, dependants, salary, and so on.
  - **Service contract management**: This commercial add-on module (for Sugar Open Source version 3.5 or later) provides the ability to track products on service contracts and subcontracts, link them to the related accounts, and list their service case history.
  - **Receiving POP email**: While Sugar Open Source 4.0 offers limited incoming email support for company mailboxes (such as support@company.com, info@company.com), this commercial add-on module for version 3.5 or later extends the Emails module to include the ability to receive email from one or more POP3 accounts per user. Emails are filed in the user's inbox, and automatically linked to related contact and account records. This automatically builds account and contact history. Each user can also define personal folders for filing email.

- Sugar Pro Add-Ons
  - **Product catalog and products module**: These two modules within Sugar Pro provide a product catalog defining the products handled by your business, and a products module that lists physical products in your inventory, on order, or sold to clients.
  - **Quotes module**: This Sugar Pro module uses data from the product catalog module above to prepare customer quotations.
  - **Forecasting**: This module within Sugar Pro provides the ability to generate individual and roll-up sales forecasts.
  - **Standard and custom reporting**: Reporting is likely the single most important feature that differentiates Sugar Pro from the Open Source version. The reporting module in Sugar Pro gets better with each release, and is now a very capable system.
  - **Sales Teams**: A key feature of Sugar Pro, Sales Teams provides you with the ability to create teams of users who can share data between themselves, which other users may not access. Combined with the Access Control Lists from release 4.0, they provide a good solution to data security.
  - **Sugar Wireless**: Part of Sugar Pro, Sugar Wireless is a separate application (sharing the same database), which provides a sub-set of Sugar functions for small form-factor wireless devices with browser support.

At the end of this chapter we also have a section about the SugarCRM web presence, and its online forums, as they are a great place to find more extensions for Sugar Open Source.

Let's dive right in to these many and varied extensions to the Sugar Open Source feature set. By the time we're done, I think you will be surprised and impressed at the range and capability of the features available to you, some free and some commercial, to grow your Sugar Open Source system to meet your evolving business needs.

As we go through the various add-ons, we will see how they relate to a small business such as RayDoc, and what real business value they bring to the table.

Free Add-Ons

I think most people in small or mid-size businesses will feel that free is the sort of price they would like to see more often. These three free options for Sugar Open Source are just a few examples of the many free add-ons you can find on SugarForge. And in many cases, although they may be free, these add-ons provide important new capabilities for your CRM. In particular, check out the many free add-ons from Marcelo Leite (also known as Mr. Milk, with AnySoft Informatica in Brazil)—their name usually starts with CallRooM.

Role Management Extension

This patch may be freely downloaded from the forums at http://www.sugarcrm.com and applied to your Sugar Open Source system. Once you download and apply this patch, your system will behave as described below.

Different patches have been developed for different versions of Sugar Open Source as the SugarCRM architecture has evolved and begun to offer some access control capabilities of its own. In addition to the patch presented here, another called Team Security from Marcelo Leite (known in SugarCRM circles as Mr. Milk) is a valuable contribution, and you should have a look at it too, on SugarForge (http://www.sugarforge.org). And as the Sugar world moves so quickly, by the time you read this, there will no doubt be others to choose from.

The principal business problem this patch addresses is a fundamental issue with the basic Sugar Open Source—everyone can see everybody else's data if they are to share data with anyone. In a sales environment this is frequently not a viable approach—sales people can be very protective of their contacts, as they generate their livelihood. While in Sugar Open Source 4.0 some access control capabilities have been added, they still do not offer the ability to define teams that can share data, while not exposing data to all users of the system.

Even in an organization the size of RayDoc this was an issue, and the availability of this patch stimulated much broader adoption of the system in that business. As lack of adoption is the most common cause for the failure of a CRM implementation, this is a critical issue.

With this patch installed, Roles within Sugar Open Source serve a dual purpose—however both are associated with limiting the access of certain users within the system. When you select the Role Management option within the administration area, you will see the Roles List view screen. It lists the roles defined within the system, and also offers shortcuts to create a new role, or define the system's default access restrictions.

Roles List View

You can define roles for groups of users to specify which modules those users should have access to. For example, sales staff will want access to the Opportunities and Dashboard modules, marketing staff will want access to the Campaigns module but not all staff will need access to these modules. As you can see in the figure opposite, each role defines the tabs that will be visible to the users assigned to the role.

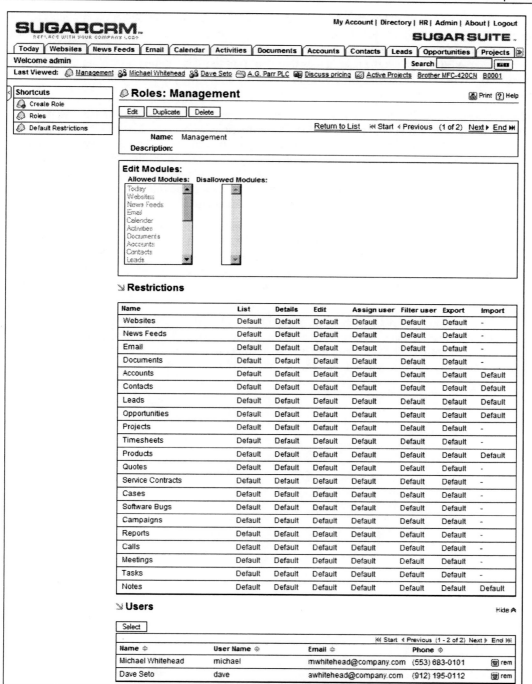

Role Detail View

To create a role, click the Create Role shortcut, type a name for the role, select the modules to include for the role from the Edit Modules sub-panel, and then save the role. To assign users to a role, go to the detail view for that role. In the Users sub-panel, click the Select button to display a list of users. You can check the user names that you want to assign to this role. Note that when a module is excluded from a role, access is also removed to the sub-panels in other modules that relate to the excluded module.

Next we need to describe the more *fine-grained* access restrictions that the system uses, what their default settings are, and how to associate different restrictions with a role. In the first place, you should know that users with system administration capability can see all data in the system. For all other users, access restrictions are initially controlled by the default restrictions defined for the system, and then managed by additional system roles. These additional roles must have names exactly the same as a user name, or as a department name (user name roles take precedence). Note that you should not use these roles for the purposes of hiding tabs like the roles we discussed earlier.

For example, if we define a role called management, and two users Michael and Dave both have their department set to management (upper and lower case matters), and are both assigned to the management role, then both of them can see all data which is assigned to either Michael or Dave. If we then define a role called Michael, and we assign another user, Steve, to that role, then Michael can also see all the data assigned to Steve. (Note that Steve cannot see Michael's data in this example.)

Click on the Default Restrictions shortcut. You will see a list of the default restrictions, formatted much like the Restrictions sub-panel shown in the figure overleaf. In the Name column are the names of all the principal modules in the Info At Hand commercial superset of Sugar Open Source. Click on a module name to edit the default restrictions for that module.

SUGARCRM.
REPLACE WITH YOUR COMPANY LOGO

My Account | Directory | HR | Admin | About | Logout

SUGAR SUITE

| Today | Websites | News Feeds | Email | Calendar | Activities | Documents | Accounts | Contacts | Leads | Opportunities | Projects |

Welcome admin   Search [   ] [GO]

Last Viewed: Management Michael Whitehead Dave Seto A.G. Parr PLC Discuss pricing Active Projects Brother MFC-420CN B0001

Shortcuts
- Create Role
- Roles
- Default Restrictions

⬘ **Restrictions : Management : Accounts**

[Save] [Cancel]

List:	○ Restricted	○ Public	⦿ Default
Details:	○ Restricted	⦿ Public	○ Default
Edit:	○ Restricted	○ Public	⦿ Default
Assign user:	○ Restricted	○ Public	⦿ Default
Filter user:	○ Restricted	○ Public	⦿ Default
Export:	○ Restricted	○ Public	⦿ Default
Import:	○ Restricted	○ Public	⦿ Default

⬘ **Subpanels**

Meetings	○ Restricted	○ Public	⦿ Default
Tasks	○ Restricted	○ Public	⦿ Default
Calls	○ Restricted	○ Public	⦿ Default
Notes	○ Restricted	○ Public	⦿ Default
Email	○ Restricted	○ Public	⦿ Default
Contacts	○ Restricted	○ Public	⦿ Default
Opportunities	○ Restricted	○ Public	⦿ Default
Leads	○ Restricted	○ Public	⦿ Default
Cases	○ Restricted	○ Public	⦿ Default
Documents	○ Restricted	○ Public	⦿ Default
Quotes	○ Restricted	○ Public	⦿ Default
Member Organizations	○ Restricted	○ Public	⦿ Default
Bugs	○ Restricted	○ Public	⦿ Default
Projects	○ Restricted	○ Public	⦿ Default

Default Restrictions—Accounts

What the above screen means is that by default, until you change the default access restrictions, access to Account List View data, Account Details View screens, or Account Edit View screens (and a few other items we will discuss in a moment) are restricted to those users with permission to see them. The sub-panel settings mean that even when looking at an Account Details screen to which you have permission, the information shown on all the associated sub-panels will also be limited to information, to which you have permission. This patch is shipped as standard with the default restrictions set to Restricted for all modules and all sub-panels.

If you would prefer not to have any restrictions on who can see what data within your Sugar Open Source installation, simply edit the default restrictions, and set every setting for every module to Public.

When your system is new, all users have access permissions as determined by the default restrictions. These restrictions will continue to be in effect for any users not assigned to any other roles that may be defined.

When a new role is defined, all permissions are set to Default. This means that this role inherits whatever the setting is in the default restrictions. Set a permission to Public or Restricted to over-ride the default setting.

This is what the various restriction settings mean for each module:

- **List**: If this is set to Public, all records for the module will be shown on the list views for any user. This has the effect of disabling the security for this module (only for the list view). If it is set to Restricted, the module will show list view records respecting the security scheme.

- **Details**: If this is set to Public, all users will be permitted to access the detail view for any record in the module. If it is set to Restricted, the module will show detail view records respecting the security scheme. While in theory, setting list view to Restricted and detail view to Public would make the record inaccessible, this is not actually the case since the user can access the detail view via an explicit link or via a sub-panel link in another module. Setting detail view to Restricted will block unwanted access even through links on the other sub-panels.

- **Edit**: If this is set to Public, all users may edit, delete and duplicate any record in the module. If it is set to Restricted, unwanted users will be unable to click on those buttons that are found on the detail view. This will also get rid of the list view checkboxes and disable the mass-update mechanism for restricted records. Therefore you can set up a Public List view and Restricted Edit view to allow read-only access to certain users.

- **Assign User**: If this is set to Restricted, the drop-down list of users displayed on the Assigned To field on the edit view of this module will have only those users whose data you are permitted to see. If it is set to Public, the drop-down list will show all users. Setting to Restricted is valuable, so that a sensitive item of information cannot be mistakenly assigned to a user outside of a controlled group.

- **Filter User**: Filter User is similar to Assign User, but relates to the drop-down list of users presented in the Search/Filter panel at the top of the list view in most modules.

- **Import**: If Import is set to Restricted for a module, then only a user with administrator permissions can import data into this module.

- **Export**: If Export is set to Restricted, then only a user with administrator permissions can export data from this module. If it is set to Public, then any user can export the data to which they have access.

- **Sub-panels**: There is a setting for each sub-panel on the detail view of each module. If it is set to Restricted, data shown in the sub-panel will be limited to data to which the user is permitted access. If it is set to Public, the sub-panel will show all related data without respecting any restrictions.

Photographic Company Directory

This patch for Sugar Open Source (derived from the Info At Hand commercial superset of Sugar Open Source) replaces the Employees module with a photographic company directory, complete with thumbnail and business card views. It also includes a red/green online LED indicator for each user, plus links to send users email or text messages. This patch provides a handy way to recognize and contact all the employees in a business.

The business benefits of this patch are in the same area as the Interface Consolidation features discussed in Chapter 5. It helps keep people within the system, and gives them one more reason to always keep a browser window to their SugarCRM system open on their PC desktop.

The rest of this section describes a Sugar Open Source system that has had this patch applied.

To view the directory, click the Directory link that appears at the top right of your screen whenever you are logged in to the system. Note that the Admin link just next to it is only displayed for users with administrator capability.

The figure below shows the Directory Thumbnail View screen. To see more information about a specific employee, simply click on the image of the employee within the Thumbnail View, to bring up their Business Card View. There are also shortcuts to choose Thumbnail or Business Card View for all selected employees.

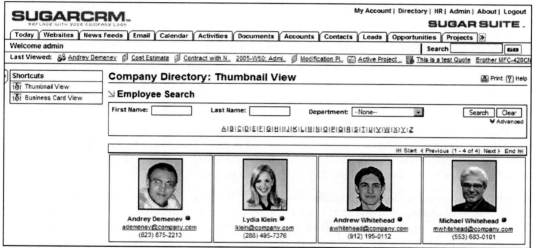

The Directory, Thumbnail View

Like most of the modules within Sugar Open Source, the Directory provides 🖨 (Print) and ❓ (Help) icons on the title bar at the top of the main screen, followed by a search capability, and a list of all or selected employees. Those employees with no photo in their profile will have a standard *no photo* image displayed. Camera-shy employees are encouraged to personalize this *no photo* image for submission.

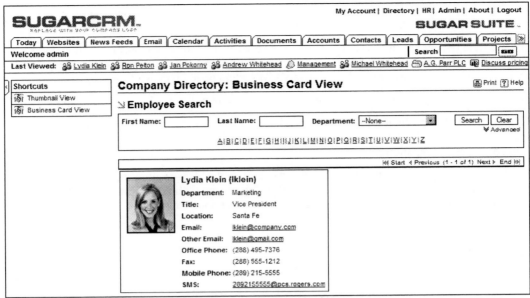

The Directory, Business Card View

The employees list may be filtered using the search controls, to see only those employees in a given department for example—or to find people by first or last name.

As well, the Directory Thumbnail View also has a red/green indicator light for each employee, to show if they are online within the Sugar Open Source system. Note that when employees do not log out of the system (but simply close their browser), they may be incorrectly shown as online until their session times out—usually about 10 minutes or so.

The employee list is paginated if it contains more items than can be listed on the display and controls are provided to go to the start or end of the list, or step to the next or previous page. Clicking on an email or SMS address for any employee in the list brings up your email client to send either an email or a text message to that employee.

Constant Availability

Clearly, not all employees of any business spend all day together in the same office. Some staff travel to make sales and to provide customer services. Others may be spread out over multiple offices. Having more than one office is not a problem for a web-based system. Wherever the server may be, all employees can access it via the Internet, as long as their location has Internet access, and they have a PC, Mac, or laptop connected to the Internet.

But when employees range outside the office, a solution often needs to be found to ensure they stay in reach of the data in the CRM system.

Overnight travel is not usually an issue any more. Employees slated for this type of work are issued company laptops, and most hotels now offer high-speed Internet access—often wireless access as well. If sales persons organize themselves well, they can usually access all the client information they need before leaving the room in the morning, and update new information to the system upon their return at night.

But what about unforeseen needs during the day for access to CRM data for both sales and service personnel? One solution is to carry a mobile device with a small format web browser, and then make sure that SugarCRM supports this type of small browser. This approach has been developed by SugarCRM as Sugar Wireless, a part of Sugar Pro, and we will discuss it later in this chapter. The alternative is to permit wireless synchronization from an Internet-capable handheld device directly to the SugarCRM server.

While you may wish to explore both avenues, my personal choice is the synchronization route. This is because handheld web access is so desperately slow—both the data transmission, and the screen navigation on the device. With a sync solution, once the data is on your device, you are using the regular calendar and contact applications within your device, at their regular speed. And as they reside in local firmware, that speed is normally extremely responsive.

Your choice may depend somewhat on your balance of remote data lookup versus remote data entry. For users who are mostly doing remote data lookup, the sync solution is likely to be far more satisfactory.

The Sync4j Open Source Project

To address the need for a direct wireless synchronization capability, there is a third-party solution available for SugarCRM (both Open Source and Pro) from an open source group called Sync4j. Its website is at www.sync4j.funambol.com (Funambol is the principal corporate sponsor of the Sync4j project).

Sync4j is a certified implementation of the Open Mobile Alliance Data Synchronization and Device Management protocols (OMA DS and DM, formerly known as SyncML). Sync4j is supported by one of the very largest communities of mobile developers.

The full Sync4j system consists of these components:

- **Sync4j server**: A Java-based mobile application server with connectors to SQL relational databases, Microsoft Exchange, Lotus Domino, and SugarCRM.
- **Sync4j clients**: Applications for Outlook, Windows Mobile PocketPC, BlackBerry, Palm, and iPod that you can use to synchronize your PIM data (address book and calendar) with the Sync4j server. Many Java phones have native support.
- **Sync4j email gateway**: A POP, IMAP, and SMTP gateway, to support mobile email.
- **Sync4j software development kit**: Tools to develop (in Java—J2SE and J2ME—and C++) sometimes-connected mobile applications.
- **Sync4j device management**: An OMA DM (Device Management) server to remotely manage mobile devices.

The protocol framework behind OMA DS & DM works like this:

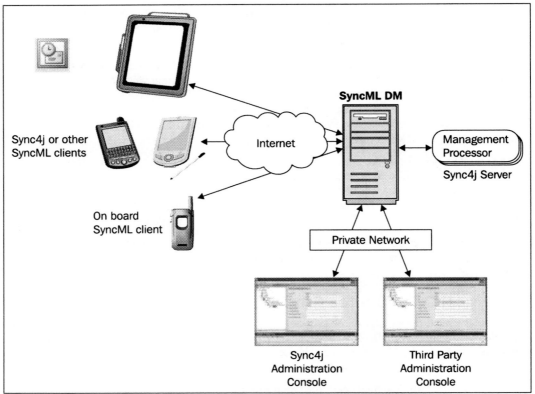

Sync4j Framework (Courtesy: Stefano Fornari, Funambol CTO)

What we see is that Internet-connected mobile devices connect to the Sync4j server via the OMA DM protocols, which are either built into the devices (such as many Java phones) or available for free download at the Sync4j website (Palm, iPod, Outlook, BlackBerry). Note that not every device can synchronize all possible data. Some are limited to synchronizing contacts and calendar data, while others are able to synchronize notes, tasks, and even files.

How does that Sync4j server have your SugarCRM data available to it? Via the OMA DS (Data Synchronization) protocols, with which it connects to the SugarCRM server and synchronizes data—with each server passing data modifications to the other, and conflicts being resolved jointly.

Now while Sync4j is built using Java, and SugarCRM is built using PHP, the two servers can peacefully co-exist on the same server messaging each other happily. So when a user away from the office uses Treo or BlackBerry to perform a sync back to the SugarCRM server, they are in fact connecting via the Internet to the Sync4j server, which then performs the synchronization with the SugarCRM server. Given that the two servers will usually reside within the same physical server, the distinction is perhaps moot.

Some representative phones that offer native support for OMA DS/DM include (check online at the Sync4j project to see the latest list):

- Alcatel: One Touch 715
- Ericcson: T39, T68
- Motorola: V300, V400, V500
- Nokia: 3300, 3595, 3650, 6108, 62xx, 6600, 6800/20, 7200/50/50i/70/80, 7650, 9500, N-Gage, …
- Panasonic: X70
- Siemens: M55, M56, S55, SL56, C65, SX1
- Sony Ericcson: P800, P900, 700, 700i, T68i, T610, T618, T630, Z600, Z1010

On the Sync4j site there are a number of documents that describe the installation and management of the Sync4j DS server, and the administration of the DM functionality. I recommend you to have a look at this project, which is currently at the 2.3Beta 4 release.

Commercial Open Source Add-Ons

Just as SugarCRM offers three versions of its software, two of which have commercial licenses attached, so there are many more commercial products that are built to add on to Sugar Open Source. Some of these commercial products (like our own Info At Hand at The Long Reach Corporation, and like Sugar Pro itself) are complete pre-configured CRM systems built on top of the base Sugar Open Source, with extended capabilities. Others, like the modules presented here, and other notable products such as the ZuckerDocs document management client, and the JRabbit Outlook plug-in, are designed to add on to Sugar Open Source to provide exciting new capabilities.

Human Resources Management

One aspect of business management that has not been explored by Sugar Open Source or Pro is **Human Resources Management**. In many states and countries around the world, businesses—even quite small ones—have a statutory responsibility to securely maintain records on their employees. The required data includes information such as health benefits information, emergency contact name and number, dependants, salary history, performance evaluations, and official warnings. In addition, a CRM system is a fairly convenient place to track information like attendance and sick days.

The Human Resources Management patch adds a link in the top right hand of the screen, near the links for My Account and Logout. Like the Administrator link, it only displays for users who have been given permission to access HR data.

Upon first entering the HR module, a list of employees is displayed:

HR: Employee List View

There is no shortcut to create a new employee. Employee records are automatically created for all users in the system, and they are created in the user management section of the Administrator area.

To view an employee's records, you simply click on their name in the list shown in the figure opposite.

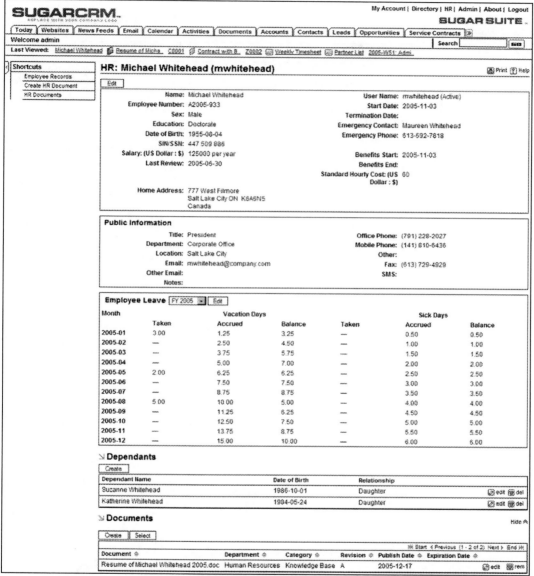

HR: Employee Detail View

To edit an employee's data, you can either click on the Edit button at the top of the screen to edit data in the top panel, or click on the Edit button in the Employee Leave sub-panel to edit leave data.

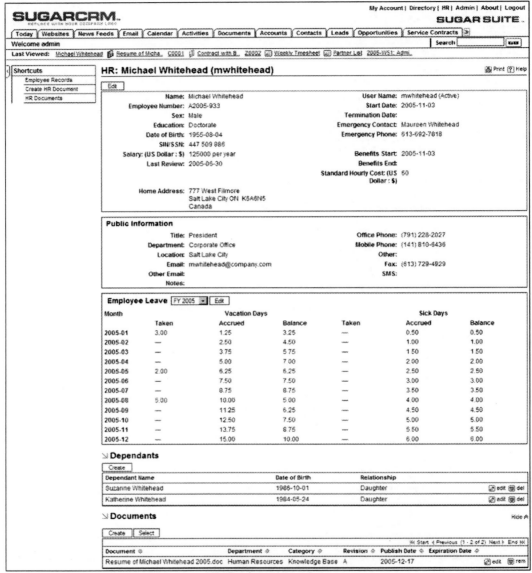

HR: Employee Leave Data

The leave data shown on the detail view is calculated from the data seen in the edit view. Annual vacation days are accrued at the appropriate rate each month, and start from the number of vacation days carried over from last year. Then any vacation days actually taken in each month are subtracted, always showing the vacation entitlement going forward.

Sick days are calculated in a similar way, and for each, the numbers are displayed in red when they go negative.

Service Contract Management

For businesses with an emphasis on customer service and support, the capabilities of Sugar Open Source (or Pro for that matter) are somewhat lacking. Many businesses have a help desk, or a customer service desk, at which customer calls are received and questions or complaints are received and dealt with. In addition, these calls frequently concern a product the business has sold, which may have a warranty or service contract in place.

Since the way the call needs to be handled will differ if there is, or is not, a service contract in effect, the customer service staff needs a quick way to determine the support status of the product in question.

To meet this requirement, Sugar needs a product catalog capability to describe the products the company is selling, and a Products module to keep track of the specific items it has sold, plus their serial numbers, details of who bought them, and their service history.

Also required is a Service Contract Management module, which keeps track of a master service contract for each account in the system, plus multiple service subcontracts for each master contract, and multiple products that are linked to each subcontract.

The patch that provides all these needs adds tabs for Products and Service Contracts, plus product catalog management functions in the Admin area. It also beefs up the Cases module somewhat, optionally linking each service case to the specific defective product and the service contract involved.

To explore this patch, let's look at the Service Contracts module.

Service Module: List View

Each master service contract has an automatically generated name—such as A0001 in this case—indicating that the account name begins with A, and that this was the first such account to open a service contract (contracts for accounts beginning with non-alphabetic characters get Z as their first letter). Each contract also has a status indicator LED, showing the status of all the subcontracts under it. Green means they are up to date, yellow means one or more are within a month of expiry, and red shows that one or more have expired. Accounts that you know have expired, but which might still be renewed one day, may be suspended so that their LED status is not sampled.

There are shortcuts available to create a new service contract, to look at a list of the types of service contracts available, or to define a new type of service contract.

To see the subcontracts linked to a master service contract, and to view the details of the master service contract, simply click on the name of the master contract.

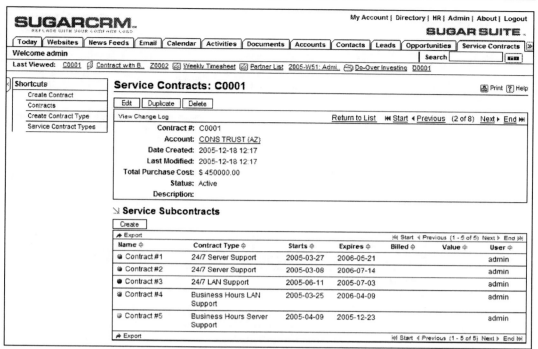

Service Contract: Detail View

To view the details of a specific subcontract, and to see the products that are under contract (and whose values sum to the totals shown), the user simply clicks on the name of a subcontract.

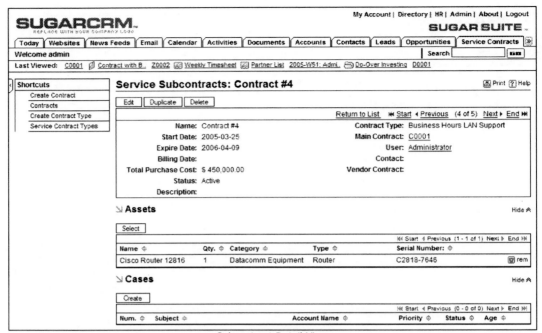

Subcontract Detail View

At this level we see the individual products, or assets, that are under contract, as well as their value. We also see the full service case history for all of the products on this subcontract.

In use, when a service technician receives a service call, they typically ask for the serial number of the unit (after first trying the simple solutions to avoid recording a service case).

Using this system, they would search for the serial number on the Products module, and when found the product would show its associated service subcontract and account.

The technician then typically checks if the service subcontract is active (and not expired), and can review the service history. A new case can then be entered for that product if need be—and it will automatically join the service history for both the product and the service subcontract.

Receiving POP Email

While the Emails module in Sugar Open Source is very handy for sending the occasional email that you want to be saved in account, contact, or opportunity history, and while the email marketing campaign capability is extremely useful, many businesses have complained that they wanted to be able to receive email within the system as well.

With the release of Sugar 4.0 some inbound email capability has been added, but to date only to support company email boxes of the form support@company.com, or info@company.com, and the associated workflow allowing a group of employees to share the responsibility of processing these emails.

In terms of interface consolidation considerations, inbound email for general user emails has the potential to have very positive effects on the number of employees who have the CRM system up in a browser on their notebook or PC all the time.

As well, it has a special bonus. Each incoming mail can have the sender's address matched against the email addresses for all contacts in the system, and an association automatically made if it is found. And if a related contact is found, then if that contact is related to an account, then the email is also automatically associated to the account too. The net effect of this is that contact and account history is automatically generated by the incoming email—just as it now is by the outgoing emails.

Throw in the fact that if you do your email inside the Sugar CRM you can now throw away Microsoft Outlook and the Exchange server (as all calendaring, contact management, and email services are now provided by Sugar), and you can see that the potential business benefits from this add-on are significant.

In addition to the patch described here, you should also have a look at the ZuckerMail module, a free open-source module that provides many of the same capabilities.

Once you apply the patch to receive POP Email, the Emails module display changes, and as well, the My Account screen gains a sub-panel for entering the information for the POP email accounts you want checked for email.

Email Inbox List View

Notice that in the shortcuts area, there are now shortcuts for the four standard folders—Inbox, Sent, Drafts, and Trash. Clicking on any one of them shows the list view of all emails in that folder. When the module is first entered, all the emails are displayed. An email may be moved from folder to folder for filing by selecting it using the checkboxes to the left of each email, selecting a new folder on the drop-down control within the mass-update panel at the bottom, and then clicking on the Update button within the mass-update panel at the bottom. Notice that even the email in the Inbox has already been linked to the contacts and accounts to which it relates.

There are also shortcuts to create personal email folders. These are viewed on the Folders list view screen, and created by using the Create Folder shortcut:

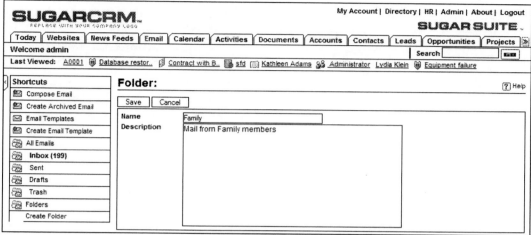

Email: Create New Folder

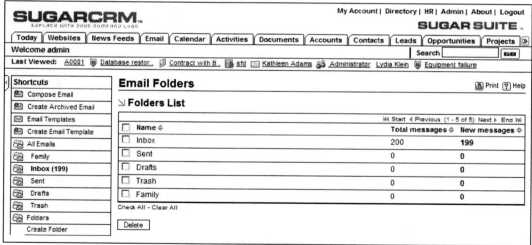

Email Folders List View

To read an incoming email from your Inbox, simply click on the subject of the email. This displays the email detail screen, which now includes buttons to Delete, Forward, or Reply to the email. Note that HTML email is displayed complete with rich fonts and graphics.

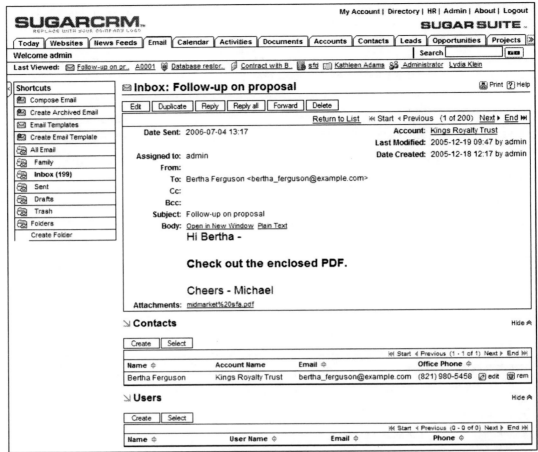

Email Detail View

If the incoming email has any attachments, they are shown and accessed just below the text of the email.

> There is a known problem with many web-based email systems, caused by Microsoft Outlook when it sends attachments as part of rich email (such as HTML email). Receiving those emails (and especially their attachments) with Outlook is not an issue, but it does often cause problems for web-based email systems. Hotmail for example suffers from this problem, whereas Google's Gmail takes care of it properly. If you receive a file attachment with the generated name `winmail.dat`, which you cannot open, you are witnessing the problem. This Outlook issue is taken care of properly by this email patch for Sugar.

Users specify the email boxes to be polled for email by using the My Admin page. Only POP3 email transfer is supported at the time of writing, not IMAP for instance.

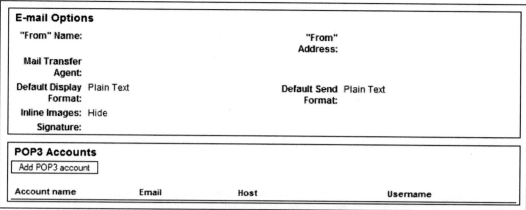

My Admin Screen: New POP3 Sub-panel

To add a POP3 email account to be polled for email, simply click on the Add POP3 account button, and fill out the information required, as shown in the figure below:

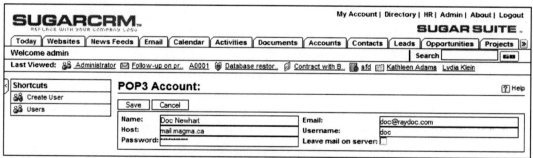

Adding a POP3 Email Account

The Sugar CRM system actually receives email for all users by periodically running a task that looks for email for every user in the system, for all of their POP3 email accounts they have listed. This scheduled task (or Cron job in Unix terminology) is set up in a similar manner to the mass emailer used in marketing campaigns. It typically runs every 5 minutes, to make sure everyone has their email available to them in a timely fashion.

Sugar Pro Add-Ons

SugarCRM is not your average open-source project, backed as it is by a Silicon Valley business with over 25 Million USD in funding. One thing we all know about venture capital firms—they need to see how the money they put in will produce more money coming back to them. For some commercial open-source businesses, that means making money providing support services for their software. But increasingly, and certainly true in SugarCRM's case, the commercial open source model includes some extended commercial versions of the software.

SugarCRM produces Sugar Pro and Enterprise versions, which cost 239 and 449 USD per user per year to license, respectively. These are products that offer significantly increased capabilities over those of the Open Source version—and several of those capabilities are discussed in this section.

Product Catalog and Products Module

CRM systems like Sugar Open Source, Saleforce.com, or NetSuite are all referred to as **front-office** applications. The front of the business is the customer facing part of the business, and it is run by applications such as these.

The **back-office** applications are those that interface with internal operations and suppliers, and which prepare financial statements and results.

Integrating front- and back-office operations into one application is the goal of expensive ERP systems for large enterprises (such as SAP). These solutions typically cost millions of dollars. Arguably, NetSuite (the name of the company and also the name of its premium product) is the best of the systems targeted at smaller businesses in terms of being able to integrate front- and back-office activities into a single system—but even it is quite expensive, and only available as an on-demand solution!

Personally, I believe that a smaller business can gain most of the benefits of an integrated system by simply adding the most frequently and broadly used aspects of the back-end activities into the front-end application—having it also cover what we might perhaps call the middle. By the middle, I mean activities such as preparing customer quotations, invoices, and sales orders—and potentially even order processing. If your CRM can help you do this, then the *wide* parts of your company—the customer-facing and customer-affecting parts—have been made much more efficient.

If you have such an extended CRM system (now covering front and middle), and link the resulting invoice or sales order data to your accounting system (by data export, or by web-service linkages to online systems), you can create a very effective solution at a bargain price.

You can also create a situation where only a limited number of user licenses are required for the accounting software. Only the real accounting people who are posting transactions to ledgers need licenses—which is not the case with an integrated system. This approach also relegates the accounting function truly to the back office—minimizing that part of the business which has no direct involvement with the customer or profit creation.

Sugar Open Source has none of these back-office (or perhaps, middle-office) capabilities, but Sugar Pro does have some initial modules that support this approach. And there are plans to add more of these capabilities in future releases.

The initial two modules of this type within Sugar Pro are the Product Catalog and the Products module. The Product Catalog is in the Administrator area of the system, and keeps track of what types of products you have available for sale, and the quantity in stock. The Products module then keeps track of the movements of those products—any units that have been quoted, ordered, or shipped to customers. If you license Sugar Pro, these two modules are included, and function as described next.

Product Catalog

There are four product catalog administration functions, which are used for maintaining the items in the Product Catalog, as well as the product categories, product types, and manufacturers to be used when defining items in the Product Catalog.

- The Product Catalog administration option displays a list view of all current items in the product catalog. You can choose to click on the name of an item in the list to see the detail view for that item, and potentially edit it. Or you may use the shortcuts menu to create a new item in the Product Catalog, or switch to viewing manufacturers, product categories, or product types. You may also import product items from Salesforce.com or via a custom field mapping.

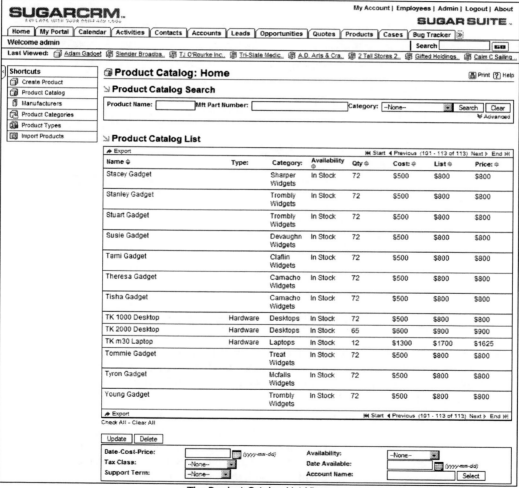

The Product Catalog List View

Note that product type is a high-level classification of items within the product catalog, and product category is a lower-level classification. One might have a product type for the broad area of software, and a product category for a more narrow area such as spreadsheet, word processor, or CRM Software. With version 3.5, a tree structure was introduced for the category organization of products, allowing for a much more detailed breakdown of products in the catalog, making the type field largely useless.

When creating a new catalog item, or editing an existing item, you enter data including the item name, associated URL, tax class, availability, the supplier, category and type, as well as the cost, list and purchase prices, and their currency. There is also a default pricing formula, which may be set to Fixed Price, Profit Margin, Markup over Cost, Discount from List, or Same as List.

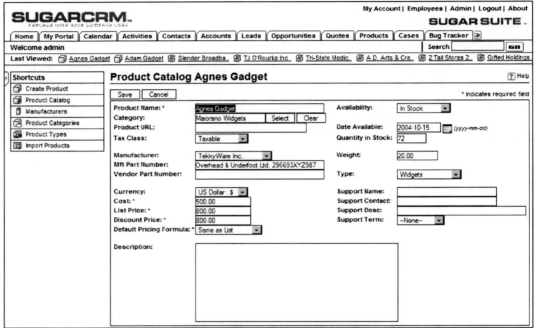

The Product Catalog Edit View

- The Product Types administration option lets you maintain the product types that are available for the classification of items in the product catalog. Each product type consists of a name and a description, as well as the order in which the entry is to appear in the drop-down list.

- The Product Categories administration option lets you maintain the product categories that are available for the classification of items in the product catalog. Each product category consists of a category name, the name of the parent category, and a description, as well as the order in which the entry is to appear in the drop-down list (largely irrelevant now with the category tree).

- The Manufacturers administration option lets you maintain the manufacturers that are available as selections within the Products module. Each manufacturer entry consists of a name and a status (Active or Inactive, where inactive will remove it from the drop-down list for manufacturer), as well as the order in which the entry is to appear in the drop-down list.

Products Module

The Products module keeps track of products that have been quoted, ordered, or shipped—as defined within the as yet somewhat limited order management framework of Sugar Pro.

Take care not to confuse the Products module with the product catalog functions within the Administration area, which define the products that are available to be sold.

A product may be created from an item in the product catalog, or may be custom-created by simply entering any name desired as the product name.

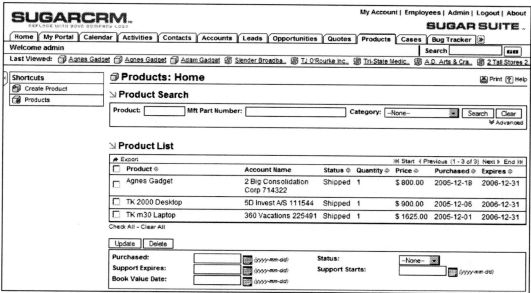

Products List View

By checking the list of products, employees can determine the activity for products—what quotes, orders, and shipments have been taking place.

Quotes Module

The Quotes module is another feature of Sugar Pro that broadens the reach of the CRM towards back-office type capability. This module uses data from the Product Catalog module described above to prepare customer quotations.

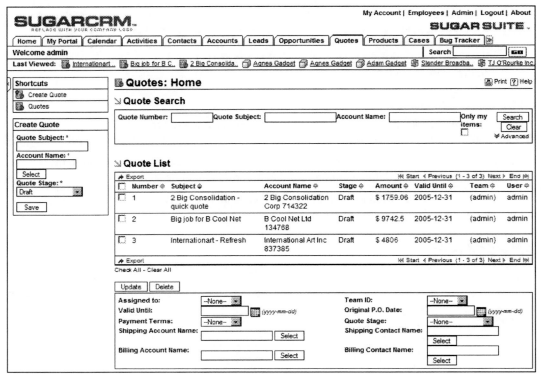

Quotes List View

Upon entering the Quotes module, you see the Quote List view screen—showing all quotes currently in the system. You can click on a quote to see the details of the quote, and further click on the detail view to edit the quote.

Preparing a quote is simple. Click on the Create Quote shortcut, and on the screen that comes up, enter a subject for the quote, the date to which the quote is valid, and select the Bill to and Ship to accounts (with a handy button to copy one to the other if they are the same).

SUGARCRM.
REPLACE WITH YOUR COMPANY LOGO

My Account | Employees | Admin | Logout | About

SUGAR SUITE

| Home | My Portal | Calendar | Activities | Contacts | Accounts | Leads | Opportunities | Quotes | Products | Cases | Bug Tracker |

Welcome admin

Search [_____]

Last Viewed: Internationart... | Big job for B.C... | 2 Big Consolida... | Agnes Gadget | Agnes Gadget | Adam Gadget | Slender Broadba... | T.J O'Rourke Inc...

Shortcuts
- Create Quote
- Quotes

Quotes: Internationart - Refresh

Help

| Save | Cancel |

* Indicates required field

Quote Subject: *	Internationart - Refresh	Opportunity Name:	
Quote Number:	3		Select
		Quote Stage: *	Draft
Purchase Order Num:		Valid Until: *	2005-12-31 (yyyy-mm-dd)
Payment Terms:	--None--	Original P.O. Date:	(yyyy-mm-dd)
Team:	admin		
Assigned to:	admin	Select	

Bill to

Account: *	International Art Inc 837385
	Select
Contact:	Bianca Uchida
	Select
Address:	48920 San Carlos
City:	Kansas City
State:	NY
Postal Code:	85538
Country:	USA

Ship to

Account:	International Art Inc 837385
	Select
Contact:	
	Select
Address:	48920 San Carlos
City:	Kansas City
State:	NY
Postal Code:	85538
Country:	USA

>>
<<

Line Items

| Currency: | US Dollar : $ | Tax Rate: | 8.25 - Cupertino, CA | Shipping Provider: | FedEx | Display Grand Total: ☑ | Display Line Numbers: ☑ |

Group Name: Hardware Items   Group Stage: Draft

Quantity	Product		Mft Num	Tax Class	Cost	List	Unit Price	
8	18	Reflective Mirror Widget	Select	2.0	Non-Taxable	200.00	325.00	267.00	Remove Row
8	2	TK m30 Laptop	Select	ABCD123	Taxable	1300.00	1700.00	1625.00	Remove Row

| Add Row | Add Comment |

Subtotal:	8056.00
Tax:	268.13
Shipping:	0.00
Total:	8324.13

| Delete Group |

Grand Total
Subtotal: 8056.00
Tax: 268.13
Shipping: 0.00
Total: 8324.13

| Add Group |

Description Information

Description:

Creating a Quote

Then simply click on the Add Group button to define the initial product grouping on the quote, and then click on the Add Row button to add items to that group. On each row, use the Select button to select a product from the catalog—then set the quantity and if you need to, edit the unit price from the default.

You can create additional groups to organize sections of your quotation, because they address different needs, are to be delivered on different schedules, or for a variety of other reasons.

When you are done, simply click on Save. The quote may now be used to create an opportunity (if the request for a quote came out of the blue), or a PDF may be generated from the quote—presented either as a proposal, or as an invoice. Standard PDF templates are provided with Sugar Pro, which may be edited to include your company logo and address details.

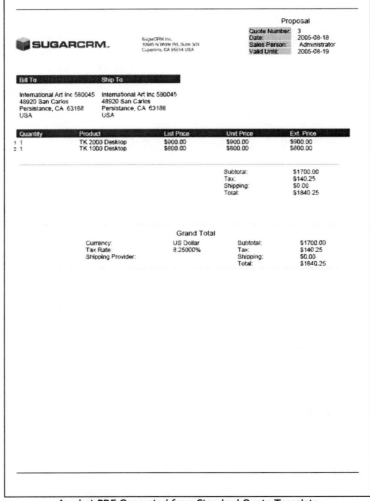

Acrobat PDF Generated from Standard Quote Template

Forecasting

Sales people (account executives, account managers, sales representatives, whatever the preferred title of the day may be) who work in organizations with a substantial sales group that is overseen by a sales manager or VP of Sales, are generally all too familiar with the phrase—"What is your commit number?" And missing your commit number is getting all too close to being a shooting offense!

While Sugar Open Source has opportunities and pipelines from which to estimate sales in a coming month, or the current quarter, Sugar Pro has a mechanism that allows the sales manager to formalize the commit number for each sales person, and roll them up to the regional or organizational level. These commit numbers are known by their polite name—the forecast.

The forecasting process begins with the definition of the forecasting periods—typically, financial quarters, or months. This is done in the Administrator area of the system.

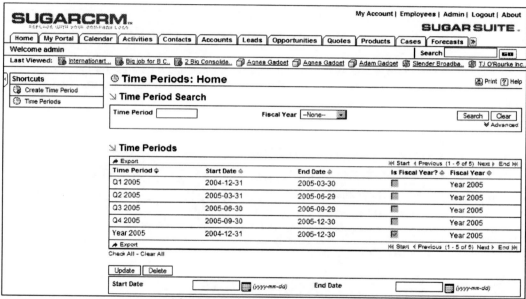

Administration of Forecast Time Periods

Once the forecasting periods have been defined, each sales person can set their forecast commitments by using the Forecasts tab. Upon entry, this module shows the forecast history. This displays a list of the time periods available to the user, and all historical commitments that the user has made for those time periods.

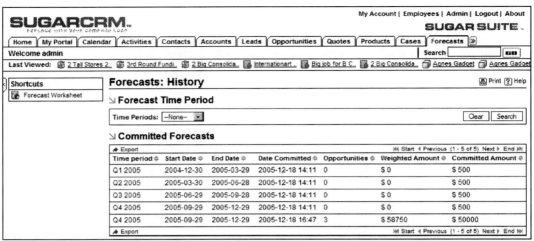

Forecast History

On the screen above, for example, we can see that the user once had a forecast for Q4 of only 500 USD—but that it has now been raised to 50,000 USD—on the basis of three opportunities whose weighted values total $58,750 USD.

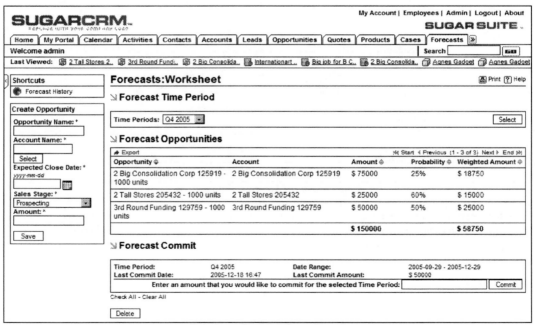

Entering a Forecast Commitment

That forecast was entered on a forecast worksheet, accessed from the Forecast History shortcut. On it, the user selects the time period to be forecast, and all opportunities for that period are automatically displayed, with their weighted value. The Commit button is used to enter a new commitment for the forecast time period. Note that a history of prior commitments for that time period is also displayed.

If the user supervises any other sales people (each user's profile has a setting for Reports To, which defines their supervisor) then they see a variant of the above screen that allows them to see a forecast roll-up of their own forecast plus that of all their direct reports. The radio button at the top allows the user to select between My Forecasts (which shows a screen like the previous figure), or My Team's Forecasts, which displays a screen like the figure below:

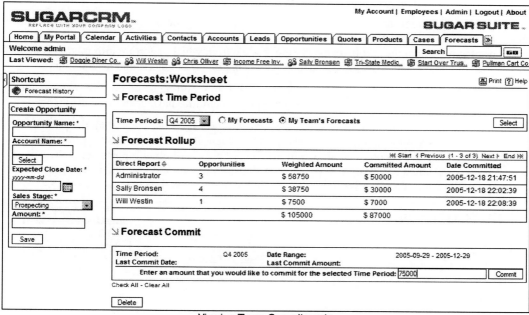

Viewing Team Commitments

This system provides a good hard commitment record for sales forecasting, and a solid, undeniable audit trail! As well, the roll-up system provides a practical and quick way to scale sales forecasting even to quite large organizations.

Standard and Custom Reporting

There are several important weaknesses in SugarCRM Open Source—and the complete lack of reporting is probably the biggest of all. In its absence, users of the Open Source system must manage by using the list views in each module, and the Dashboard. For smaller companies, this is just about acceptable. But as organizations get larger and the data becomes more complex, reporting becomes mandatory and not just a nice-to-have feature.

Some of the simple reports you might want from a CRM would include:

- **List of Accounts**: Filtered by, say, account type—just customers, just partners, just suppliers, and so on
- **List of Contacts**: Filtered by, say, the user to whom they are assigned
- **List of Opportunities**: Filtered and sorted by such criteria as sales stage, probability percentage, the user they are assigned to, and the estimated closing date (so you can report by the month or quarter)

Typically, reporting capabilities within business systems fall into two categories: standard reports and custom reporting. Standard reports are just as they sound—a series of pre-defined reports that the creators of the system are certain will be relevant to you—at least from time-to-time.

Custom reporting systems are more difficult to create (especially good ones!), and they provide the ability for the user to define their own reports. In the case of Sugar Open Source or Pro the user would want at minimum the ability to specify the module from which reporting information is to be drawn, the columns of data to be presented, and if any columns are numeric and need totaling,

Historically this is just about exactly what Sugar Pro's custom reporting could do. But with versions 3.5 and 4.0 of the Pro product, more advanced reporting capabilities have been made available.

When you first click on the Reports module in Sugar Pro, you see a list view of all the published reports in the system. So what is a published report? In Sugar Pro, the system is supplied with very few (in fact, 6) standard reports—as shown in the figure below. All other reports begin their lives as custom reports. Once you design, save, and run a custom report, and you like it, you may choose to publish that report so that it is made available to others in the company.

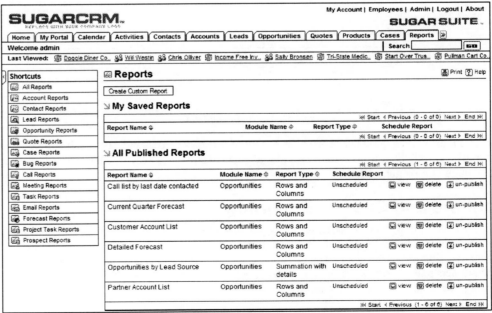

Published Reports List View

To get a feel of this process, let's see what it is like to build a custom report, and then publish it.

To start off with, you should notice that the Reports module has a long set of shortcuts in it. Each shortcut displays a list of the published reports of that particular type—reports on accounts, opportunities, contacts, and so on. All the reports shown opposite happen to be opportunity reports.

For our sample report, we will build a very useful report that lists all the accounts in the system that are classified as customers, and then within each of those accounts, lists the name and contact information for each contact at that account.

So to build this report, first we click on the Create Custom Report button.

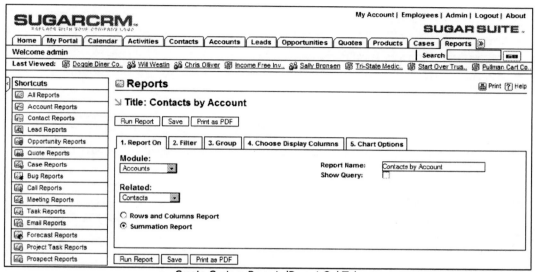

Create Custom Report: 'Report On' Tab

We see a screen with five tabs, Report On, Filter, Group, Choose Display Columns, and Chart Options. In the first tab we specify the module(s) we wish to report from, and the report name, and choose if this is a summation report or a rows and columns report. Since we will be listing contacts grouped by their account, this is classified as a summation report.

Even though it is the contacts that we are most interested in for this report, we must start with the Accounts module information, as the first thing we do is limit ourselves to those accounts that are marked as customers. So we choose Accounts as our first module, and Contacts as the related module.

If we now click on the Filter tab, we see a system for filtering which accounts are to be included in the report, and we simply specify that the Type field should hold the value Customer.

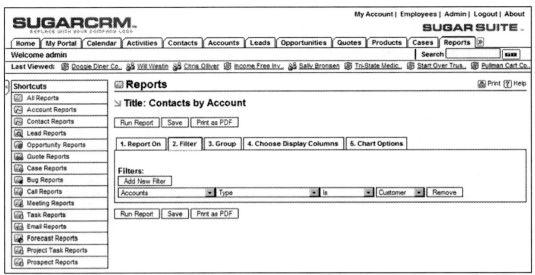

Create Custom Report: 'Filter' Tab

As we proceed to the Group tab, we see that we can group contacts together that have the same account name.

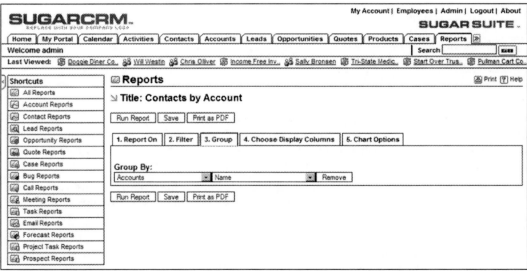

Create Custom Report: 'Group' Tab

On the Choose Display Columns tab, we actually assemble the real information of the report.

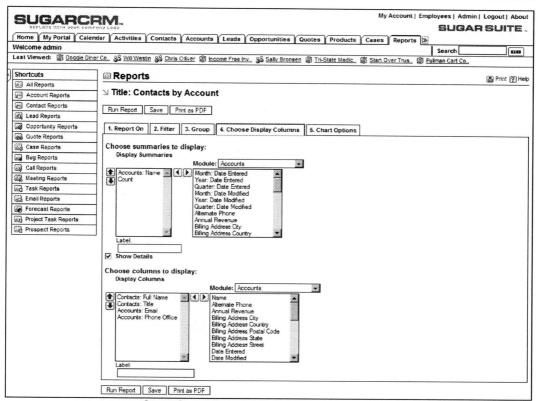

Create Custom Report: 'Choose Display Columns' Tab

In the figure above, we specify that on the summary line for each account, we will display the account name and the count of the number of related contacts, and that under each account group, we will display the details of the contacts for each account. (It would not be much of a report if we did not—as we would only list the names of the customer-type accounts, but no contacts!)

Then underneath that, we specify the fields from the Contacts module that we want to have listed in the report. There are controls on the left to change the order of those fields as you prefer. And when you click on a field in the list on the left, you may type in a name below for the label to be used for that column of the report.

On the fifth tab, Chart Options, we can choose the chart type to be displayed and the data series to be plotted on that chart, as well as entering the description for the chart. In our example, Count is the only data series which may be plotted on the chart.

Note that a summation report with a group-by column and one summary column is required within a report definition before an associated chart may be rendered.

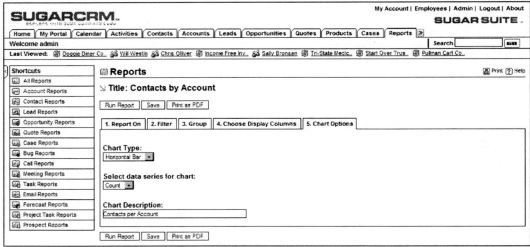

Create Custom Report: 'Chart Options' Tab

When you have completed the last tab, click on **Save** or **Run Report**, and the report is executed, and displayed like this (only the beginning of the report is shown in the figure opposite):

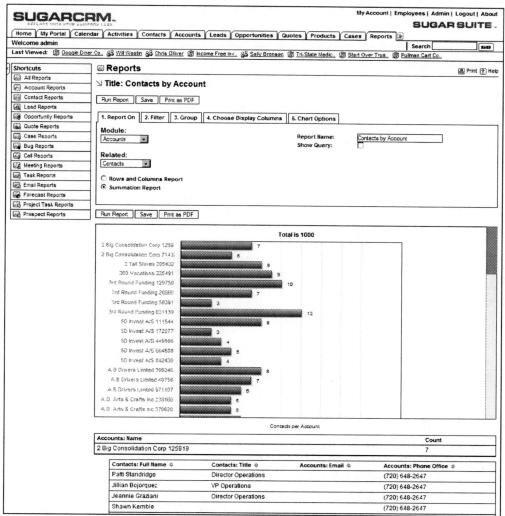

Sample Custom Report

Notice the option to print the report as an Acrobat PDF file, which is extremely useful.

If the user now clicks on the shortcut for Account Reports, the system shows a new report there, like this:

Account Reports

Note that the new report is classified under My Account Reports. By clicking on the publish link to the right of that report, the report may be published and made available for everyone in the company to run. Once that is done, the new report is displayed in the list of all published reports view which is the default view upon entering the reports module.

Sales Teams

As noted in the section about the role management extension, SugarCRM Open Source has a significant weakness in the areas of permission management and data security. To address this weakness, in Sugar Pro SugarCRM chose to define teams for information sharing.

Each data item in the system has its structure changed, to include a field that says which team owns the data—much like an extension of the field that assigns the data to a user. Note that the Assigned To field still exists as well.

In the Administrator area there is a team management feature added, in which teams are defined.

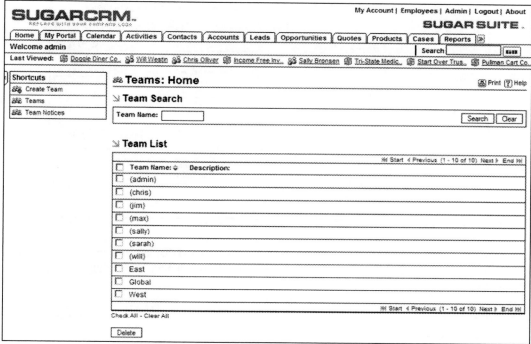

Team List View

Users may be assigned to one or more teams, giving them the ability (say as a Sales Manager) to see sales opportunities and customer information from perhaps the Western, Central, and Eastern regions, if there were a team defined for each region.

A team may also be defined with the same name as a user, to create a team that private or personal information may safely be assigned to.

The rules for data access are very simple—you can see data if you are on the team to which that data is assigned. If data is assigned to a team to which all employees belong—then everyone can see that information. One drawback of this system is that if you can see a data item, you can also edit it or delete it—there is no *grey-scale* of permissions, such as read-only access. With Release 4.0 of Sugar Pro, this drawback was addressed with the enhancement of the role management system—more on this shortly.

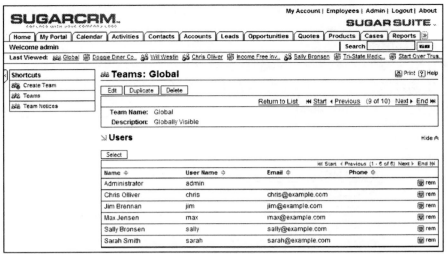

Team Detail View

One very handy function associated with teams is the creation and display of team notices. On the Home tab within Sugar Pro, a new section is created that shows an animated rolling display of team notices:

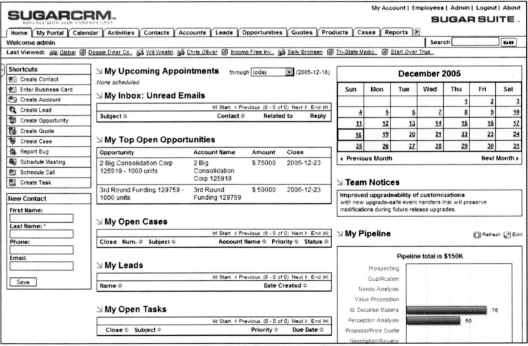

Home Page with Team Notices Section

There is also a shortcut available to create team notices. Clicking on this shortcut shows a list of all existing team notices, plus a form to create a new notice. Notices can be created with a start and stop date, and may also link to a URL for more details.

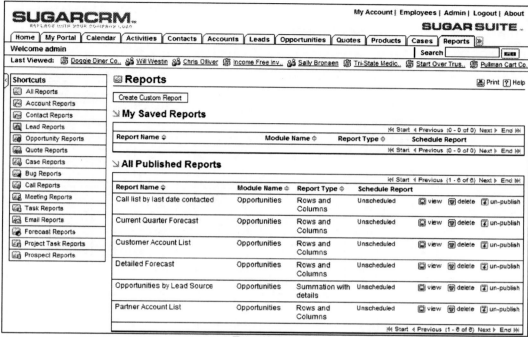

Team Notices

Enhanced Role Management: Access Control Lists

Role Management within Sugar Open Source, up to and including release 3.5, was a rather weak function—simply allowing the system administrator to create roles that could limit which tabs each user could access within the system based upon the roles to which each user was assigned.

With the release 4.0 of Sugar Open Source and Pro, role management was expanded significantly, and addresses the lack of a rich permission management or access control system within Sugar. In the case of Sugar Open Source (which lacks the teams feature of Sugar Pro) this enhanced role management feature was an improvement, but still not complete. But within Sugar Pro it combines with the teams feature to produce a very effective access control system.

The **Access Control List (ACL)** mechanism manages the actions (Read, Write, Delete, Update, Import, and Export) that a user can perform within each module. Each user may be assigned to one or more roles, and when they have multiple roles the most restrictive permissions will determine their actual capabilities. The following screen shows the role of a Junior Administrator who can read, write, and update, but cannot delete, import, or export, the data from any module.

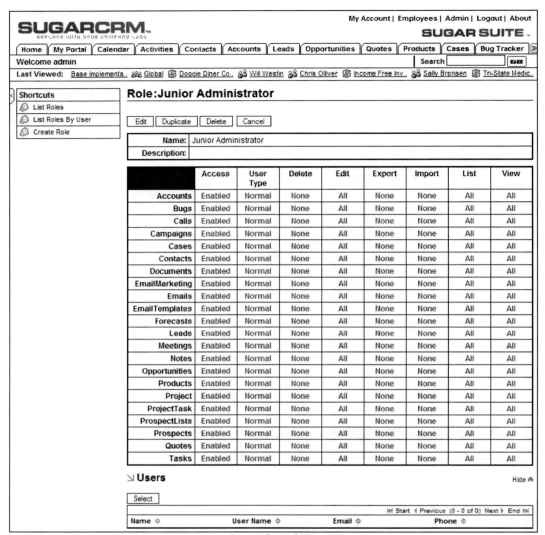

Access Control List

Sugar Wireless

Sugar Wireless is a separate application (sharing the same database) that provides a sub-set of the Sugar capabilities, but with screen layouts that are formatted for small form-factor wireless devices with web browsers.

The value of this sort of application is quite clear—the ability to access Sugar data when you are not near an Internet-connected PC. You can access data for contacts, leads, accounts, opportunities, calls, and meetings.

With a device such as a Treo 650, PocketPC, or BlackBerry, you can browse to a web address that is a little different from your usual CRM access address, and see small, unadorned screens with simple Sugar layouts. Try the demo at `http://demo.sugarondemand.com/wireless/`, preferably from your handheld, and see it for yourself.

Like the regular Sugar CRM, you will first need to log in to the system. You use the same username and password as you do for the usual system.

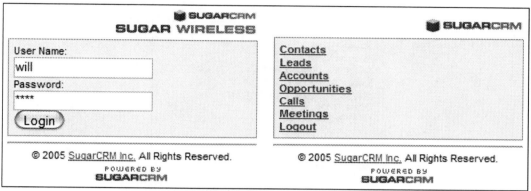

Wireless Login and Menu

Then you see the abbreviated menu, with the options available to you in the wireless version. You just click on a link (or roll the wheel to select and then click on a BlackBerry) to choose one of the modules. If you choose Contacts, for example, you will see this:

Wireless Contact List View

Eight contacts are listed with their details. Previous and Next buttons are provided to go to the next or previous page of contact data. If you have a lot of contacts, this won't be very productive, so a search capability is also provided:

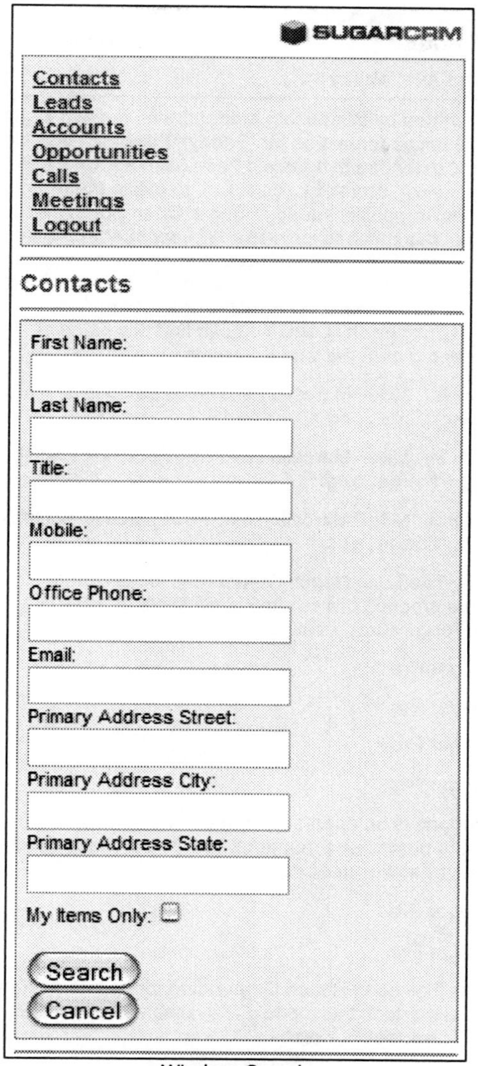

SUGARCRM

Contacts
Leads
Accounts
Opportunities
Calls
Meetings
Logout

Contacts

First Name:

Last Name:

Title:

Mobile:

Office Phone:

Email:

Primary Address Street:

Primary Address City:

Primary Address State:

My Items Only: ☐

(Search)
(Cancel)

Wireless Search

Only you can decide which you prefer—handheld browser access to your Sugar data, or handheld wireless Sync of your data from the handheld back to your server. I find that applications native to the handheld device operate so much more responsively, and make so much better use of the screen layout, that I almost always prefer to do the Sync, and then use the local applications.

Moreover, speed is an issue. Between poor wireless bandwidth, and poor processing power on the handheld creating a slow browsing experience, I have not generally enjoyed using Sugar Wireless nearly as much as I had hoped to.

Add-on Summary Table

Name	Author and Availability	Sugar OS Support
Role Management	Originally written by Badarinath Medendravu, (known in the SugarCRM online forums as Mr. Baddy), this patch was later revised and extended by Marcelo Leite (also known as Mr. Milk, of AnySoft—www.anysoft.com.br), to utilize the Roles management capability added in Sugar Open Source v3.0. An extension of this patch to include a full user interface within a heavily modified Role Management module (which also eliminated Mr. Baddy's original Hierarchical security approach) was developed by The Long Reach Corporation (www.thelongreach.com). You can find this patch at SugarForge.org or in the Sugar Forums.	3.0C & later
Team Security	Created by Mr. Milk—Marcello Leite—this patch is available from www.sugarforge.org.	3.5 & later
Project GANTT Charts	Created by Mr. Milk—Marcello Leite—this patch is available from www.sugarforge.org.	
Organization Charts	Created by Mr. Milk—Marcello Leite—this patch is available from www.sugarforge.org.	
Company Directory	Created by The Long Reach Corporation for its Info At Hand commercial product, this module is available at www.thelongreach.com.	3.5 & later
Products	Part of Sugar Pro	2.0 & later
Quotes	Part of Sugar Pro	2.0 & later
Forecasting	Part of Sugar Pro	3.0 & later
Reporting	Part of Sugar Pro	2.0 & later
ZuckerReports	ZuckerReports is an open-source reporting solution that may be of interest to businesses that don't wish to purchase Sugar Pro. See www.sugarforge.org.	3.01B & later
Sales Teams	Part of Sugar Pro	2.0 & later
Sugar Wireless	Part of Sugar Pro	3.0 & later
Service Contracts	Created by The Long Reach Corporation for its Info At Hand commercial product, this module is available commercially at www.thelongreach.com.	3.5 & later
Human Resources	Created by The Long Reach Corporation for its Info At Hand commercial product, this module is available commercially at www.thelongreach.com.	3.5 & later
Sync4j Wireless Synchronization	Created by Funambol, this software is available at www.sync4j.com.	3.5 & later

Name	Author and Availability	Sugar OS Support
Receiving POP Email	Created by The Long Reach Corporation for its Info At Hand commercial product, this module is available commercially at www.thelongreach.com.	3.5 & later
ZuckerMail	ZuckerMail is an open-source email add-on solution that may be of interest to businesses that don't wish to purchase a commercial add-on. See www.sugarforge.org.	3.5 & later

Participating in the Sugar Online Community

Now that you have seen some examples of the extensions available for Sugar Open Source, it is useful to know where to look for more of them. On the Internet, the SugarCRM project all starts at http://www.sugarcrm.com. This is the home of the open-source CRM business, SugarCRM Inc., which is based in Cupertino California. While the early days of the open-source project were lived out at http://sourceforge.net, and SugarCRM still maintains an open-source project on this site, it is no longer the best place to find current information about the SugarCRM open-source project.

One of the best places to look these days for Sugar info, tips, and add-on modules is on the SugarCRM forums (accessible from the menu system at http://www.sugarcrm.com, or directly at http://www.sugarcrm.com/forums/.

A very useful index of all the Sugar sites is held at http://sugarcrm.net. As explained on this site, the various Sugar-related sites and their characterizations are as follows:

- SugarCRM.com (http://www.sugarcrm.com): Home of the SugarCRM business.

- SugarForge.org (http://www.sugarforge.org): Home of open-source add-on downloads for SugarCRM—themes, modules, and various widgets and gadgets that bolt onto SugarCRM—as well as a home for a number of projects for Sugar add-ons whose development is ongoing.

- Demo (http://demo.sugarondemand.com/sugarcrm): This is where you want to go for a demo of the latest version of Sugar Pro. Use /sugarcrm_os for the Open Source demo, and /sugarcrm_ent for the Enterprise version, which began with version 3.5.

- Downloads (http://downloads.sugarforge.org): This is the basic download site for Sugar Open Source, and its related themes, documentation, installers, and language packs.

- Forums (http://forums.sugarcrm.com): Home of the Sugar user forums, where you can give and get hints and tips from the thousands of Sugar users in the community.

- Store (http://store.sugarcrm.com): This is where you go to buy Sugar Pro or Enterprise, as well as the various Sugar On-Demand services.

SUGAR NETWORK

Sugar Network is the gateway for all things Sugar. Visit SugarCRM.com to learn about the company and its products. Develop or participate in projects at SugarForge.org. Experience Sugar Suite's rich functionality and intuitive user interface at Sugar Demo. Deploy Sugar Open Source at Downloads. Discuss CRM with experts at Sugar Forums. And buy Sugar Suite Enterprise or Professional at the Store

SugarCRM.com

http://www.sugarcrm.com

SugarCRM.com is the corporate homepage of SugarCRM Inc. Learn about the company, its growing customer base, and career opportunities; explore Sugar Enterprise and Professional product lines and our flexible deployment options; evaluate how quickly and affordably you can migrate your existing CRM implementation to SugarCRM. Most importantly, have fun exploring the company that is rethinking CRM.

SugarForge.org

http://www.sugarforge.org

SugarForge.org is the destination for SugarCRM's open source community to share ideas and innovations from CRM developers spanning around the world. Contributed by SugarCRM Inc., SugarForge.org offers Sugar Suite extensions, modules, language packs and themes. In addition, SugarForge.org provides a range of support and information services to benefit all SugarCRM users, including development and implementation advice, user forums and customer feedback.

Demo

http://demo.sugarondemand.com/

Sugar Demo is the place to get your hands on the hottest app in the CRM marketplace. We are so proud of the ease-of-use and speed of our product that we offer a live version of Sugar Suite. No sales people, screen shots or mock-ups. See for yourself why SugarCRM offers the best user experience with deep functionality across sales, marketing and service. When you're done, ask other software providers to do the same.

Downloads

http://downloads.sugarforge.org/

Are you ready for Sugar Suite? Download Sugar Suite Open Source. Forget the project scoping and consulting fees typical when deploying CRM applications. Click download and you will be humming in 15 minutes. Yes, it is that easy! Oh yeah... and it's free!

Forums

http://forums.sugarcrm.com/

Would you like to praise, vent, discuss or collaborate on CRM or Sugar? Sugar Forums is the place. Meet-up with CRM experts and Sugar users from around the world. Learn best practices; discuss module extensions and upcoming functionality. Become a part of the community and make Sugar Forums a better place!

Store

http://store.sugarcrm.com/

Sugar Store is the Commerce destination for SugarCRM. Purchase Sugar Enterprise or Professional and gain the advanced CRM functionality and support that has made SugarCRM the fastest-growing provider of Commercial Open Source CRM.

The Sugar Network Site

Sugar User Forums

The Sugar forums are frequented by both experienced and technically knowledgeable users, as well as those who are new and bewildered. Within the Open Source forums (there are Pro forums as well, which only become visible to customers of Sugar Pro or Enterprise), there are major sections dealing with:

- Announcements
- General Discussion
- Feature Requests
- Developers
- Translators
- Downloads
- Classifieds
- Help

There are also specific forums for business-oriented discussions on a range of topics, and for users in specific foreign languages.

New users typically frequent the General Discussion and Help areas within the Open Source forums. Once you get a little better grounded, the Feature Requests and Downloads areas become very useful and interesting as well. The Developers and Translators areas are rather specialized as indicated by their names. And the Classifieds area is one way to look for a CRM partner—although typically it is frequented by people in the technology business looking for Sugar-skilled sub-contractors.

While you may read forum posts without registering as a member, to make posts of your own you must register. You can provide a minimum of personal information, or add a photo, signature file, and other personal data to help other people know who they are interacting with. The figure overleaf shows how to log in to the forum if you are already registered, and also the link to use to register on your first visit.

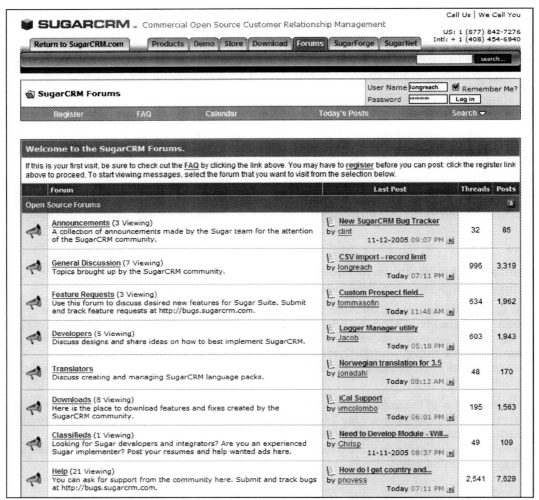

The Sugar Forums

Summary

In this chapter we have looked at over a dozen popular commercial and open-source add-ons to Sugar Open Source. Each of them extends the system in a direction that enhances the value of the Sugar Open Source CRM system to your business.

- The Role Management patch lets groups or teams share data, rather than all data being visible to and editable by all users, making the system much more popular with sales representatives and their managers.

- The Company Directory patch provides a photographic company directory, always at your fingertips.

- Direct wireless synchronization of handheld devices such as Palms, BlackBerrys, Pocket PCs, and SyncML-compliant mobile phones to the SugarCRM database—permitting sales and service personnel out of the office to access updated information, and to update account, contact , case and other information back to the SugarCRM system for all employees to share.

- The Human Resources module lets your company securely track employee details online—their salaries, their dependants, their emergency contacts, their résumés, and performance reviews, as well as their vacation and sick day history.

- The Service Contracts module allows businesses to support their service desk by tracking products sold against service subcontracts and main contracts, as well as linking all service case histories to both the products and service contracts involved.

- The POP Email add-on allows incoming email to be received by all users in Sugar Open Source, and automatically adds incoming mail to account and contact history. Attachments are handled automatically, and users may create personal email folders for filing.

- The Product Catalog and Products Module let you keep track of the products you have available for sale, as well as how many are in stock, on order, or sold to customers.

- The Quotes module let you prepare customer quotations using data from the Product Catalog, and even generates Acrobat PDFs from them.

- The Forecasting module allows each sales person to enter a hard commit number for each forecasting period, and these forecast commitments roll up through reporting lines to create forecasts at the region and organization levels.

- The reporting module allows custom reports to be designed and run—with Sugar Pro 3.5 onwards these reports can be quite complex. Reports may also be published in order to be available to all users.

- Sales Teams are a mechanism in Sugar Pro that allows data to be shared within teams, secure from other users.

- Sugar Wireless is an add-on that lets users access a sub-set of Sugar data wirelessly using a browser on their mobile phone or PDA.

We also introduced the various SugarCRM websites—a great place to keep up with the Sugar online community and get more free SugarCRM add-ons—and learned how to use the User forums. The forums can help you find others with similar customization and extension needs with whom to compare notes, and even free open-source solutions developed by other users.

In the following chapter, we shall look at the critical issue of introducing your new CRM to its users, and making sure that the system is received as an easy-to-use, capable, and valuable addition to your business management process. For any CRM system to improve your business efficiency people have to use it, and there are a number of techniques available to ensure that they do.

7

Managing Your CRM Implementation

So far, this book has dealt with the topics of introducing CRM concepts, understanding why CRM requirements differ from one organization to the next, and then studying CRM in detail by installing and using Sugar Open Source (and an array of add-ons) as a candidate CRM solution for your small or mid-size business.

In this chapter, now that you have a good background in CRM terminology and capabilities, we will study some of the real-world challenges of introducing a new CRM solution into an organization. The goal of this chapter is to leave you with a good understanding of how to approach and structure your own CRM implementation project, with a focus on these important topics:

- The key steps to a successful CRM implementation
- Some common pitfalls
- It takes a team to win (Getting the whole company on board)
- Setting project goals and specifications
- Selecting a CRM development partner
- System development
- Pilot testing
- The CRM training process—awareness, familiarity and buy-in
- CRM training materials (the content for a CRM training slideshow is included)
- Going live: Stepwise introduction—evolution, not revolution
- Continuous feedback and enhancement

As you will discover, one of the keys to a successful CRM implementation is to approach it in a stepwise manner. A great way to get the CRM ball rolling is a first phase implementation that minimizes disruption and re-training requirements, and maximizes perceived benefits for all key stakeholders.

In the following chapter, we will be discussing some fairly complex but important CRM issues, such as integrating your CRM system with your public website and with a customer self-service portal. These are not typical goals of the first phase of a CRM introduction. As such, you may choose to regard the topics that follow this chapter as an overview to those business processes that you may address with future phases of your CRM implementation program.

Key Steps to a Successful CRM Implementation

As you undertake your CRM implementation, before we get into a lot of specifics, you should understand that there is one overriding attribute to any successful CRM implementation. This common factor is open and frequent communication and collaboration.

The typical groups that are going to be significantly affected by a new CRM system, and therefore will need to be involved in its selection, development, and delivery are the following:

- Executive sponsor
- Project manager
- Implementation team
- Lead trainer
- Internal or external network administration and MIS
- Finance management
- Sales management
- Sales general staff
- Administration management
- Administration general staff

This group will be your CRM implementation team.

Successful CRM implementations share another important factor. The implementation team should manage the project relatively conservatively—set realistic goals, phase the implementation in modest steps, and view the entire process as one of continual improvement and not as a one-time event. To quote Clint Oram (a co-founder of SugarCRM) "Think big, start small, and move quickly."

Another critical factor in any successful CRM implementation is to review the different user groups—especially the last five groups listed above—and make sure that in your first implementation each of these groups perceives some value to them personally in making the effort and commitment to support the development and to use the system once it is implemented.

For example—sales general staff may be motivated if the system calculates commission reports—and will be receptive to the argument that the numbers will only be correct if all opportunities and closed sales are in the system.

Planning the Implementation

Now that we have these very important principles in the front of your mind—let's plan your implementation.

First—you need to look at the list opposite, and translate it into the right people, and the right number of people, in your organization. Clearly, the size of the group and the planning effort should be appropriate to the size of the business. For a ten-person organization, it is likely that 3-4 people need to be involved in the implementation. For a company the size of RayDoc—about 25 people—probably 6 or so people have a role to play. This quickly tapers off, and in a 200-person business you will need no more than 10-12 people to be involved in the CRM implementation process.

Your two most important players are the executive sponsor, and the project manager. Your project manager will provide the drive to ensure the project is executed successfully, and your sponsor will provide the encouragement and resources to all other participants to play their part as well.

Commonly, the executive sponsor may be the President or owner, the finance chief, or sometimes the sales manager. If you have an in-house MIS group, the sponsor should not be someone from that group. You need the business and people part of this equation to work out properly, as well as the technology—and frankly, the technology part is not the biggest risk. You need to be sure that the CRM implementation is being undertaken because of perceived business process shortcomings, and that the chosen solution will be selected because it best addresses them. Your project should not be driven by a technology push, but by a business pull.

Your project manager needs to be someone inside your organization, not someone contracted for the job. They can work closely with their opposite number on a vendor's implementation team, but they need to be someone that all the stakeholders know and trust. As well as being a person known for being very competent and detail-oriented, you need someone who is also known for communicating openly, taking suggestions, and not being overly political. If the people participating in the implementation team feel they are just window dressing, and not really involved in the process, they will quickly turn negative. If the solution feels *imposed*, staff will react with cynicism, resistance, and at best low commitment.

Your project manager needs to be your champion—someone with the people skills to get employees throughout the organization excited about the new CRM system. And as the implementation will require a lot of work from your project manager, you need to address their normal workload to make room for the CRM-related work.

Like any initiative, it is best to work from something other than a blank sheet of paper. While you do not want to present the CRM implementation team with a fait accompli at the first meeting, neither do you want to simply ask them "What you think should be done? What are the goals? What are the potential technology solutions?"

In order to focus and manage the process of agreeing upon a specific set of goals, a specific technology solution, and a particular vendor for customization, it would be advisable for the project manager and the executive sponsor to prepare an initial briefing note for the first meeting—stating what some of the key perceived shortcomings are in the current business processes, some of the potential solutions, the make-up of the CRM implementation team, the proposed timeline, and candidates for the technology to be used.

In terms of the technology candidates, it is best if all solutions on the short list of candidate systems have demo versions available for members of the team to try out. Clearly, from the title of this book, I feel that for smaller businesses, Sugar Open Source is a very good cost-effective candidate for that technology. By now, with luck, so do you. But it is essential that other opinions on the subject be heard.

By having the CRM implementation team meet regularly for a few weeks, and do offline investigation and preparation between meetings, you should quickly get to a set of business goals, as well as an agreed-upon technology base and specifications for customization. These specifications can be as simple as printed copies of screen layouts with changes marked on them.

This is where you need to get to before you talk to anyone outside your company.

As a checklist, here is what your planning needs to achieve:

- Executive sponsor identified
- Project manager identified
- Members of the CRM implementation team agreed
- Initial briefing note generated for the first team meeting
- First meeting held
- Responsibilities assigned for investigation and team briefing on key topics—these topics include:
    - Business processes needing improvement
    - Suggested improvements
    - Identifying the top three goals for the implementation
    - Base technology to be used
    - Candidates for vendor to perform implementation and customization
    - Suggested goals for phase one of the implementation
    - Suggested implementation schedule for multiple phases
    - Approach to data migration
    - Approach to training
    - Approach to stepwise introduction within the organization
- Briefings delivered at later meetings, and key decisions made on the topics above

Clearly, a larger organization will perform a more comprehensive and slower version of the process above, and a smaller one will have a more abbreviated and faster process.

Some Common Pitfalls

Just to underscore the points made in the section above, and to highlight the importance of planning and communications to the CRM implementation process, here is a list of some of the classic mistakes we unfortunately see at more client sites than not:

- Failure to get someone to take ownership of the process from start to finish.

- Failure to involve your stakeholders, especially the end users, right from the requirements gathering stage.

- Not having a focus on the current business process, the intended business process improvements, and the specifications for a system that will effect that change.

- Thinking that implementing a CRM means buying CRM software, installing it on a server, and then telling the people who need to use it.

- Not making a particular and continuing effort throughout the project to communicate the benefits specific to each user and stakeholder, to ensure their buy-in.

- Biting off too big an initial project phase, or simply proceeding as if phases are for sissies. This will load too much expenditure up front, delay implementation, and make the gap in time between initial good will and early project successes too great to bridge.

- Pursuing too rigid a development process. CRM systems are more about people than they are about technology. A process such as **Agile Programming** (Google will show you a nice article on the topic by Martin Fowler) is the sort of approach that you should use. In this approach early prototypes are used to generate feedback, and successive iterations of the user interface ensure that users feel involved, empowered, and happy. Few business users can picture every last detail of a system or screen at the outset. And few system architects know exactly what users want. Get fairly close, then try it out, and make adjustments. Repeat if necessary.

- Not training your trainer early enough, not giving them enough resources to train all users thoroughly, and not planning the roll-out to allow for sufficient training time.

- Failing to define what a successful implementation looks like at the beginning of the project.

- Failing to institute a periodic review of the CRM system, and continuing phases of development, to further improve business processes and user satisfaction.

It Takes a Team to Win

As we saw above, a CRM implementation needs the involvement of a whole team of participants. Yes, the executive sponsor and the project manager are of particular importance, but each person or group represented on the team is important, and must be continually involved in the process from beginning to end.

This continual involvement, and the ongoing effective and frequent communications between all team members, is the one thing all successful CRM implementations have in common.

Like the introduction of any new business initiative, people know when they are truly involved, or just being invited to meetings guided by an elite few in an attempt to win their cooperation.

The team members that are in management positions should typically be involved in the odd *pre-meeting-meeting* to ensure they are familiar with a specific CRM system, or a solution to a business problem, in advance, so that they can back it up in front of the whole group, or help make a change before it goes to the whole group.

One of the most common errors seen on CRM implementations is not paying enough attention in the team collaboration process to input from general sales, operations, and admin staff. The whole nature of a CRM system is that management will have no data to analyze if these people do not use the system regularly. These people need to be onboard for two very good reasons. One is the functional reason that they can best determine what an efficient data entry process is and what list views and reports are needed for everyday use. The second is the human element—the implementation needs to win these people over, and everyone reacts more positively when they are involved and have their input heeded, than when a solution is imposed on them.

Some of the techniques you may wish to use in managing the CRM implementation team (depending on the size of your business) will include:

- Define email groups to keep the entire team up to date—psychologically it makes everyone on the team a peer.

- Have the team meet physically once a week throughout the requirements definition process, and have the entire team physically sign off on the requirements.

- During development, the team can meet once every two weeks to review progress against the schedule, and to review any escalated issues.

- Once the first pass of development has been completed, the team should again meet once each week. Continue this until the entire organization has been deployed.

- Assuming there are no critical issues, have the team meet again a month after deployment has been completed, to review initial feedback, and make or plan adjustments.

- Meet again, three months and six months after initial deployment, to perform further reviews.

Setting Project Goals and Specifications

In the initial briefing note presented at the first meeting of the CRM Implementation team, you should include suggested project goals, couched in terms of current business processes and the manner in which they should be improved. If required, you should also suggest timelines and phases to the implementation process.

After some initial discussion, and depending on the scale of your business and the CRM implementation, one or more team members should be given the task of documenting in detail the suggested project goals. These can be presented and agreed at later meetings.

It will help to first simply agree upon the manner in which each business process can be improved, and not focus on any specific CRM technology.

This approach enables the team to first address the business requirements, and then assign one or more members to identifying a suggested shortlist of candidates for the core CRM technology to be used for the project.

That shortlist should then be presented to the entire team, and a winning candidate agreed, that appears best suited to satisfying the agreed business requirements, and which also has credible references.

Then the team can generate and choose some sketches and specifications of suggested screen layouts for list, detail, and edit view screens. These may only be minor variants of the existing CRM screens, or they may require heavy customization. The overall project timeline and phases foreseen to complete it should also be discussed and agreed at this stage.

Once the team has developed and agreed upon a set of detailed project business goals, identified the desired project timeline and phases, agreed a core CRM technology, and developed detailed drawings and specifications, it is time to look for the CRM development partner who will put your CRM all together for you, and will in effect join the (previously internal members only) CRM implementation team.

Selecting a CRM Development Partner

If you think you can do this without external help—think again. Ask yourself these questions:

- Have I worked through dozens of CRM implementations and gained insights into what can go wrong and why?
- Have I got experience in data import and massaging techniques gained from years of CRM implementations?
- Am I comfortable with my ability to interpret a business process into software workflow and screen designs?
- Will I inspire the confidence internally that an external domain expert can?

Your first task in the process of finding the right partner is to assemble a short list of candidate firms. Look in the yellow pages under *Customer Relationship Management*, by all means, to get started.

One of your best sources of good information is your peers who are running their own businesses—ask your professional colleagues if they have any positive recommendations of firms focused on this type of work.

Another way to find potential partners is to look on the website of the CRM software you intend to implement, and look for its approved development partners. Make sure you find a partner focused not just on selling or hosting the software, but also on the development of custom enhancements to the standard software—as you will need some without doubt.

SugarCRM, for example, on www.sugarcrm.com, has a list of its partners organized by country, with links back to the homes pages of each of those organizations. Note that you shouldn't necessarily rule out a partner because they are not in your city or country.

A final suggestion for building your shortlist of candidates to become your CRM development partner is to simply search for the name of the CRM you intend to use, on Google, and look at the advertisements on the right, as well as the links on the left.

Once a member of the team has the shortlist of candidate firms assembled (about 3-4 is the most you want), then they should bring the list back to the CRM implementation team to be approved, and to assign the evaluation work.

Do not split up the evaluations—the same one or two people should speak to all candidate firms, and come up with a report and a recommendation to the team. Emphasis should be placed on personal compatibility with the internal Project manager, demonstrated competence and knowledge, high quality reference implementations, a credible and acceptable proposed project timeline, and acceptable pricing with perceived high value for the budget.

Before you make your final selection of a partner, the team should make a tentative selection, based on initial specifications and the candidate firms' estimated development budget. Then you should work together to jointly develop a final agreement with a very detailed specification, and a fixed development cost. If you can do that successfully, you have your CRM development partner.

Once you make the final selection of your CRM development partner, you will likely have to make a substantial initial deposit against the development work to be undertaken and then you are up and running.

System Development

The typical CRM development process, even within a single phase of an overall CRM implementation program for your business, is broken down into a number of major areas—such as enhancements to be made to the accounts model, to contacts, to projects, and so on, as well as the custom reports and charts you may need.

While some of these alterations may interact with each other, many of them will not, and clusters of functionality can typically be identified that are fairly independent of each other.

Usually the best practice is to have the partner develop these off site, and then introduce each new function-cluster to you for evaluation one at a time (typically through a development website that is exposed just to you). Unless you have spent the time and money to develop a remarkably detailed specification, there will always be issues such as "I thought that control would be a dropdown, not a radio button", or " I wanted the tab order to go like this ...", or "When you select a value in that field—this other field is meant to be pre-populated."

Performing initial acceptance testing on each function-cluster one at a time lets the internal CRM implementation team focus on it clearly, and ensure that they get it implemented exactly as they need it. Then they can move on to the next function-cluster, and so on until a full first pass of the application has been implemented and accepted.

Now full acceptance testing on the integrated CRM application should be performed by your team and a formal sign-off performed against a specific revision of the software on the evaluation website.

Once that has been done, the CRM application is either hosted by a hosting supplier (which may be your CRM development partner again), or the now custom CRM application software is delivered to you for installation on your own server hardware. If the latter, you will need a further brief acceptance test of the application as installed on your own server.

Data Import

While the acceptance testing is going on, any past CRM or contact manager data that you wish to import into your CRM solution should be getting prepared, converted, and imported. Data import, checking and cleanup can itself easily take weeks to perform (when there is lots of data, and it comes from an awkward and complex source format)—so make sure to allow sufficient time.

Do not think that the big job is to get the data into the CRM, and that you can clean it up afterwards. The big job is to get the data cleaned up. Ask yourself—are there any transformations that should be performed on the data while it is outside a CRM—the assignment of accounts to users, for example—by postcode perhaps? Will you design and run a scan for duplicates?

When you have approved the software customization and development process, and your imported data looks just right, you are ready to start introducing your new CRM to the most important people in the process—its users.

Pilot Testing

Pilot testing of the CRM is a critical step of the process. Each section of the CRM should be tested by one of the user that are most dependent on that section working optimally. Sales management should test the pipeline charts. Sales staff and Finance should test the commission reports. Sales, service, and admin general staff should test the usability of account, contact, opportunity, lead, and case screens. Administrators should evaluate management reports, and so on.

I always look at it this way. A year after your implementation, no one will remember clearly if it was on time, or on budget. All they will remember is if you produced a system that is now a critical part of the organization's business processes, if they like the system, and if they felt like a part of its introduction.

Project managers should not be afraid to send the system back for re-work if the initial pilot testing indicates significant dissatisfaction with the usability of the system, or the accuracy with which it adheres to the desired business processes.

The CRM Training Process

CRM training has two goals and making the users familiar with the system and teaching them how to use it is only one of them. The other goal is to generate positive momentum for the implementation, and enthusiasm in the user base.

To accomplish this latter goal, you need to make sure people like what they see—especially the general sales staff, and to some degree the general administrative staff—as these are the two most likely sources of resistance and negative reactions.

Therefore your approach should be as follows:

Session 1: Initial Management Training and Product Exposure

Goals:

- To create awareness in Senior Management, to stimulate questions, and to discover any shortcomings early, within a controlled group that consists of those individuals most likely to be supportive of the CRM implementation and its goals.
- To finalize and clarify all system access details with MIS.

Attendees:

- Lead trainer
- Project manager
- Executive sponsor
- Internal or external network administration and MIS
- Finance management
- Sales management
- Administration management

After the first session, all the attendees should be encouraged to go and use the system, enter live data, and take note of any problems, questions, or dislikes.

Next Steps:

- A week later, this same group should re-assemble for session 2.

Session 2: Management Training Completion and Issue Management

Goals:

- To complete the management training, so that senior management has a good understanding of the system's capabilities, and how to operate the system.
- To make management enthusiastic about the system.
- To ensure management's full support of the broad introduction of the CRM system.
- To allow management to answer questions about the system knowledgeably, and to correct any misinformation later on from staff.
- To address any management concerns about the system function, clarify any misunderstandings, and identify any last-minute system shortcomings that must be addressed prior to general introduction of the system.

Attendees:

- Same as session 1. MIS optional.

Next Steps:

- Any mandatory fixes must be identified, documented, summarized, agreed by the CRM implementation team, and then developed and applied.
- If any fixes were required, this same group should re-assemble for session 3 to review the fixes.

Session 3: Present Final System Adjustments (Optional)

Goals:

- To reinforce the perception that the system will evolve over time, and will genuinely be guided by the needs of its users.
- To ensure management's full support of the broad introduction of the CRM system.

Attendees:

- Same as session 1.

Next Steps:

- Schedule session 4 a week later.

Session 4: General User Training Session

Goals:

- Note that there may be multiple classes scheduled for session 4. No class should have more than 6 users in it. Separating users by department is a good idea—Sales will have questions on different topics than Administration.
- To present the CRM system capabilities and method of operation in a comprehensive and logical manner.
- To stimulate class participation and questions.
- To record user feedback and open questions.
- To define initial goals for scope of use. (Departmental management participation is mandatory for this.)

Attendees:

- Lead trainer
- Project manager (not all sessions if there are many)

- Sales management
- Sales general staff
- Administration management
- Administration general staff
- All other general staff that will use the system

Next Steps:

- Optional follow-up session 5, two weeks later.

Session 5: Training Completion (Optional)

Goals:

- To close off any open questions
- To address any questions that have arisen in the last two weeks
- To re-present training sections where users seem uncertain
- To ensure a positive attitude on the part of of all users
- To record any outstanding concerns or issues

Attendees:

- Lead trainer
- Project manager
- All staff that wish to participate

Next Steps:

- Presentation of training results to CRM implementation team, including any outstanding issues identified.

CRM Training Materials

The most important prerequisites for the CRM training sessions are:

- A good trainer that can understand the business context, as well as relate to the users at their level.
- A quiet training room, with overhead projector connected to the laptop/PC of the trainer, a meeting table, and plenty of room for all attendees.
- A group of no more than six attendees, to create a constructive learning environment, and to prevent any impersonal *mob rule* negative feedback events from having a chance to start.

- All users to have been pre-configured in the system prior to the session, so they can see themselves already set up as users, and so they can use the CRM system immediately after the session if they wish.

- Optionally, you may wish to allow users to have their own PCs or laptops in the training session, to experiment with the system. If so, only allow laptop/PC use after initial orientation in the system is complete. Be prepared with slips of paper with sign-on URL, user names and passwords if you do this.

Expect each training session to be 75-90 minutes long. Any longer and attendees will want to avoid them—attention spans will only stretch so far.

While the various sessions outlined above have different goals and attendees, the material to be presented at the main sessions (1 and 4) as well as used for backup material at the reinforcement sessions (2 and 5) is largely common.

The remainder of this section contains suggested content to be used to make up a set of overhead slides for use as training material for these sessions.

While you present these slides, it is a useful technique to switch back and forth between the slideshow software, and the web browser with a live session on the go, to illustrate general points with specifics from the live software.

Always be prepared to stop the presentation to answer (somewhat sane and valid) questions—the users must always feel that the company is listening to them.

Slide 1: What is a CRM System?

- A system that manages the information and processes surrounding your organization's relationship with its customers

- Principle goals are to improve customer satisfaction and retention, plus sales efficiency and performance

- Sales as well as service/support, plus administration and even finance

- Not a contact manager—it is typically based on the distinction between an Account and a Contact

- Includes opportunity tracking and sales pipeline, lead source analysis

- Even corporate calendar, RSS news feeds, to-do lists, and email

Slide 2: CRM Deployment Options

- On Demand
- Self Hosted Application Software
- 3rd Party Hosted Application Software

Slide 3: What are our Business Goals?

- For you to fill in the goals identified by your CRM implementation team
- On your list you may want to include—
    - To improve customer satisfaction and retention
    - To improve sales efficiency and performance

Slide 4: What Functional Areas of CRM will we Use the Most?

- Again—you need to fill in the key areas of focus for your organization
- Will you use simply the core basic CRM capabilities, or broaden its use to include Marketing Campaigns, Project Management, Document Management, and so on?

Slide 5: What is SugarCRM?

- A leading CRM implementation from a commercial open-source vendor in California
- Based on the LAMP platform
- Delivers CRM capabilities (and more) into any web browser
- Are you using the Open Source or Pro version?
- What are the customizations you have had developed?
- What vendor developed those changes?
- Where do users go for support— internally and externally?

Slide 6: CRM Basics 1—System Access, Screen Layout, Navigation

- Logging In—user name, password, selecting language and theme
- Principal Screen Layout Elements
- Navigating SugarCRM—tab or side panel navigation, shortcuts
- List, Detail and Edit Views
- Main panel and sub-panels
- Logging Out

Slide 7: CRM Basics 2—Accounts and Contacts

- Account information content
- Contact information content
- Relating Contacts to Accounts
- Permissions and Security—who sees my information?

Slide 8: CRM Basics 3—Opportunities and the Sales Pipeline, Home Tab

- Opportunity information content
- Home Tab—My Pipeline, My Top Opportunities
- Dashboard Charts

Slide 9: CRM Basics 4—Calendaring

- Home Tab Calendar
- Calendar Module—Day, Week, Month, Year Views
- Shared Calendar
- Making a Quick Appointment

Slide 10: CRM Basics 5—Activities (Calls, Meetings, Tasks, Notes)

- Creating a Task
- Scheduling a Call
- Scheduling a Meeting
- Making a Note—file attachments
- My Upcoming Appointments
- My Open Tasks

Slide 11: CRM Basics 6—Email

- Entering Your Email Settings
- Sending a Single Email
- System Email Reminders
- Email Templates

Slide 12: CRM Basics 7—Advanced Interface Features

- Printing
- Getting Help
- Data Import and Export
- Mass Update
- Quick New Item Box
- Input Business Card
- Create from vCard

Slide 13: Extending CRM 1—RSS News and External Sites

- Interface Consolidation Concepts
- RSS News Feeds
- External Websites

Slide 14: Extending CRM 2—Marketing Campaigns

- Targets versus Leads and Contacts
- Target Lists
- Marketing Campaigns
- Email Marketing Program
- Mass Emailing Queue

Slide 15: Extending CRM 3—Document Management

- Document Information content
- Document Revisions
- Document Upload
- Document Download

Slide 16: Extending CRM 4—Project Management

- Project Information Content
- Project Tasks
- Monitoring Project Status

Slide 17: Extending CRM 5—Customer Service Management

- Service Cases
- Bug Tracker
- Case and Bug History

Slide 18: Extending CRM 6—Always in Touch

- Pros and Cons of Various Remote Access Techniques
- Offline Access and Synchronization
- Wireless Handheld Sync—Palm, PocketPC, BlackBerry
- Wireless Handheld Browser Access

Slide 19: Extending CRM 7—Reaching Out

- Website Lead Collection
- Customer Self-Service Portal

Going Live: Stepwise Introduction

Once employees have been introduced to the new CRM and fully trained, it is time to go live.

A common technique is to conduct general user training in sections by department, and to take each department live after they have been trained. If you adopt this approach, be sure to allow enough time after each department is trained for them to come to grips with the system and get any questions they have answered by support staff, before the next group goes through and the support staff is overwhelmed.

This is typically the approach we ourselves use at The Long Reach Corp. with our clients. The only caveat I would recommend is that you make absolutely sure that you have an accurate reading on user acceptance in all departments and roles of the organization (from acceptance testing and pilot testing) if you are going to use this approach. Once you have taken one group live, if another group provides significantly negative feedback in their training session, you have a serious problem.

Continuous Feedback and Enhancement

Just as every business itself does, every CRM system needs continuous evaluation and enhancement. As your business changes, so must your CRM system. And as the competitive business environment gets steadily more intense, your CRM must evolve and improve to maintain and advance your competitive standing in your industry.

Until the CRM system achieves a high level of internal user satisfaction, it should be reviewed at least once every business quarter for usability improvements, and any potential extensions to automate additional business processes.

Once the system is popular internally, it should be reviewed at least once every six months for potential improvements and enhancements. In particular, opportunities should be sought for more advanced methods (typically involving external connectivity) of improving your customer relationships and satisfaction, such as customer self-service portals, automated website lead collection, automated client emails advising of product shipments and problem resolutions, as well as email marketing campaigns.

Summary

In this chapter, we analyzed the process of managing and delivering a CRM implementation. Some of the key topics detailed here include:

- The makeup of a CRM implementation team
- The key steps to a successful CRM implementation
- How to plan your CRM implementation
- Some common pitfalls to avoid in your CRM implementation
- The importance of genuine team involvement
- How to set CRM implementation project goals and specifications
- How to select a CRM development partner
- Managing your data import process
- The CRM training process, for both management and staff
- CRM training materials—suggested content for a CRM training slideshow was provided
- Stepwise introduction of your CRM system as a key to a successful initial CRM implementation and overall long-term CRM program
- Continuous user and customer feedback and resulting improvement of the CRM system as key to keeping your business operating at its competitive best

In the following chapter we will go on to study more advanced CRM topics, which increasingly link your CRM to all your key business processes, as well as to your existing customers and future prospects. Typically an organization will address these capabilities after the initial phase of the CRM implementation is complete, as part of its ongoing program of continuous improvement.

8
Linking SugarCRM to Your Customers

Surely the most important goal of any CRM system is to make your customers feel positive about your company, and to make them feel that exciting things are happening at your company such as:

- That the employees they are in contact with are caring and well informed
- That new and better information systems are coming into place
- That your company is keeping them better informed about their orders and shipments, their service issues, and new product and service introductions

When a CRM is limited to interacting with only the employees of a business, it will certainly affect the first item above positively, but not necessarily the other items. To really improve a customer's perception of your organization, one of the biggest improvements can be to let them interact almost directly with your CRM system. Some of the activities that this makes possible are:

- Capturing customer leads and requests for information from the public website, directly into the CRM.
- Developing email auto-responders within the CRM to send out requested information, and to advise clients of activities involving their orders and shipments—such as order receipt notices, advice of expected delivery dates, and shipping advice notes.
- Developing a customer self-service portal in conjunction with the CRM system, to allow clients to file their own service cases, to check on the latest status on a case, and to update their own customer profile.
- Linking an email marketing campaign to a public website, which then captures client requests for information and inserts the lead data directly into the CRM, complete with lead source information.

Most of us in our own lives can forgive or understand when a family member, friend, or supplier lets us down a bit, or makes a mistake—as long as they communicate with us honestly and effectively. In addition, with early detection of any errors, corrective action can always be put in place more quickly. Integrating your CRM more directly with your customer is no more complicated than this—promoting more effective, more accurate, and timelier communications with your customers, in order to make them feel informed, valued, and empowered.

Capturing Customer Leads from a Public Site into your SugarCRM Installation

Capturing leads from a public website directly into your CRM is one of the greatest early initiatives you can implement in terms of streamlining business processes to save time and effort. In this section we will show you how to do this with SugarCRM.

As our working example here, we will use the public site for **The Long Reach Corporation**. (By rights, we should really use RayDoc as our example here, but as RayDoc is not a real company, and as it was important that there be a live site you could go to look at and capture code from, we will have to make do with my own site.) On this site, there is a page that offers a free 30-day trial of Info At Hand software (a commercial extension of SugarCRM Open Source, by the way).

One key advantage of the lead capture method described here is that your public site does not need to have access to PHP scripting capabilities which many inexpensive site hosting options do not include, reserving it for higher priced offerings.

The sample lead capture page looks like this:

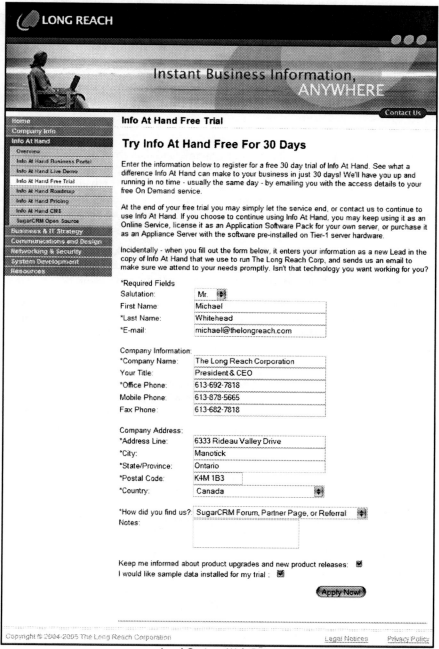

Lead Capture Web Page

> The code for the page overleaf defines and captures the data into a form. It assumes that it is sending the form data to a SugarCRM installation at the URL http://demo.longreach.net—where it is received by a PHP file called leadCapture.php in the root directory.
>
> This code can be found in the code bundle or you can browse to http://www.thelongreach.com/iah_free_trial.html and go to View | Source in your browser.

If you have several pages on your public site that capture lead data from people interested in different topics, then each page can set one field in the form data to a specific value, to indicate that the lead captured is a person interested in a particular topic. Alternatively, each lead capture page on your public site could be the same, but post its form to a different lead capture module on your SugarCRM server, which could *hardwire* the *referred by* value, as seen in the code in the next section.

One thing you will need to be careful of—the options offered for Lead Source (seen in the code above as Partner, SugarCRM forum, Google Search, and so on) need to be added to (or pre-existing) options in the drop-down list lead_source_dom. If they are not they will appear as blank.

The software that receives the form data from your public website (you can see a reference to it about one page down from the top of the code segment discussed above) is the leadCapture.php file, which is in the root directory of your SugarCRM installation. It should be edited to include certain important blocks of code that are mentioned below (the entire code file can be found in the code bundle).

At the line immediately under the comment about MODIFIED CODE, you see the reference to username and password—these must be a valid username/password combination within the SugarCRM installation. It is a good practice not to use a normal username here, but a special one like leadCapture, which is only used for this purpose. Case (upper or lower) matters here.

```
$users = array(

    // MODIFIED CODE
    'leadCapture' => array('name'=>'username', 'pass'=>md5('password')),
);

$current_user = new User();
$current_user->user_name = $users[$_POST['user']]['name'];
if($current_user->authenticate_user($users[$_POST['user']]['pass'])){
    $userid =
        $current_user->retrieve_user_id($users[$_REQUEST['user']]['name']);
    $current_user->retrieve($userid);
    $leadForm = new LeadFormBase();
    $prefix = '';
    if(isset($_POST['prefix']) && !empty($_POST['prefix'])){
        $prefix =    $_POST['prefix'];
    }

    if( !isset($_POST['assigned_user_id']) ||
!empty($_POST['assigned_user_id']) ){
        $_POST['prefix'] = $userid;
    }
```

```
$_POST['record'] ='';

if( isset($_POST['_splitName']) ) {
    $name = explode(' ',$_POST['name']);
    if(sizeof($name) == 1) { $_POST['first_name'] = '';
$_POST['last_name'] = $name[0]; }
        else { $_POST['first_name'] = $name[0];  $_POST['last_name'] =
$name[1]; }

//       die('first name is: '.$_POST['first_name'].'<br/>Last name
is:'.$_POST['last_name'].'<br/>');

}
```

The block of code between the comments START ADDED CODE BLOCK 1 and END ADDED CODE manipulates some of the form values from their captured post values into the right form for saving in the leads table.

```
// START ADDED CODE BLOCK 1
$_POST['status']        = "New";
$_POST['refered_by']    = "Lead Capture Webpage";
// convert 'opt in' checkbox into 'opt out' value
$_POST['email_opt_out'] = empty($_POST['email_opt_in']) ? 'on' : 'off';
// test_data is a custom field used by Long Reach
if(!empty($_POST['test_data']))
        $_POST['description'] = "Please set up test data on this account!";
else
        $_POST['description'] = "Do not populate this account with test
data.";
$_POST['assigned_user_id'] = $userid;
// END ADDED CODE

$return_val = $leadForm->handleSave($prefix, false, true);
```

The block of code between the comments START ADDED CODE BLOCK 2 and END ADDED CODE sends an email to sales@thelongreach.com indicating if the lead capture has been successful or not. Assume that the public site is at http://www.thelongreach.com, and that there is a file in the root directory of that site called success.html to which the user is transferred if his or her lead data has been successfully captured.

```
// START ADDED CODE BLOCK 2
if($return_val) {
    mail(
        "sales@thelongreach.com",
        "Lead Capture Success",
        "Lead Capture New Lead ID# ".$return_val->id
    );
    header("Location: http://www.thelongreach.com/success.html");
}
else {
    mail(
        "sales@thelongreach.com",
        "Lead Capture Failed",
        "Lead Capture Failed"
    );
    header("Location: http://www.thelongreach.com/failure.html");
}
exit();
// END ADDED CODE

if(isset($_POST['redirect']) && !empty($_POST['redirect'])){

    //header("Location: ".$_POST['redirect']);
```

```php
        echo '<html><head><title>SugarCRM</title></head><body>';
        echo '<form name="redirect" action="' .$_POST['redirect'].
'" method="POST">';

        foreach($_POST as $param => $value) {

            if($param != 'redirect') {
                echo '<input type="hidden" name="'.$param.
'" value="'.$value.'">';
            }

        }

        if( ($return_val == '') || ($return_val  == 0) || ($return_val < 0) )
    {
            echo '<input type="hidden" name="error" value="1">';
        }
        echo '</form><script language="javascript"
type="text/javascript">document.redirect.submit();</script>';
        echo '</body></html>';
        die();

    }else{
        echo "Thank You For Your Submission.";
    }
}
```

The block of code between the comments START ADDED CODE BLOCK 3 and END ADDED CODE transfers the user to failure.html if the lead data is not captured successfully.

```php
else
{

    // START ADDED CODE BLOCK 3
    header("Location: http://www.thelongreach.com/failure.html");
    exit();
    // END ADDED CODE

    echo "We're sorry, the server is currently unavailable, please try again
later.";
    echo '<html><head><title>SugarCRM</title></head><body>';
    echo '<form name="redirect" action="' .$_POST['redirect'].
'" method="POST">';
    echo '</form><script language="javascript"
type="text/javascript">document.redirect.submit();</script>';
    echo '</body></html>';
    die();
}

?>
```

> If you want to capture a different set of data fields than that shown in this worked example, you simply need to change the set of fields used in the page on the public site.

An example of a page to display upon a successful lead capture is as follows:

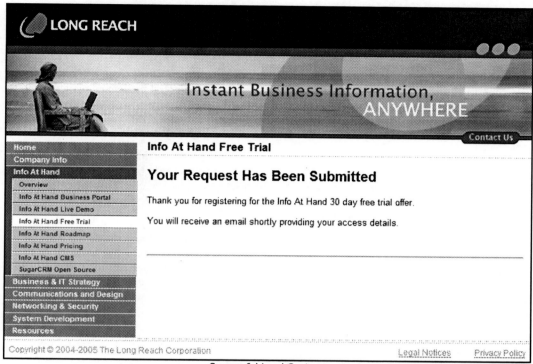

Once your public site is successfully sending leads to your CRM, and they are being captured there, and notification emails are going out to sales to follow them up—you will really begin to feel like you are making progress in your efforts to modernize and automate your organization.

There are few things quite as satisfying as driving along in the car, and receiving an email on your BlackBerry telling you that a new lead has been received. Especially when you know that it took no effort at all from anyone in the company!

And from a process perspective—having every new lead automatically entered into the CRM makes it quick and easy to convert that lead into a contact, enter details of new sales opportunities, and include them in email marketing campaigns—all without any data transcription errors, or lost leads, due to human errors.

One note of caution—most lead capture sites capture as much as 50% bad data—people who just enter anything they fancy in the form for a lark. It is handy that all new leads above are captured in a way that they are assigned to an easily identified special leadcapture username. This way the leads list view can easily be filtered to show just these leadcapture leads, and they can be checked for data quality before they enter (and potentially pollute) your general data pool.

Customer Self-Service Portals

After automating the lead capture process, the next step in linking your customers into your CRM, and therefore into your business and its processes, is the self-service portal.

Much as it sounds, this is a software system that enables your customers to exchange information with your organization in a completely autonomous manner. In this initial implementation, we will show you how to implement a system that allows customers to file service cases and software bugs within your CRM system, and then to check periodically for their updated status. The system is designed to be extensible to support customer interaction in almost any area covered by the CRM.

The fundamental capability that the self-service portal provides is to enable customers to add information into the CRM, and retrieve that information later on when it has been updated by company staff, without allowing them access to the CRM system as a whole. That information can also be provided in the context of other customer-focused information and services, creating a very positive impression and experience.

The key business value provided by such self-service portals is that customers need not wait for support staff to be available in order to report problems they are experiencing, or to check on the latest progress in resolving them—speeding the process, reducing call volumes in customer services, and allowing support staff to focus on resolving problems, not just talking about them. It also allows customers to file new issues, or check on status of existing issues, 24 hours a day, not just within business hours.

A word of caution: At the time of writing, SugarCRM 4.0 is the current Sugar version. However, it does not yet support the Mambo portal integration. Sugar 3.0 integration works solidly, and Sugar 3.5 integration seems to be just being tidied up by several contributors. Check in the SugarCRM Open Source forums for the latest information on this integration. Additionally, with the split of the Joomla portal from Mambo portal, there is now some Joomla integration work going on, so you may wish to check into that as well.

Installing the Mambo Portal

Assuming you have already installed SugarCRM Open Source on your server, you have the perfect environment already established to receive the Mambo portal. Like SugarCRM, it uses the LAMP or WAMP system software platforms.

Download the ZIP file for Mambo (versions 4.5.1 or 4.5.2 are supported by the Sugar portal components you will be installing shortly). You can find the Mambo download at `http://mamboforge.net/frs/?group_id=5`.

You can refer to the following books by Packt Publishing (www.packtpub.com) for more information regarding the Mambo open-source content management system.

- Building Websites with Mambo [ISBN 1-904811-73-6]
  (http://www.packtpub.com/mambo/book)

- Mastering Mambo : E-Commerce, Templates, Module Development, SEO, Security, and Performance [ISBN 1-904811-51-5]
  (http://www.packtpub.com/mastering_mambo/book)

Unzip the Mambo package—it produces a single main directory structure. Place this directory within your web server's document root, or within your public HTML directory. For our purposes here, it is assumed that we are installing into /mambo off the root directory of the web server. If the web server is serving the principal URL of http://longreach.net, then you would access the Mambo portal by going to the web address http://longreach.net/mambo/—and that is how we shall document the installation process here. Clearly, your server will be on a different URL, and you should change any references to the URL within this documentation appropriately.

Set the permissions on the files in the /mambo directory just the same way as you did the files in the sugar directory when you installed that software.

Now you need to create a new database, and a new database user, that will be used within MySQL for the Mambo installation. For the purposes of this chapter, assume that both of these are to be called mambo. For a Linux server, you can follow the same process that you did in the *Configure MySQL* section of Appendix A. For a Windows server, use phpMyAdmin or a similar utility to create the new database mambo, and then create the new database user, mambo and assign that user full rights to the new database.

Now—point your browser to your Mambo installation—for our example here that is http://longreach.net/mambo/. You will see the pre-installation check screen (shown overleaf) of the Mambo web-based installer, which will guide you through the balance of the Mambo installation process.

Installing Mambo Portal: Pre-Installation Check

If you have set all the file permissions correctly, and all other supporting files required by the installation process are present, all the entries in the top section of the screen should be green, allowing you to proceed with the installation. When they are, click on Next.

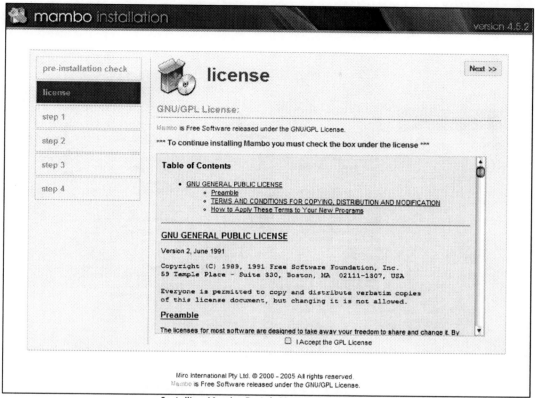

Installing Mambo Portal: License Acceptance

On the screen above, you simply accept the Mambo GPL license, and then click on Next.

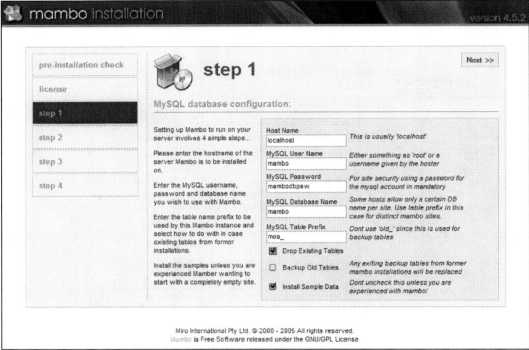

Installing Mambo Portal: Step 1: MySQL Database Configuration

Assuming that you created your new MySQL database and MySQL database user as mambo, then the setting shown in the figure above should be fine for your installation. Enter them, and click on Next.

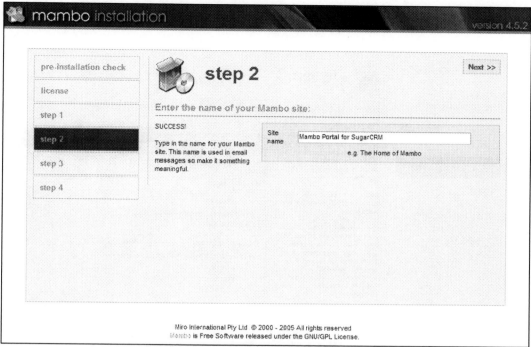

Installing Mambo Portal: Step 2: Naming Your Site

Once you get to this screen safely, you are in great shape. Simply provide a name for your Mambo site, such as the one shown above, and click on Next.

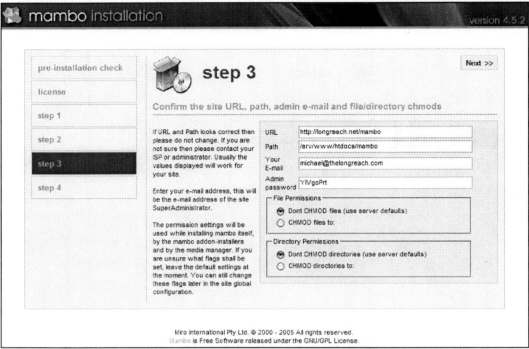

Installing Mambo Portal: Step 3: Confirm Installation Settings

Now set the URL that will be used to access your portal, and the path on your server to the root directory of the Mambo installation. Add an email address that the portal can send any important messages to, accept all other defaults, and click on Next.

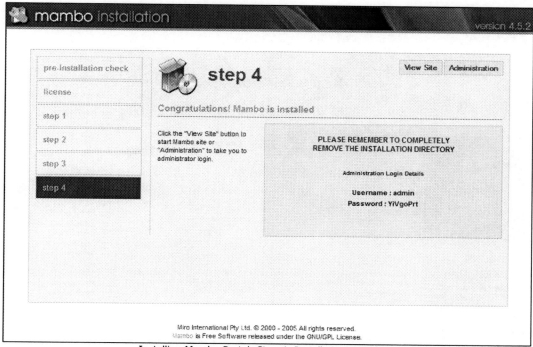

Installing Mambo Portal: Step 4: Installation Complete

The basic Mambo installation is now complete.

You should now erase (or at least rename) the installation directory within the Mambo root directory on your server.

Take note of the administration username and password information—you will need it shortly.

Now click on the View Site link to see your customer portal for the first time.

First Login to Mambo Portal

Here is your customer portal. Mambo includes an entire content management system that allows you to define the content, appearance, and navigational structure of your customer website, and that is a subject that needs its own book to describe properly. For now, just accept that you can use Mambo to create whatever company graphics and menu system you want for your customer portal. You can log in to this screen using the administrator username and password provided on the last screen.

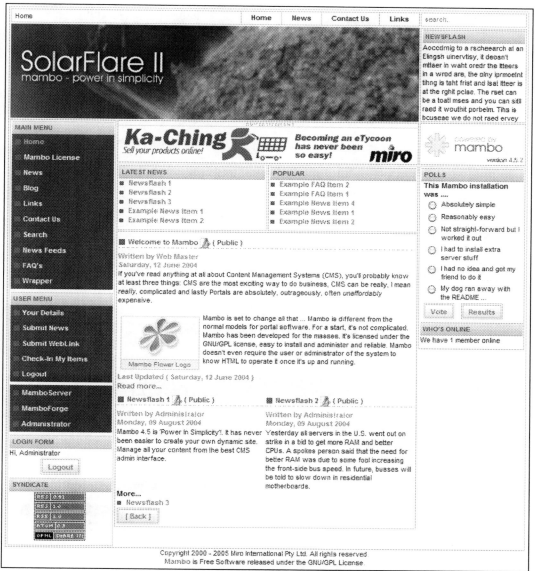

Logged in to Mambo Portal Site as Admin

Here you are logged in to the customer portal as a regular user. As of yet, the special features that link the Mambo portal to the SugarCRM system are not installed. In order to install them, we will need to use the administration functions provided within the Mambo portal. To access them, click on the Administrator link just above the login form.

Now you see the administration login screen. Use the same administrator access information to login here.

Login to Mambo Portal Admin Console

And finally, we see the Mambo administration menu screen.

The Mambo Admin Console

Installing the SugarCRM Portal Components for Mambo

With Mambo now fully installed, you are ready to go on to the next step—that of installing the SugarCRM portal components for Mambo.

The Sugar self-service portal for Mambo consists of three Mambo portal components, and one Mambo portal module (components and modules are different sorts of add-on elements within the Mambo framework). The new components are:

- com_sugarregistration: This component links from the Mambo portal to Sugar Open Source to create an authenticated session between them. A user defined within the Sugar Open Source CRM is used for this purpose, and must be defined within the Sugar system.

- com_sugarbugs: This links from the Mambo portal to Sugar Open Source using the Sugar's SOAP communications facility to provide searching, creating, and editing of software bug reports.

- com_sugarcases: This links from the Mambo portal to Sugar Open Source using Sugar's SOAP communications facility to provide searching, creating, and editing of services cases.

The new module for Mambo portal is:

- mod_sugarlogin: In Mambo terms this is a *helper* module that works with the com_sugarregistration component to provide login services to Sugar from within Mambo.

In order to install and use these objects within Mambo, you will first want to define a portal user within Sugar Open Source, for the Mambo modules to use to *talk* to the CRM system.

Within the admin area of Sugar Open Source, create a new user—typically with the username Portal, and the Portal Only User checkbox selected. This user will be used uniquely for this role, and will not be a valid login for Sugar Open Source as a normal user.

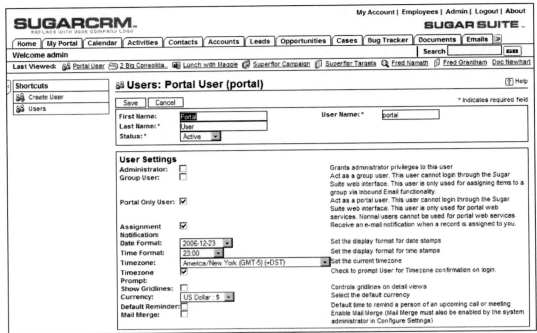

Definition of Sugar's Portal User for Mambo

While in the Sugar admin area, choose Configure Settings, and click on the checkbox for Enable Self-Service Portal Integration. This turns on the portal integration services, and also adds a new Display in Portal checkbox for any notes attached to cases. This checkbox is used to enable notes to be exposed to customers if they do not contain sensitive information.

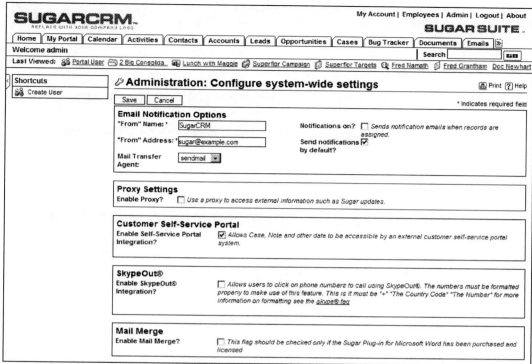

Enabling Sugar's Portal Services

Next, you use the administration area within Mambo to install the various components and module for Mambo to link to Sugar. First, you will need to download these objects from SugarForge.org. These are currently at `http://www.sugarforge.org/frs/?group_id=10&release_id=11`.

Each of these four objects is downloaded in the form of a ZIP file and you need to keep these files as ZIP files and not expand them.

The process of installing these four objects within Mambo is rather sensitive—in particular, they need to be loaded in a specific order, as documented here.

First, you need to install and configure the com_sugarregistration component. Use the drop-down menu system at the top of the page in the Mambo administration system to select the Components menu item, and the Install/Uninstall option on that menu.

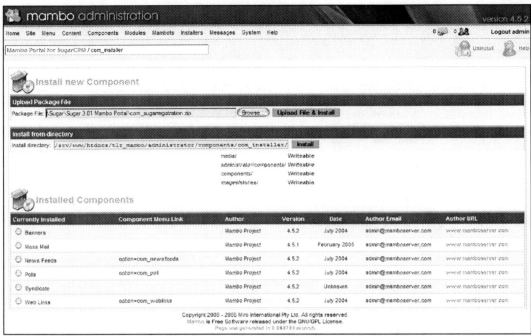

Installing Mambo com_sugarregistration Component

Now you need to set the configuration information for this component. Type in the values for the Sugar portal username and password you created earlier for portal access within Sugar. Also enter the URL of the server, and then click on Save Configuration.

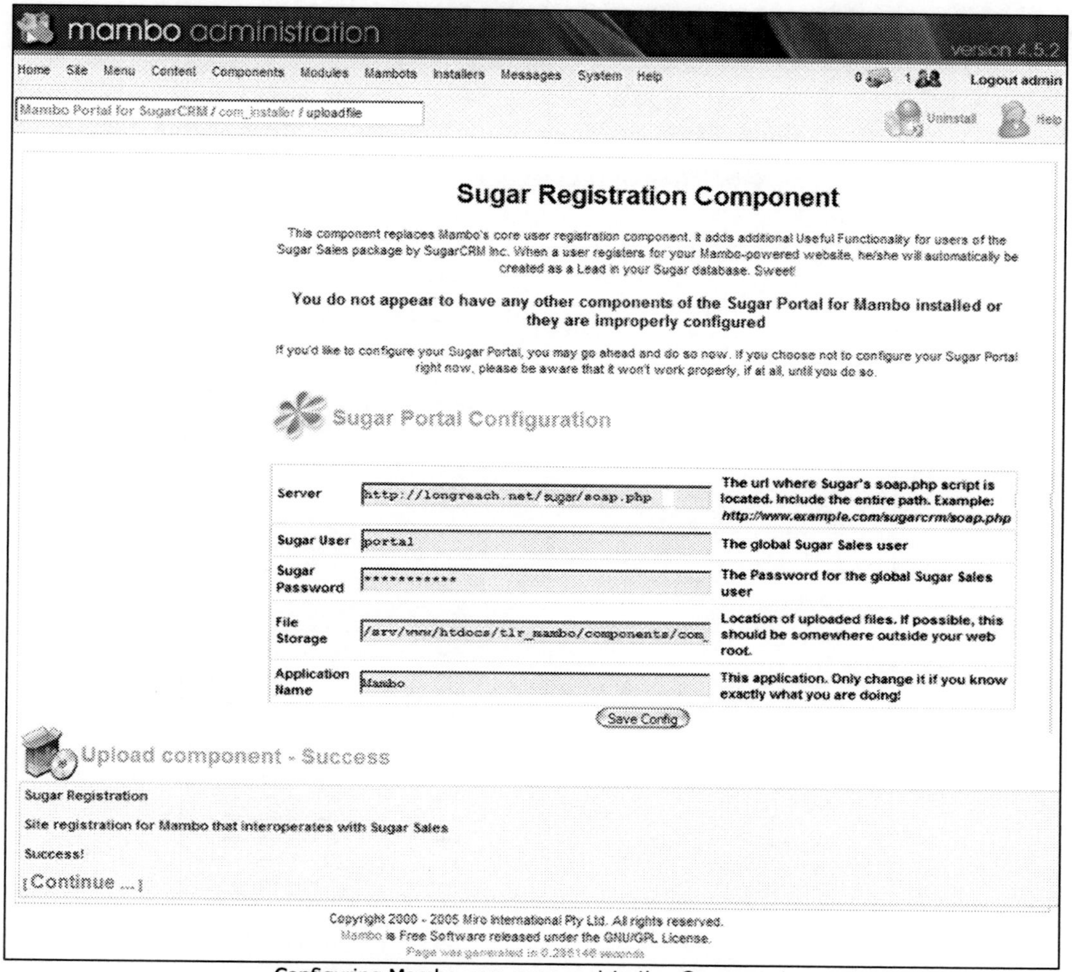

Configuring Mambo com_sugarregistration Component

Next you will need to configure the form fields to be used within the com_sugarregistration component. You should see the next screen automatically displayed. If you do not, you can use the menu system within Mambo administration to navigate to Components | Sugar Registration | Form Fields. Make the screen look like the figure that follows, and click on the Save icon at the top right.

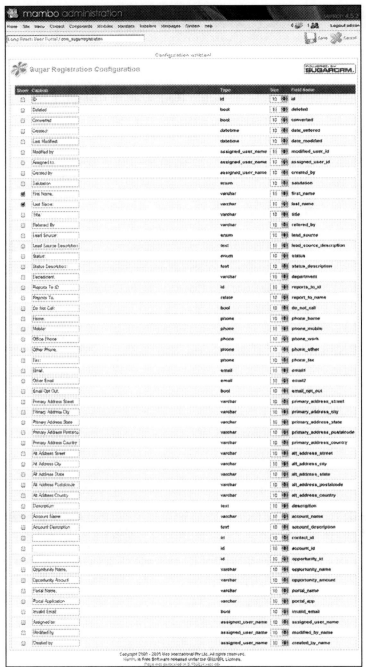

Configuring the Sugar Registration Form Fields

Next, you will need to install the com_sugarcases component. It will make use of the configuration data already provided for the com_sugarregistration component. Use the menu system within Mambo administration to navigate to Components | Install/Uninstall, and then browse to the ZIP file for this component and click on Upload File and Install. All being well, you will see a screen confirming Upload component—Success. Click on Continue.

Go to the administration menu option, Components | Sugar Cases | Configuration and check that all the configuration data is set correctly.

Now do the same again for the com_sugarbugs component—installing the component, and then checking that the configuration values are correct.

Adding Cases and Bugs to the Mambo User Menu

Now that the three Sugar components have been loaded into Mambo and configured, we need to make these capabilities accessible to Mambo users.

From the Mambo administration screen, select Menu | User Menu. Then click on the icon for a New Menu item. On the screen that appears next, select the radio button for Component, and then click on Next.

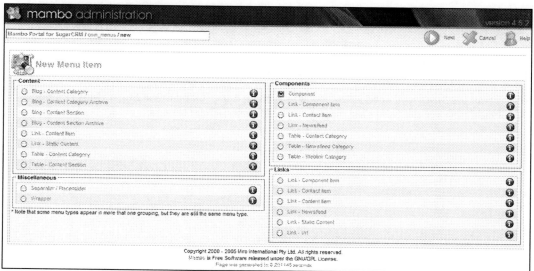

Adding a New Mambo Menu Item

On the next screen, type in the name Your Cases for the name of the menu item, and select Sugar Cases from the list. For access level, specify Registered. Then click on the Save icon.

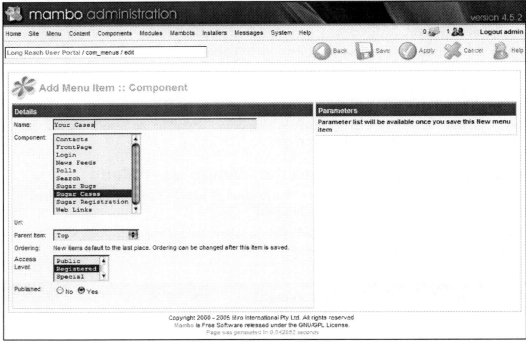

Adding Your Cases as a Menu Item

Now repeat the process, and add Your Bugs as a menu item, linked to the Sugar Bugs component.
You should now see the following display in the Mambo Menu Manager:

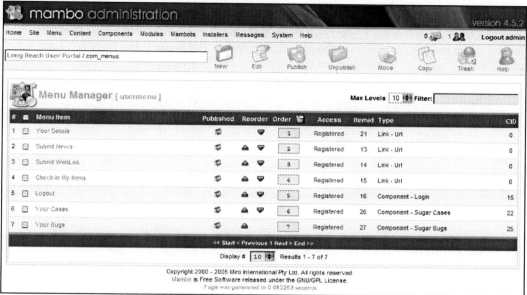

The Mambo Menu Manager

Next, you need to install the mod_sugarlogin module from the Modules | Install/Uninstall menu within Mambo administration. Just browse to the ZIP file for that module, and click on Upload File and Install. You should see the following screen. Once you do, click on Continue.

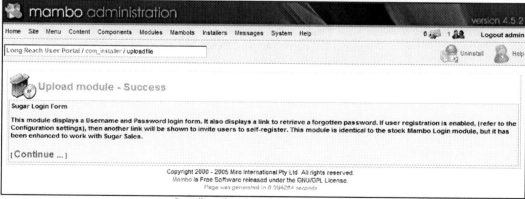

Installing the mod_sugarlogin Module

Publish the Sugar Login Form

Next, you need to publish the Sugar Login Form provided by this module. Use the Mambo administration menu to navigate to Modules | Site Modules. The Sugar Login Form is likely on the second page of modules listed. Click on the red X to publish the form.

The Mambo Admin Console

Create a New Mambo User

Now use the Mambo administration menu to navigate to Site | User Manager, and then click on the New icon to create a new user. Once you have entered the user information (note that you need to set Group to Registered), click on the Save icon.

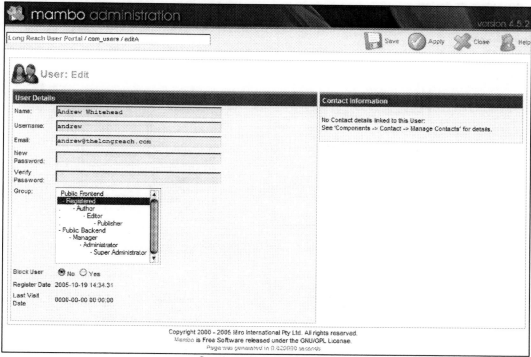

Creating a New Mambo User

Create a New Sugar Contact Linked to the Mambo User

Lastly, create a new contact within Sugar Open Source, link it to the Mambo username you have just created, and mark it as active within the portal.

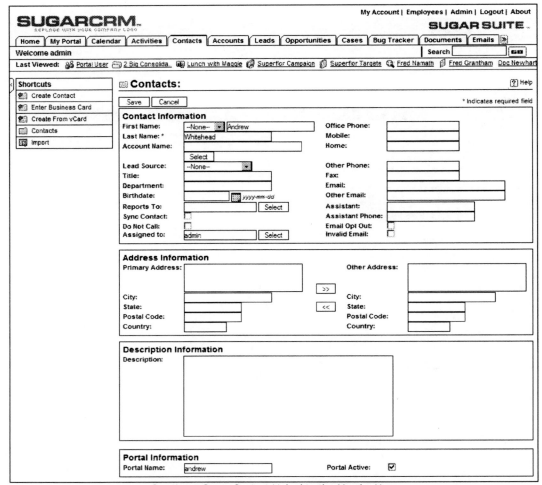

Creating a Sugar Contact Linked to the Mambo User

Using Your New Self-Service Portal

You should now be able to use your self-service portal. Log out of the system, and log in to the regular Mambo site (not administration) as the new Mambo user you just created.

Logged in to Mambo, with New Cases and Bugs Menu Items

Click on the link to Your Cases. From here, you have choices for Home (which lists all cases that relate to your user), New (to create a new case), and Search (to look for a specific case). Click on New to create a new case. Enter a name for the case, and a description.

Creating a New Case, Using the Mambo Self-Service Portal

Click on **Save**. Now you see the full form for a new case, and can enter the details of a note to be attached to the case and optionally a file attachment.

Now you can look at the cases within Sugar Open Source, and see that the case has been entered there automatically.

Similarly, you can click on the link to **Your Bugs**. From here, you again have the choices for **Home**, **New**, and **Search**. Click on **New** to create a new bug report. Enter a name for the bug, select the release, and enter a description. Once you have saved this record, check within Sugar that it has been entered as a new bug.

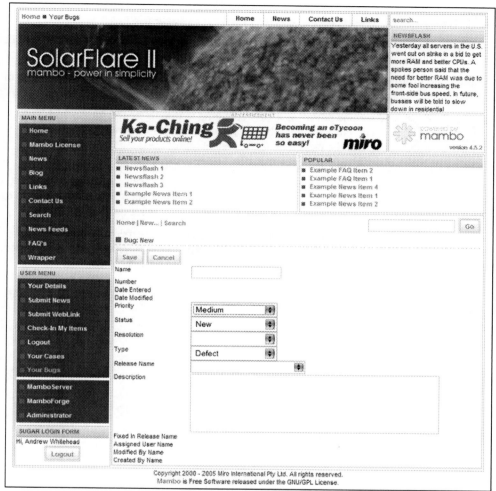

The Mambo Admin Console

While we have only illustrated self-service bugs and cases capabilities here, with the development of new components you can use the generalized SOAP interface to Sugar Open Source to create all sorts of customer self-service applications, including such applications as document sharing portals, project tracking portals, and so on.

This sort of technology use is only going to grow faster and faster in the coming years. Now that you have seen what it can do for a business, do you really want to compete without these tools against companies that are using them to their full potential?

Summary

In this chapter, we have covered two key techniques for linking your CRM to the outside world, and more specifically to your current and potential customers.

Lead-capture applications are simple to set up, and have immediate impact on the bottom line in terms of both creating revenue, and cutting administration costs.

Developing customer self-service portals is a key technique to maximize the return from your CRM investment. They keep your customers better informed and happier, while improving efficiency and reducing costs in the customer service and support areas.

From here, the sky is the limit. The future will hold many new developments in the CRM field. One widely anticipated trend is CRM systems that act as their own portal—offering carefully controlled and regulated direct access to the CRM for customers and suppliers, allowing them to see only that information and navigation capability that the system is set up to allow them.

At the current speed of evolution and development in the CRM field (especially in the red-hot field of CRMs for smaller businesses), we can expect this type of development, and many others, within the next year or so. I look forward to updating this book to describe them.

A

Installing SugarCRM on Linux

To install SugarCRM on Linux, I recommend, and have documented here, the use of SUSE Linux. It is one of the two top Linux distributions, and owned by Novell. SUSE is particularly friendly to use for the novice, offering an excellent graphical user interface through which most system management and maintenance functions can be performed.

SUSE has different versions of its Linux product, and several of them will be fine for you to use as an operating system platform for SugarCRM. SUSE Linux Enterprise Server 9 is currently the flagship SUSE server operating system. SUSE Linux Professional 9.2 or 9.3, or the newer SUSE Linux 10 will be fine as well. The important thing is to watch the versions of Apache, MySQL, and PHP that you use. My personal favorites have been PHP 4.3.8 with MySQL 4.0.21 and Apache 2.0.50. The balance of this chapter documents the installation using SUSE Linux 10.

You will need the SUSE Linux 10 installation DVD, as well as the SugarCRM installation Zip file.

An ISO image of a SUSE installation DVD (actually a cut-down evaluation version, but it will work for these purposes) may be downloaded (although it is 3.5 GB, so be ready to wait a while) from ftp://SUSE.cs.utah.edu/pub/SUSE.com/SUSE/i386/current/iso/. The filename is SUSE-10.0-EvalDVD-i386-GM.iso.

Once downloaded, you must use a DVD burning program capable of burning a disk from an ISO image—such as Record Now! Deluxe from Sonic, which may be purchased for download at http://estore.sonic.com/enu/recordnow/.

We would recommend, however, that you simply purchase SUSE Linux 10, either online at http://www.novell.com/products/linuxprofessional/pricing.html, or at your local retailer or distributor. For 59.95 USD you will get a full installation image, and over 1000 pages of documentation.

Basic SUSE Linux Installation

1. Insert the SUSE Linux boot DVD and re-boot your server from the DVD drive.
2. Choose Installation from the DVD Boot Options Menu.
3. Wait for a few minutes during Initializing Hardware.
4. Choose the SUSE installation language, most often English (US).

5. On the Installation Settings screen, choose New Installation. Note that this screen does not appear if a brand new, unformatted hard drive is being used.

6. Make any necessary changes to Installation Settings—including the formatting of disk partitions, setting the Time Zone, and adjusting the software to be installed (do not install Office Applications).

7. Confirm the package license for the Macromedia flash player.

8. Confirm the installation by clicking on the Install button.

9. The system then goes on to prepare the hard disk and performs the installation—this should take 10-15 minutes.

10. The system then reboots—and you must choose Boot from Hard Disk. Congratulations—your basic SUSE Linux installation is complete. You will now go on to configure your server installation.

Configure the SUSE Linux Installation

1. Enter a root password, and confirm it.

2. The system then performs its network configuration. This usually goes quietly and when it completes, just click on Next.

3. The network configuration is saved, and the internet connection is tested. Connect the server to the Internet, select Test Connection to the Internet, and click on Next.

4. The server then downloads the latest release notes, and checks for the latest updates. If all is well, a Success message is displayed, and you should click on Next.

5. You are offered the opportunity to download online updates—choose to skip this, and click on OK.

6. For Authentication Method, choose Local (/etc/passwd), and click on Next.

7. Enter User Data, Full User Name (for example Michael Whitehead), User Login (for example michael), Password (enter it once, and then again to confirm). Select Auto-Login, and click on Next.

8. You may read the displayed release notes, and then click on Next.

9. Browse to Hardware Configuration | Graphic Cards and ensure that the correct monitor type, resolution, color depth, and other settings are selected. Then click on Next.

10. Click on Finish—the system then boots into the graphical desktop. You may remove the DVD from the drive at this time.

Updating the SUSE Linux Installation

Now you need to update the system software packages already installed, and add in several more that need to be installed in preparation for receiving SugarCRM. This section starts with two different sets of instructions for beginning this process, depending on the type of DVD you are installing from.

If you are using the free SUSE evaluation DVD image from a download, use Version 1, provided here. Otherwise, skip to Version 2 if you are using a full installation DVD from a retail copy of SUSE Linux 10. Version 2 is much faster, as it eliminates a lot of downloading!

Version 1:
Using a Downloaded DVD of SUSE Linux 10

1. From the SUSE button, choose System | YAST (YAST is an acronym for Yet Another Setup Tool). You will need to provide the root password. From YAST, click on Change Source of Installation. Click on Add, FTP, and enter the server name SUSE.cs.utah.edu, and the directory name pub/SUSE.com/SUSE/i386/current, with anonymous authentication. This will take a moment or so to complete. Once it has been added, promote it to become the first source on the list, and then click on Finish.

2. Now select Install and Remove Software within YAST. The system will display Reading Package Information; One Moment Please... for a while, as it is reading this package data over the Internet.

3. Now skip over Version 2, and proceed to Continuing the Update.

Version 2:
Using a Full Retail DVD of SUSE Linux 10

1. From the SUSE button, choose System | YAST (YAST is an acronym for Yet Another Setup Tool). You will need to provide the root password. Now select Install and Remove Software within YAST. The system will display Reading Package Information; One Moment Please... for a moment, as it is reading this package data from the DVD.

Continuing the Update...

1. In the Search box, enter apache—and when a list of packages is displayed on the right side of the screen, select apache2-mod_php4 and apache2-prefork, and click on Accept. Several additional packages will be selected to satisfy dependencies— apache2, libapr0, and php4. Click on Continue. The various packages will now be installed.

2. You will be prompted Would you like to install more packages?. Click on Install More.

3. In the Search box, enter mysql—and when a list of packages is displayed, select mysql, mysqlcc, mysql-client, php4-mysql, and phpMyAdmin, and click on Accept. Many additional packages will be selected to satisfy dependencies. This is fine, so click on Continue. The various packages will now be installed.

4. You will be prompted Would you like to install more packages?. Click on Install More.

5. In the Search box, enter php—and when a list of packages is displayed, select php4-session, and click on Accept. The package will now be installed.

6. You will be prompted Would you like to install more packages?—Click on Finish.

7. Now select Online Update within YAST. Under Update Configuration, select User-Defined Location, and enter the location: ftp://SUSE.cs.utah.edu/pub/SUSE.com/ SUSE—then click on Next. (Note that if you experience difficulty downloading updates from this location, you may need to try one of the pre-defined locations,

available from the drop-down menu.) Update information will be retrieved. If at any point the system seems to stall for several minutes, abort the update process, and re-try it—it should recover from where your last try left off.

8. Typically, simply accept the list of packages to be updated, by clicking on Accept. You may receive a message suggesting that you are updating the kernel, and should re-boot after the update process is complete. This is OK. Remember to click on Remove Source Packages after Update.

9. The various patches are now applied. This will take 5-10 minutes on a high speed connection. When the update is complete, click on Finish.

10. Re-boot the server by clicking on SUSE | Logout | Restart Computer.

11. Using YAST, select System on the left-hand menu, and click on Run Level Editor. Maximize the window, and find the Apache2 module in the list displayed. Select Apache2, and then click on Enable, to run the Apache server now, and in future on each boot. Now do the same for MySQL. Click on Finish to exit the Run Level Editor, and also close YAST.

12. Congratulations—you have now installed the latest Apache, MySQL, and PHP system software for use with SugarCRM. You have also updated the SUSE Linux operating system to the latest software patches available.

Test Apache and PHP

1. Click on SUSE | Utilities | Editor to start the Kate editor. Enter <?php phpinfo() ?> and perform a File | Save As ... and store the file in your desktop for now, using the filename index.php.

2. Click on SUSE | System | File Manager | File Manager—Super User Mode, and enter the root password when prompted. From file:/root, navigate upwards one click to file:/. Click on the srv folder, and then www, and then htdocs.

3. Drag and drop the index.php file into this directory from your desktop.

4. Run the Konqueror browser by clicking on its icon on the panel across the bottom of the screen. Enter localhost as the URL. You should see the results of phpinfo() displayed on the screen, providing a lot of configuration information about your PHP installation. This confirms that both Apache and PHP are running, and that they are getting along with each other.

Configure MySQL

1. Right-click on the SUSE button, and select Menu Editor. Select File | New Item, and enter the item name MySQL CC, then click on OK. Under command, enter mysqlcc. Click on the icon selector top right, and choose the SUSEconf icon. Close the Menu Editor, and Save Changes. Now when you click on the SUSE button, under All Applications, you will see MySQL CC. Click on this icon now.

2. You will need to register your server:
   Name: localhost
   Host Name: localhost
   User Name: root
   Password: <leave blank>
   Port: 3306
   Then click on Test | Add.

Steps 3 and 4 are optional—you may create the database and database user name as you use the SugarCRM Installation Wizard if you prefer.

---

3. Within MySQL CC, use the Action drop-down menu to connect to the localhost server. Then, on the left-hand side, click on Databases to expand the list of databases, then right-click on Databases to add a new database. Use the name sugarcrm. Similarly click on User Administration to show all users, and then right-click on Users to add a new user.

4. In the dialog box for New Users, enter the username as sugarcrm, host as localhost, and a password of your choosing (suggestion—sugardbpsw). On the right-hand side, click on Allow Access to: sugarcrm. Then click on All Privileges, and With Grant Option. Then click on the Add button to add the new user sugarcrm.

5. Now double-click on the user root@localhost. This is the default global user in the database, and this user currently has no password—a gaping security hole. So enter a password for this root MySQL user, and click on the Apply button, and then the Close button.

6. Doing this has now broken your connection to MySQL, as you were connected as the root user with no password, from step 2 above. In the MySQL CC Console Manager click on File | Exit. Then re-enter MySQL CC, and notice that you get an Access Denied message at the bottom of the window. Click on the Action drop-down menu item, and select Edit, to edit the localhost server connection. Enter the password from the previous step there, and click on the Apply button. Now click on the Action drop-down menu item, and select Connect. You should now be back connected to the database, but with no security hole.

7. Exit MySQL CC.

Configure php.ini

1. Click on SUSE | System | File Manager | File Manager—Super User Mode, and enter the root password when prompted. From file:/root, navigate upwards one click to file:/. Click on the etc folder.

2. Scroll down to find the php.ini file, and right-click on it. Select Open With | KWrite.

3. Search for memory_limit, and set it to 11M. This will allow SugarCRM to consume up to 11megabytes of memory as it executes. Without this setting, complex actions may run out of memory.

4. Search for max_execution_time, and set it to 90. This will allow any PHP instruction up to 90 seconds to complete. Without this, activities such as an import of large amounts of data will terminate with an error, as they exceed the maximum execution time allowed.

5. Also set max_input_time on the next line of the file to 300. This allows a 5 minute window for large files to be uploaded.

6. Search for display_errors, and set it to Off. This will suppress the display of warning messages, which will otherwise disrupt the display.

7. Search for post_max_size, and set it to 25M to allow large documents to be uploaded. Then search for upload_max_filesize, and set it to 22M. The effect of these two changes will be to allow a document file of 20 megabytes in size to be uploaded to the system. A third setting ($upload_maxsize in config.php), is automatically set to exactly 20M by the installation script.

8. Search for session.gc.maxlifetime. Note that by default it is set to 1440 seconds, which is 24 minutes. This controls the length of time a SugarCRM session can be idle before the session is terminated. Set it to 1800 for 30 minutes, 3600 for an hour, and so on.

9. Make sure that when setting the above values in php.ini, that the entire line is not preceded by a semi-colon—as this indicates that the line is merely a comment, and not to be processed.

10. Perform a File | Save, and exit KWrite.

Install SugarCRM

1. Put the SugarCRM zip file on the desktop within your session on your server.

2. Right-click on the file and select rename. Change the file name to sugarcrm.zip. Then right-click on it again, and select extract to sugarcrm/.

3. Click on SUSE | System | File Manager | File Manager—Super User Mode, and enter the root password when prompted. From file:/root, navigate upwards one click to file:/. Click on the srv folder, and then www, and then htdocs.

4. Drag and drop the entire sugarcrm directory from the desktop to this directory. Confirm it is a Move when prompted.

5. Right-click on the sugarcrm folder, and select Properties. On the Permissions tab, set Ownership to wwwrun, and Group to users. Set Owner to Can View & Modify Content, and Group and Others to Can View Content. Click on the box to apply changes to all subfolders, and then click on OK.

6. We now begin the actual installation process:

7. **Installer Welcome Screen**: Run the Konqueror browser by clicking on its icon on the panel across the bottom of the screen. Enter localhost/sugarcrm/install.php as the URL. You should see the SugarCRM Installer Welcome screen. You're getting close to the finish line! Click on Start.

SugarCRM Installer Welcome Screen

8. **License Acceptance Screen**: The SugarCRM license acceptance screen is the next one you will see. Click on the I Accept checkbox, and then on the Next button.

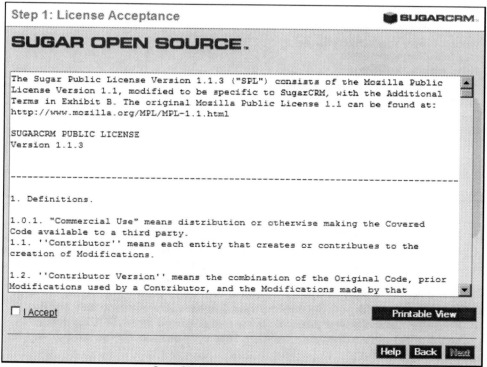

SugarCRM License Acceptance Screen

9. **System Check Screen**: Next you see the SugarCRM system check screen. The SugarCRM installer checks several aspects of the installation environment, and reports their status to you on this screen. You will see a series of green (and perhaps a few red) status messages down the right-hand side of the screen. They need to be all green for the installation to proceed. Now click on the Next button to proceed to the next step of the SugarCRM installation process.

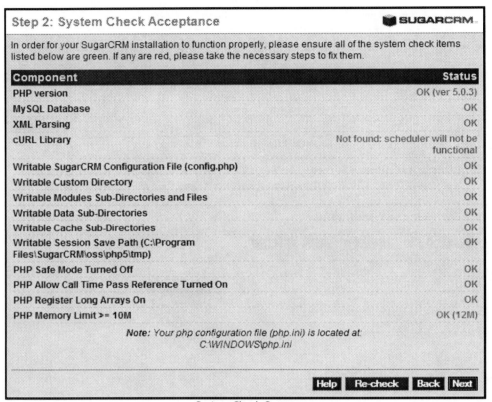

System Check Screen

10. **Database Configuration Screen**: Set Host Name to localhost, Database name to sugarcrm, Database User Name to sugarcrm, and Database User password to whatever you chose above (sugardbpsw was suggested). Set the Admin password to your choice of password. Click on Drop & Re-create Existing Tables if this is a re-installation. Click on Populate Database With Demo Data if you would like some test data created for you. Set the Privileged Database User Name to root, and the Privileged Database User password to the root password for MySQL (as defined in step 5 of the section *Configure MySQL*). Then click on Next. (If you see a prompt re: Kwallet, cancel it.)

Step 3: Database Configuration   SUGARCRM

Please enter your database configuration information below. If you are unsure of what to fill in, we suggest that you use the default values.

* Required field

Database Configuration

* Host Name	localhost	
* Database Name	sugarcrm	☑ Create database
* User Name for SugarCRM	sugarcrm	☑ Create user
Password for SugarCRM	••••••••••	
Re-Type Password for SugarCRM	••••••••••	

Drop and recreate existing SugarCRM tables?   ☐
Caution: All SugarCRM data will be erased
if this box is checked.

Populate database with demo data?   ☑

Database account above is a privileged user?   ☐

* Privileged Database User Name   root
This privileged database user must have the proper
permissions to create a database, drop/create
tables, and create a user. This privileged database
user will only be used to perform these tasks as
needed during the installation process. You may
also use the same database user as above if that
user has sufficient privileges.

Privileged Database User Password   ••••••••••

Help   Back   Next

Database Configuration Screen

11. **Site Configuration Screen**: Enter the new password you wish for the SugarCRM Admin user, and confirm it. Then click on Next to proceed to the Confirm Settings screen.

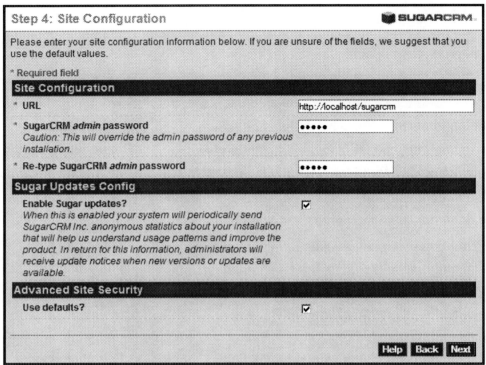

Site Configuration Screen

12. **Confirm Settings Screen**: This screen simply shows you all the settings you have provided for the SugarCRM installation. If they look correct, click on the Next button to proceed with the actual SugarCRM installation.

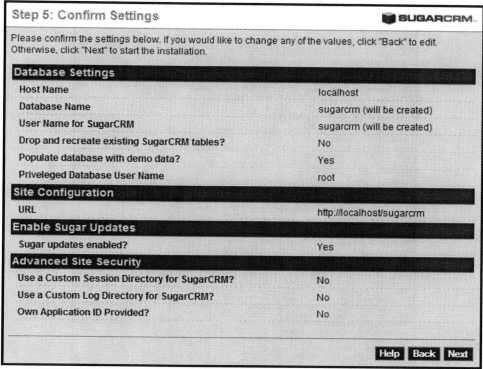

Confirm Settings Screen

13. **Perform Setup Screen**: You should see a screen like the one opposite generated. Note it will take a minute or two to complete—so be patient! Your database tables have now been created. If all goes well, this step will end with the message—The Setup of SugarCRM 4.0 is now complete.

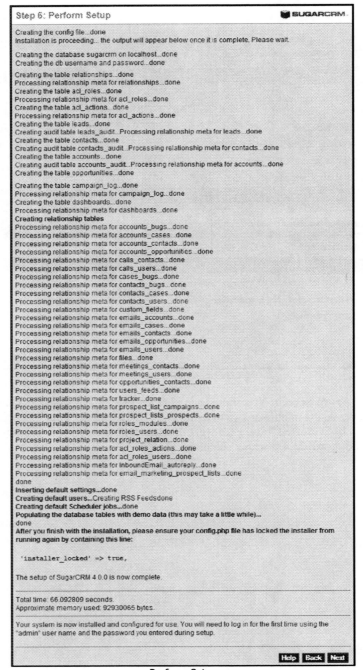

Step 6: Perform Setup

Creating the config file...done
Installation is proceeding... the output will appear below once it is complete. Please wait.

Creating the database sugarcrm on localhost...done
Creating the db username and password...done

Creating the table relationships...done
Processing relationship meta for relationships...done
Creating the table acl_roles...done
Processing relationship meta for acl_roles...done
Creating the table acl_actions...done
Processing relationship meta for acl_actions...done
Creating the table leads...done
Creating audit table leads_audit...Processing relationship meta for leads...done
Creating the table contacts...done
Creating audit table contacts_audit...Processing relationship meta for contacts...done
Creating the table accounts...done
Creating audit table accounts_audit...Processing relationship meta for accounts...done
Creating the table opportunities...done

Creating the table campaign_log...done
Processing relationship meta for campaign_log...done
Creating the table dashboards...done
Processing relationship meta for dashboards...done
Creating relationship tables
Processing relationship meta for accounts_bugs...done
Processing relationship meta for accounts_cases...done
Processing relationship meta for accounts_contacts...done
Processing relationship meta for accounts_opportunities...done
Processing relationship meta for calls_contacts...done
Processing relationship meta for calls_users...done
Processing relationship meta for cases_bugs...done
Processing relationship meta for contacts_bugs...done
Processing relationship meta for contacts_cases...done
Processing relationship meta for contacts_users...done
Processing relationship meta for custom_fields...done
Processing relationship meta for emails_accounts...done
Processing relationship meta for emails_cases...done
Processing relationship meta for emails_contacts...done
Processing relationship meta for emails_opportunities...done
Processing relationship meta for emails_users...done
Processing relationship meta for files...done
Processing relationship meta for meetings_contacts...done
Processing relationship meta for meetings_users...done
Processing relationship meta for opportunities_contacts...done
Processing relationship meta for users_feeds...done
Processing relationship meta for tracker...done
Processing relationship meta for prospect_list_campaigns...done
Processing relationship meta for prospect_lists_prospects...done
Processing relationship meta for roles_modules...done
Processing relationship meta for roles_users...done
Processing relationship meta for project_relation...done
Processing relationship meta for acl_roles_actions...done
Processing relationship meta for acl_roles_users...done
Processing relationship meta for inboundEmail_autoreply...done
Processing relationship meta for email_marketing_prospect_lists...done
done
Inserting default settings...done
Creating default users...Creating RSS Feedsdone
Creating default Scheduler jobs...done
Populating the database tables with demo data (this may take a little while)...
done
After you finish with the installation, please ensure your config.php file has locked the installer from
running again by containing this line:

```
'installer_locked' => true,
```

The setup of SugarCRM 4.0.0 is now complete.

Total time: 66.092809 seconds.
Approximate memory used: 92930065 bytes.

Your system is now installed and configured for use. You will need to log in for the first time using the
"admin" user name and the password you entered during setup.

Help   Back   Next

Perform Setup

14. **Log In Screen:** Congratulations, you're done. Just click on Finish to log in to SugarCRM for the first time. You should see a screen like the one shown below. Log in, using the user name admin, and the admin password you provided on the Site Configuration screen.

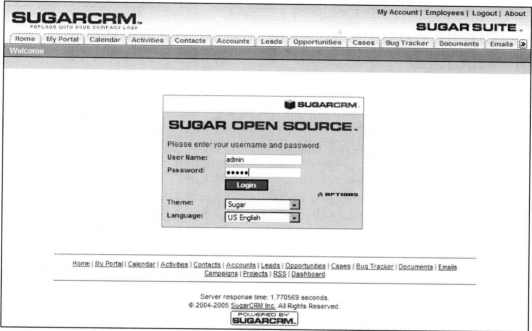

SugarCRM Log In Screen

Configure Installation Settings

This section deals with the configuration of installation settings such as how to re-run the installation, and the integration of the email server.

Re-running the Installation

1. Click on Suse | System | File Manager | File Manager – Super User Mode, and enter the root password when prompted. From file:/root, navigate upwards one click to file:/. Click on the srv folder, and then www, and then htdocs, and then sugarcrm.

2. Right click on the config.php file, and select Kate to edit the file with the Kate editor. Scroll down about one page to the entry 'installer_locked' => true, and replace the word true with the word false. Now perform a File | Save, and then exit the editor.

3. Exit the File Manager.

4. Now you may run the install.php file again, to re-run the installation.

Email Server Integration

1. Ensure that your SugarCRM installation is configured in the Admin area to use the sendmail Mail Transfer Agent (MTA).

2. Check that sendmail is running—by default it is.

Configure Apache for Multiple Virtual Server Installations

If you intend to run more than one instance of SugarCRM on a server, perhaps providing service to a number of organizations, you will need to create multiple virtual server entries on your server. If you are performing a conventional installation of SugarCRM for a single organization, you will not need to follow the instructions in this section.

1. Click on SUSE | System | File Manager | File Manager—Super User Mode, and enter the root password when prompted. From file:/root, navigate upwards one click to file:/. Click on the etc folder, and then on apache2.

2. Scroll down to find the listen.conf file, and right-click on it. Select Open With | KWrite.

3. Uncomment the name-based virtual hosting entry—NameVirtualHost *:80.

4. Perform a File | Save, and exit KWrite.

5. Open the folder vhosts.d in etc/apache2.

6. In that folder, there are two template files—vhost-ssl.template, and vhost.template.

7. Copy the vhost.template file by right-clicking on it and selecting Copy. Then right-click in an open area within the current folder, and select Paste. Enter _primary.conf as the new file name when prompted. This will be the new configuration file for your primary server entry (if your URL is example.com, then http://www.example.com will use this configuration file). Note the underscore at the start of the name—it is very important.

8. Edit your _primary.conf file, by right-clicking on it and selecting Open With | KWrite.

9. Replace all instances of dummy-host.example.com with the fully qualified domain you intend to serve—for instance example.com.

10. Within the same file, uncomment the line Include /etc/apache2/conf.d/*.conf.

11. Now find the entry beginning with DocumentRoot and edit it to read DocumentRoot /srv/www/htdocs.

12. Now look for the entry beginning with <Directory, and edit it to read <Directory "/srv/www/htdocs">.

13. Save the file _primary.conf, and exit KWrite.

14. Much the same way as in *Step 7* above, copy vhost.template to your first virtual server entry, for example new.conf.

15. Edit your new.conf file, by right-clicking on it and selecting Open With | KWrite. Replace all instances of dummy-host.example.com with the fully qualified sub-domain you intend to create—for instance new.example.com—where example.com is the URL you have defined in steps 7-13 above.

16. Within the same file, uncomment the line Include /etc/apache2/conf.d/*.conf.

17. Save the file new.conf, and exit KWrite.

18. Go to the directory /srv/www/vhosts and within that directory create the folder that will hold the content for your new sub-domain address—for instance new.example.com. When you are installing multiple instances of SugarCRM, this is the sort of folder into which it should be installed for each virtual host. As covered in step 5 of the *Install SugarCRM* section, ensure that permissions on this folder are set appropriately. Also—remember that each installation will require a new database to be defined within MySQL, and potentially a new MySQL user as well—or you will mix the data from one site with that of another.

19. For each additional virtual host you wish to create, repeat steps 14-18 above.

20. Restart the Apache web server, so that these changes come into effect.

Installing SugarCRM on Windows Server

To install SugarCRM on Windows Server, we recommend, and have documented here, the use of the **SpikeSource Windows Installer** for SugarCRM. SpikeSource (www.spikesource.com) and SugarCRM have built an integrated CRM solution based on the SpikeSource Core Stack that installs in just minutes. You can download this integrated installer from SugarForge at www.sugarforge.org/projects/spikewamp/.

Basic SpikeSource Installation

Once downloaded (the current file is about 25MB in size), you simply drop this executable file onto a server that already has Windows Server installed, and double-click on the icon to start the install. Once you do, you will see this dialog box on your display:

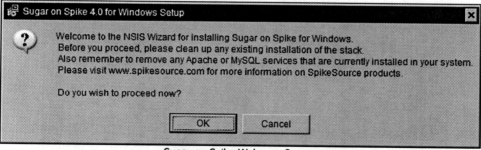

Sugar on Spike Welcome Screen

Click on the OK button to proceed, assuming you have no leftover Apache or MySQ installations on your server. You now see this SpikeSource License dialog box:

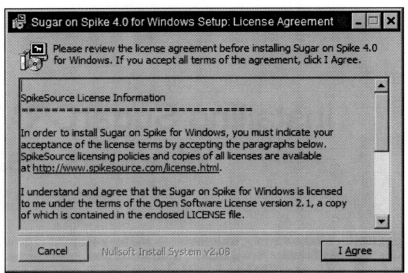

SpikeSource License Screen

This is the SpikeSource license agreement. You must click on the button labeled I Agree in order to proceed. You then see this dialog box:

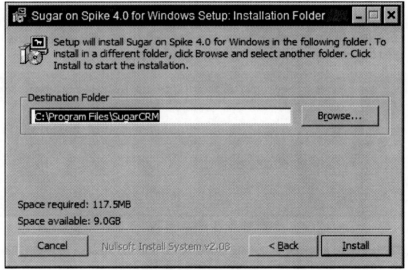

Select Installation Folder

Accept the default installation folder, or edit it to another folder you prefer. Then click on the Install button. You will see this dialog box:

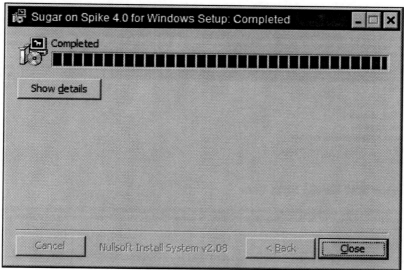

SpikeSource Install Completed

Click on the Close button to proceed to finish the installation. A black DOS CMD session dialog box will come up as the last of the installation is completed, and then you see the dialog box shown below:

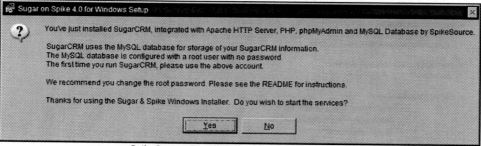

SpikeSource Install Completed: Start Services?

At this point, click on Yes to start the Apache and MySQ services. A DOS CMD window comes up again to start the services, and then two browser windows open. The first window contains the SpikeSource Sugar on Spike Readme notes, which also provide the instructions for completing this installation:

Released December 15, 2005   Certification

Sugar on Spike v4.0 for Windows   Level 1

Welcome to Sugar on Spike v4.0 for Windows

Sugar on Spike for Windows is a one-click installation file that contains SugarCRM, Apache, MySQL, and PHP. The package has been tested and configured using SpikeSource's patented automated test harness to install out of the box in 5 minutes. SpikeSource offers services and support for the underlying stack of software, the 'SpikeSource Core stack', which is tested 22,000 times per day. Visit http://www.spikesource.com for information on the SpikeSource Core Stack that supports this installation file.

Updates to the Sugar & Spike Windows Installer will be made available on SugarForge on a regular basis. The combined build will include the latest version of Sugar CRM and the latest version of SpikeSource Core stack. Please note that this installation requires a clean install of all four components. Users will need to uninstall other versions of Apache, MySQL, or PHP before using this install file.

Table of Contents

Starting SugarCRM for the First Time

After initial installation, the SugarCRM database and application requires some configuration. This is handled automatically the first time you run SugarCRM. To proceed, you'll need to know your database administrator account and password. As installed, the default account is "root" and password is blank. You can change the root password by following the instructions available in this section.

Starting Services

The shortcut "Start SugarCRM" is provided on the desktop and in the SugarCRM folder in the Start Programs Menu which could be used to start Apache and MySQL services. This script then automatically launches your internet browser to open SugarCRM.

You can also use "Apache Monitor" to check the status or start, stop and restart apache service. This is available in <InstallRoot>/oss/httpd/bin.

SugarCRM installation

- Install the SpikeSource sugar stack and run the services.

- The Setup Wizard Welcome screen will be displayed.

- Press "Start" on the Setup Wizard Welcome Screen.

- Step 1: License Acceptance

    Please read the Sugar Public License Version 1.1.3 terms carefully. If you accept the license terms click in the box "I Accept", then press "Next". You cannot proceed unless you accept the terms of the license.

- Step 2: System Check – all status should be "OK"

    Press "Next"

- Step 3: Database Configuration

    Enter "localhost" in the "Host name" field

    Enter "sugarcrm" in the "Database name" field

    Check "Create Database"

    Enter < username> in the "Username for SugarCRM" field; you can use the default username 'sugarcrm'.

    Check "Create User"

    Enter < password > in the "Password for SugarCRM" field

    Re-Type < password > in "Re-Type Password for SugarCRM" field

    Check "Populate database with demo data?"

SpikeSource Readme Notes

The second browser window that opens contains the Welcome Screen for the SugarCRM Setup Wizard:

SugarCRM Setup Wizard Welcome Screen

Click on the Start button to begin the SugarCRM installation process.

The SugarCRM license acceptance screen is the next screen you will see:

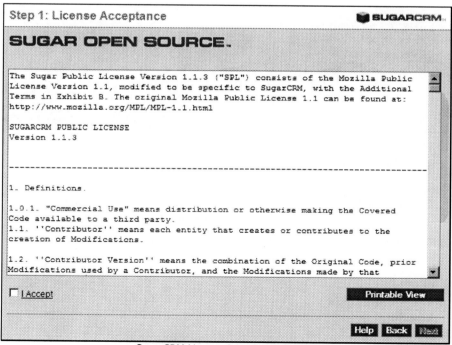

SugarCRM License Acceptance Screen

Click on the I Accept checkbox, and then on the Next button.

Next you see the SugarCRM system check screen. The SugarCRM installer checks several aspects of the installation environment, and reports their status to you on this screen. You will see a series of green (and perhaps a few red) status messages down the right-hand side of the screen. They need to be all green for the installation to proceed.

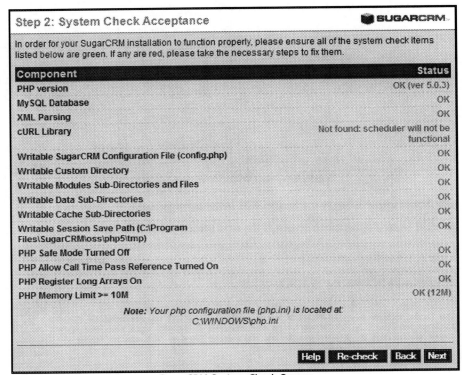

SugarCRM System Check Screen

Now click on the Next button to proceed to the next step of the SugarCRM installation process.

The database configuration screen helps you to configure MySQ properly for its role in supporting the SugarCRM installation. You need to create a database for MySQ to use for SugarCRM, and a database user name, with a password for that user as well.

The first time you install, you will likely want to install the demo data as well.

You also have to provide the name and password for a privileged database user, so that the installer has the power to create a new database and user within MySQ.

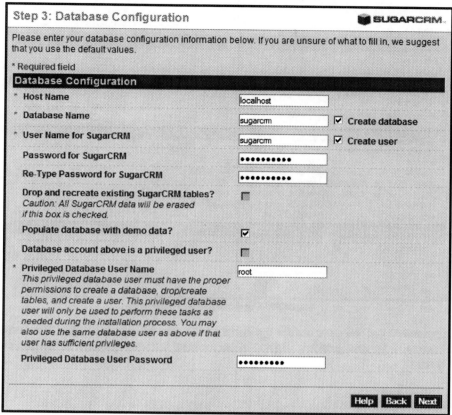

SugarCRM Database Configuration Screen

Once this screen is filled out properly (see the SpikeSource readme notes for more details on how to complete this screen if you are unsure), click on the Next button to proceed to the Site Configuration screen. Note that the Privileged Database User Password defaults initially to blank.

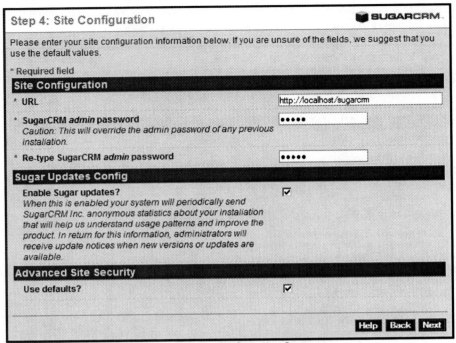

SugarCRM Site Configuration Screen

Enter the password you intend to use for the initial admin user within your SugarCRM installation, and then re-enter it for confirmation. Then click on the Next button to proceed to the Confirm Settings screen.

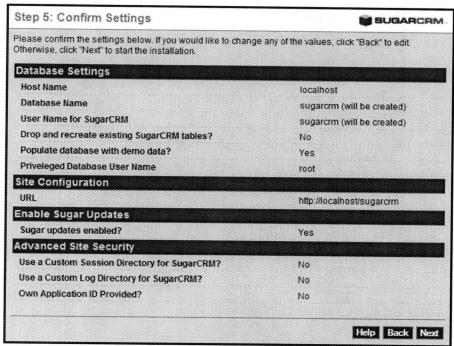

SugarCRM Confirm Settings Screen

This screen simply shows you all the settings you have provided for the SugarCRM installation. If they look correct, click on the Next button to proceed with the actual SugarCRM installation.

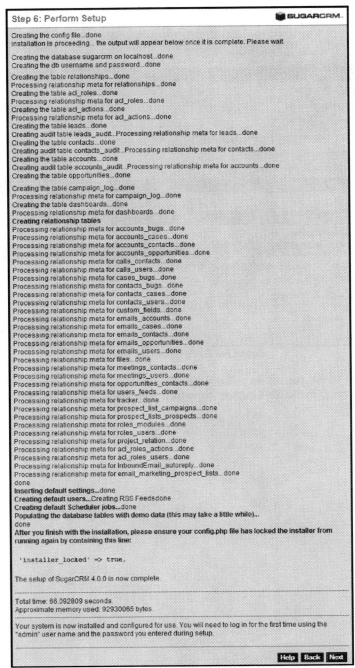

SugarCRM Perform Setup Screen

The Perform Setup screen shows you the actions taken by the SugarCRM installer as it builds the database for your SugarCRM installation. Once it completes the process (which can take up to 2-3 minutes)—congratulations, you are done. (Note that the screen image opposite has been abridged. The actual screen is even longer than shown.)

Click on the Next button, and you will see the optional Registration screen. If you wish, you may fill out the registration details, and click on the Send Registration button to register your installation with SugarCRM. Then click on the Finish button to log in to SugarCRM for the first time.

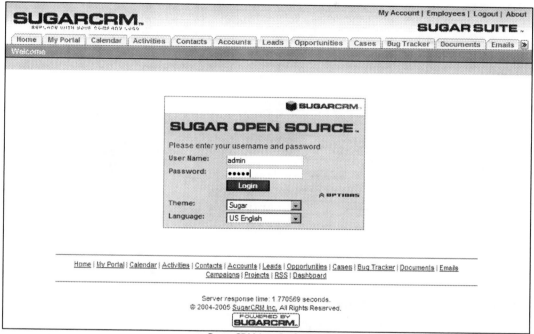

SugarCRM Log In Screen

Now type in the name of the admin user (admin), and the password you set for that user on the Site Configuration screen. You should now enter the SugarCRM application, and see the home page for the system administrator.

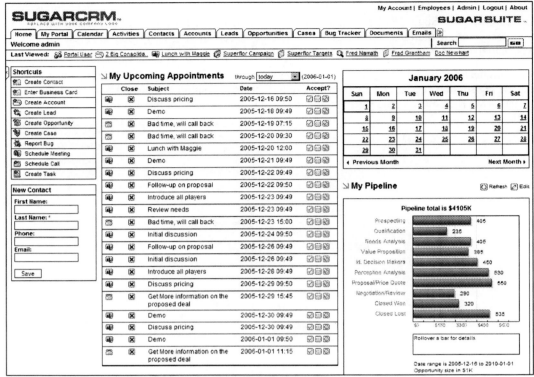

SugarCRM Home Page

Re-running the Installation

1. Using notepad or another editor, edit the `config.php` file in the root directory of your SugarCRM installation. Scroll about a screenful down into the file, looking for the line `'installer_locked' => true`, and replace the word true with the word false.

2. Save the edited file.

Now you may run the `install.php` file again, to re-run the installation.

C

Data Import and Export

One of the most important aspects of any CRM software is getting the data from your last CRM system moved across into the new one, and getting the data out of your new CRM system for use in other applications. Note that this should typically only be done by a system administrator.

SugarCRM supports the importing of various kinds of data from several different popular contact managers and full CRM systems.

- Accounts may be imported from Salesforce.com, from ACT! 2005, or from most other systems via a custom comma-delimited or tab-delimited mapping.
- Contacts may be imported from Salesforce.com, from ACT! 2005, from Outlook, or from most other systems via a custom comma-delimited or tab-delimited mapping.
- Leads may be imported from Salesforce.com, or from most other systems via a custom comma-delimited or tab-delimited mapping.
- Opportunities may be imported from Salesforce.com, or from most other systems via a custom comma-delimited or tab-delimited mapping.

Importing Accounts and Contacts

Importing contacts into SugarCRM is fairly straightforward. First you use your old CRM application or contact manager to export the data into a Comma Separated Values (.CSV) file format. Then you use the import function within the Contacts module (accessible via the Navigation Shortcuts Box) to import the data. If a contact record that is imported refers to an unknown account, then a new record is automatically created for an account of that name.

However, one thing to watch out for is that when account records are created automatically in this fashion, they are essentially empty—they have associated contacts, but no address or telephone information is recorded. Because of this, you should typically import your account data first, creating the records complete with address and telephone information (plus perhaps Account Type and lots of other information, depending on your old CRM system). This avoids creating rather empty account records, and having to manually add the rest of their information later.

See the sections below for the exact steps for exporting and importing contacts and accounts.

Export Contacts from Your Current Contact Manager

We will use Outlook 2003 as an example of exporting contact manager data. Other systems tend to work in similar ways.

1. Under the File menu, select Import and Export. The Import and Export Wizard dialog box is then displayed.

2. Select the action Export to a file, and click the Next button.

3. Choose to create a file of the type Comma Separated Values (Windows), and click on the Next button.

4. Select an Outlook folder from which to export—typically your contacts folder—and click the Next button.

5. Enter the filename and directory location for the exported file to be created, and click the Next button.

6. Confirm your intention to export this file by clicking on the Finish button.

7. The desired .CSV file is then created by Outlook 2003. You can view the file easily, using Microsoft Excel or a simple text editor, to confirm that the data you intended has been exported.

Import Accounts

If your account data is coming in from another CRM system, then typically that system understands the distinction between a contact and an account—that one account can have multiple contacts—and has separate data for each. However, if your data is being imported from a simpler contact manager—such as Microsoft Outlook, then the only data available is contact data, and you will have to be a bit creative to avoid a lot of manual data entry as described above.

If you are importing account data from a full CRM, proceed now to step 6. If you only have exported contact data, and need to massage, or manually clean it to act as account data to be imported, perform steps 1-4 shown below:

1. Copy your exported Contacts.csv file, and call the copy Accounts.csv.

2. Edit the Accounts.csv file using Excel. First, sort the file according to the company name.

3. Now the more complex part: As you scroll through your data, sorted by company name, you will see successive records that have the same company name, because there is more than one contact from that account. To avoid multiple copies of the same account within SugarCRM, you need to delete these duplicates. And to make sure that the best information is attached to the Account record, you should retain only the contact whose address and telephone information best represents the account as a whole.

4. Also look out for company names that are similar but not identical due to inconsistencies in the way the company name was entered—you should delete all duplicate records except the one with the company name spelled exactly as you wish to see it in SugarCRM.

5. Now that you have a nice clean set of account data, save the Excel file as a .CSV file type, and let's proceed to import this account data.

6. Click on the Import Accounts function within the Navigation Shortcuts Box of the Accounts module.

7. Specify the Data Source. Select Salesforce.com, ACT! 2005, Custom Comma Delimited or Custom Tab Delimited—then click on the Next button to continue. For massaged or manually cleaned Outlook files where the field names no longer match exactly what is exported from Outlook, use the Custom Comma Delimited data source.

8. Upload the Export File. Use the Browse button to locate the Accounts.csv data file, and then click on the Next button to continue.

9. Confirm Fields and Import. This screen (see the figure overleaf) shows four columns of data. Column 2 (Header Row) is the key—this contains the names of the fields being exported from your old CRM or contact manager. Columns 3 and 4 show example data from the first two records you are about to import. Column 1 (Database Field) is where you come in—you need to use all of the drop-down box controls in this column to select the fields within SugarCRM into which each incoming account field is imported.

10. Spend some time with this, exploring the names of the incoming fields, and the names of the corresponding SugarCRM fields, until you are sure you have defined the optimum mapping between them. If you are importing from Outlook, a particularly important field mapping to get right is to map the incoming Company field to the Account Name field within SugarCRM.

11. When you are satisfied you have the field mapping right, click on the Import Now button, at the bottom right of the screen. Before you do this you may choose to click on the Save As Custom Mapping checkbox, and provide a name for this mapping so that it may be used again in future.

12. The Import Results screen is displayed. It will summarize how many records were successfully imported, how many were skipped over, and the reasons they were skipped over. Below the summary are complete lists of all the data imported.

13. You can now choose to click on the Undo Last Import, Import More, or Finished buttons. Click on the Finished button if you are satisfied with the results of the data import, or Undo Last Import if you want to go back and try again—usually to improve the field mapping.

SUGARCRM.

SUGAR SUITE

| Home | My Portal | Calendar | Activities | Contacts | Accounts | Leads | Opportunities | Cases | Bug Tracker | Documents | Emails | ▶ |

Welcome admin

Search [_____] [Go]

Last Viewed: Portal User, 2 Big Consoles, Lunch with Maggie, Superior Campaign, Superior Targets, Fred Namath, Fred Grantham, Doc Newhart

Shortcuts

- Create Contact
- Enter Business Card
- Create From vCard
- Contacts
- Import

Import Step 3: Confirm Fields and Import

Print Help

* Indicates required field

In the list below, select the fields in your import file that should be imported into each field in the system. When you are finished, click **Import Now**:

Database Field	Header Row	Row 1	Row 2
-- Do not map this field --	category	Business	Personal Services
Salutation:	salutation		
First Name:	first_name	Peter	Norman
Last Name: *	last_name	Abrams	Adams
Lead Source:	lead_source		
Title:	title	Director of Marketing & B	President
Department:	department		
-- Do not map this field --	reports_to_id		
Birthdate:	birthdate		
Do Not Call:	do_not_call		
Email Opt Out:	phone_home		
Mobile:	phone_mobile		
Office Phone:	phone_work	(650) 463-0243	(613) 489-3583
Other Phone:	phone_other		
Email:	email1	peter_abrams@padg.com	norman@adamsandassociates.ca
Other Email:	email2		
Assistant:	assistant		
Assistant Phone:	assistant_phone		
Email Opt Out:	email_opt_out		
Primary Address Street:	primary_address_street	567 University Avenue	6733 Rideau Valley Drive South
Primary Address City:	primary_address_city	Palo Alto	Kars
Primary Address State:	primary_address_state	Ontario	
Primary Address Postal Code:	primary_address_postalcode	94301	K0A 2E0
Primary Address Country:	primary_address_country	USA	Canada
Alternate Address Street:	alt_address_street		
Alternate Address City:	alt_address_city		
Alternate Address State:	alt_address_state		
Alternate Address Postal Code:	alt_address_postalcode		
Alternate Address Country:	alt_address_country		
Description:	description		
Portal Name:	portal_name		
Portal Active:	portal_active		
Portal Application:	portal_app		
Invalid Email:	invalid_email		
Account Name:	account_name	Palo Alto Design Group	Adams & Associates Ltd.
Assigned User Name:	assigned_user_name		

☐ Save as Custom Mapping: [_____]

Notes:

- Either Last Name or Full Name must be mapped.
- If Full Name is mapped, then First Name and Last Name are ignored.
- If Full Name is mapped, then the data in Full Name will be split into First Name and Last Name when inserted into the database.
- Fields ending in Address Street 2 and Address Street 3 are concatenated together with the main Address Street Field when inserted into the database.

[< Back]   [Import Now]

Confirm Fields and Import Screen

Import Contacts

Now that you have a set of account records with fully descriptive data, let's import your contact data:

1. Click on the Import Contacts function within the Navigation Shortcuts Box of the Contacts module.

2. Specify the Data Source: Select Salesforce.com, Microsoft Outlook, ACT! 2005, Custom Comma Delimited or Custom Tab Delimited—then click on the Next button to continue.

3. Upload the Export File: Use the Browse button to locate the data file exported by your contacts manager, and then click on the Next button to continue.

4. Confirm Fields and Import: This screen (see the image opposite) shows four columns of data. Column 2 (Header Row) is the key—this contains the names of the fields being exported from your old CRM or contact manager. Columns 3 and 4 show example data from the first two records you are about to import. Column 1 (Database Field) is where you come in—you need to use all of the drop-down box controls in this column to select the fields within SugarCRM into which each incoming Contact field is imported.

5. Spend some time with this, exploring the names of the incoming fields, and the names of the corresponding SugarCRM fields, until you are sure you have defined the optimum mapping between them. If you are importing from Outlook, a particularly important field mapping to get right is to map the incoming Company field to the Account Name field within SugarCRM, so that contacts are associated with the correct accounts. (Be sure that you have corrected any inconsistent company names that you found in your data in step 4 of the *Import Accounts* section.)

6. When you are satisfied you have the field mapping right, click on the Import Now button, at the bottom right of the screen. Before you do, you may choose to click on the Save As Custom Mapping checkbox, and provide a name for this mapping so that it may be used again in future.

7. The Import Results screen is displayed. It will summarize how many records were successfully imported, how many were skipped over, and the reasons they were skipped over. Below the summary are complete lists of all the data imported—both Contacts, and any Accounts that were automatically created.

8. You can now choose to click on the Undo Last Import, Import More, or Finished buttons. Click on the Finished button if you are satisfied with the results of the data import, or Undo Last Import if you want to go back and try again—usually to improve the field mapping.

Importing Leads and Opportunities

Leads and opportunities are typically only tracked by a full CRM system, not a simple contact manager. If your old system is Microsoft Outlook or a similar contact manager, then you will have no data to import. If you are migrating from a full CRM system such as Salesforce.com, then the lead and opportunity data may be exported from that system and imported into SugarCRM in a very similar fashion to importing contact data, as described above.

Exporting Information

SugarCRM has flexible data exporting capabilities. Essentially all of the SugarCRM modules have an export function, accessed by clicking on the Export link in the top left corner of the list portion of each list view screen, including all of Activities, Accounts, Contacts, Documents, Leads, Opportunities, Bugs, Emails, Campaigns, Prospects, Projects, and Cases.

In each case, a Comma Separated Values (.CSV) file is produced, which contains all the currently selected records from the module in use (not just those records currently displayed on the screen). CSV files can be opened for viewing by Microsoft Excel, or Notepad, WordPad, and other text editors—and can easily be parsed as input files by most software.

CSV File in Excel

A sample portion of a CSV file, exported from the Accounts module and viewed in Microsoft Excel, is shown above. You can see that essentially the entire database table of information is exported in the CSV file with column titles, including the Record ID (a long and largely incomprehensible string of letters and numbers used as a unique reference to each account record) and other fields that SugarCRM uses internally.

D
The System Administrator Role

This section is intended for system administrators of Sugar Open Source installations. Administrators access an additional System Administration home screen by clicking on the Admin link in the top right corner of the screen. Note that the Admin link is only displayed for users that have been given administrator access privileges.

Every shared business system needs a system administrator, to perform the housekeeping tasks that belong to the system, not to any one user of the system. SugarCRM is no different in this regard, and has a number of general administrative activities that will be the responsibility of a system administrator.

Some of these duties occur around the time of initial system installation and setup. Others are general maintenance activities that are performed as new users join the system, or other users leave. In this appendix we will deal with topics such as:

- What are the system administration requirements as the time of initial system setup?
- What are the ongoing responsibilities of the system administrator?
- Who should be the system administrator?
- Should more than one person have administrative access?

System Administration Duties

System administration duties fall into two categories. Those to be performed at the time of system installation, and those that will need to be performed on a regular or ad hoc basis for the duration of the system's time in service.

At the time the system is installed, system administration duties include:

- Adding all users to the system—their first and last names, their user name and password, and their other user settings.
- Sending information to users about their user name, their initial password, and how to change their password.
- Sending information to users as to how to fill in their email options.

- Defining System Roles.
- Using the Configure Tabs feature to suppress any tabs not required, and the Rename Tabs feature to change the name of any tabs desired.
- Using the Configure Settings feature to set options for email notifications, customer self-service portal, and SkypeOut.
- Using Sugar Studio for any customizations required.
- Defining system currencies and rates.
- Using the Bug Tracker feature in administration to enter any software release information, to be used in the bug tracker module.
- The system administrator may also need to define recurring system tasks (i.e. crontab on Linux-based servers, or using the Scheduler on Windows servers) to enable the System Scheduler, which is used for email marketing campaigns, running scheduled reports, and other scheduled system activities.

From time to time after the system is installed and running, system administrators will need to:

- Add new users, suspend (mark as inactive) the accounts of users on prolonged absences, and remove (actually, recycle) or mark as inactive accounts for users that leave the organization.
- Reset passwords for users that forget them.
- Update currency rates.
- Maintain role data.
- Check for Sugar updates.
- Use the upgrade wizard to manage system upgrades when Sugar releases new version of their software.
- Use the module loader to load in add-on modules from third-party suppliers of Sugar modules.
- Create system backups from within Sugar, which back up the Sugar software (not the data).
- Use MySQL administration tools such as phpMyAdmin or a MySQL dump to back up system data.
- Check that available storage is not in danger of running out on the Sugar server.

Who Should Be the System Administrator?

As you can see from the lists above, the system administrator has a fair bit of work to do to help install and maintain the SugarCRM system.

This should tell you that whoever you choose as the system administrator needs to have some time available to discharge these new responsibilities. As well, the administrator must be someone who can be trusted with all the user access information, and with the company's most sensitive data—as the administrator can see all the data in the entire SugarCRM system.

Many businesses choose as their system administrator the same person that administers their PCs and their network. And in smaller businesses, this person is frequently a part-time contractor, not an employee.

If an outside contractor is already administering all your network access information, it doesn't really make things any worse to hand them the keys to the CRM as well—so if that's your inclination—go ahead. Just make sure you have a good non-disclosure and non-competition agreement in place with that contractor.

Otherwise, not that much technical knowledge is required to be the system administrator. With a little technical advice, a senior manager in the business can fill the role of system administrator just fine—although it may not be a good use of their time to be resetting user passwords. But at least they will have a good knowledge of and control over who is accessing the business's key data within the CRM.

Should More Than One User Be Given System Admin Capability?

The system is designed so that if there is only one system administrator, that user cannot be removed, or have those system administrator abilities removed. And a good thing too!

But normally, most businesses keep two system administrators on the system. One is typically the real administrator, doing the bulk of the work day to day. The other is typically a senior manager who keeps an eye on the system but does not typically enter much data. This is also the person who makes the administration changes to the system if the everyday system administrator is terminated or resigns and has to have their system access disabled.

Administration Duties at System Installation Time

The figure overleaf shows the top-level Administration screen. The administration capabilities referred to below can all be accessed from this screen.

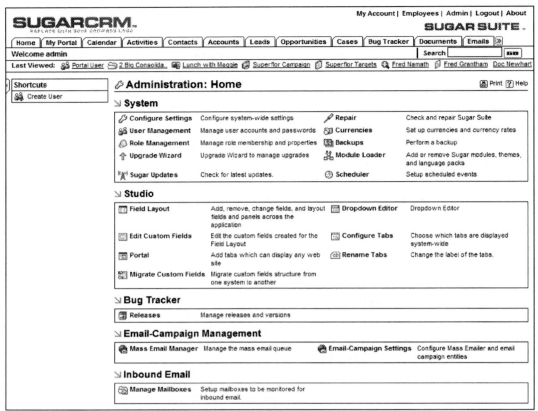

System Administration Module

Configuring System Settings

Configure Settings has five sections:

- The first section is used to define the Email Notification Options associated with the emails that Sugar Open Source can send to Users when they are assigned new responsibilities. Email notification settings include the subject line of the email to be sent, the user name and email address from which the email will be sent, as well as the Mail Transfer Agent (MTA) to be used. Note that the SMTP (Simple Mail Transfer Protocol) MTA should be selected if your system is running Windows. If your system is running Linux, either the SMTP or sendmail MTA may be selected, depending upon how your server is configured. If the SMTP MTA is selected, you must also specify the SMTP server name, and port number (default is 25) used to communicate with SMTP. If SMTP Authentication is selected via the checkbox provided, the SMTP User Name and Password to be used must also be provided. Configure Settings can also be used to enable and disable the email notification system, and establishes the default notification setting for new users.

- The second section is used to enable a proxy connection by which the Sugar server will access external information such as Sugar updates. If it is enabled, the user will also have to define settings for the proxy host and port number, and if authentication is checked, then a username and password must also be entered.

- The third section is used to enable or disable the ability of Sugar Open Source to integrate data (such as Cases and Notes) with a Customer Self-Service portal. The initial implementation of this has been created using the Mambo portal.

- The fourth section is used to enable or disable integration with SkypeOut—which enables users to click on phone numbers within the system to place outbound phone calls via the Internet.

- The fifth section is used to enable the Sugar Mail Merge option—and should be checked only if the system is using a licensed copy of the Sugar Plug-in for Microsoft Word.

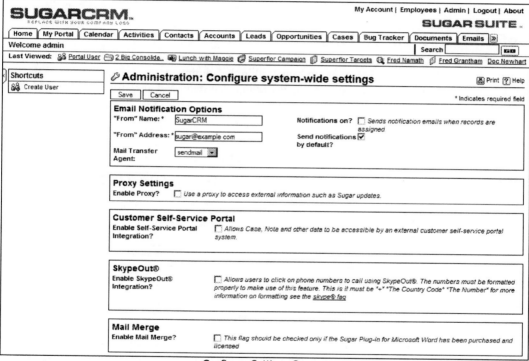

Configure Settings Screen

Defining Currencies and Rates

The Currencies screen is used to define currencies other than the US dollar. For each new currency defined, the name, symbol (for example $), exchange rate to the US$, and code (such as CAN for the Canadian dollar) must be entered. Note that each user can select his or her default currency in the User Management screen.

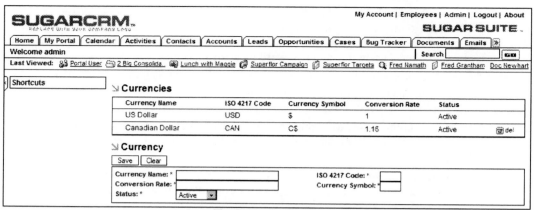

The Currencies Screen

Defining System Roles

Roles within SugarCRM serve the purpose of limiting the access of certain users within the system. When you select the Roles option from within the administration area, you will see the Roles List view screen. It lists the roles defined within the system, and also offers shortcuts to create a new role, or list roles by user.

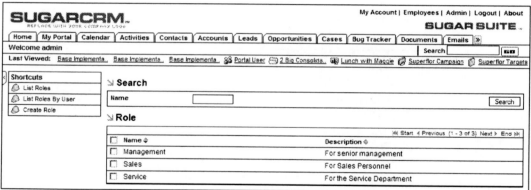

Roles List View

You can define roles for groups of users to specify which modules those users should have access to. For example—sales staff will want access to the opportunities and dashboard modules—marketing staff will want access to the campaigns module but not all staff will need access to these modules. As you can see in the figure overleaf, each role defines the modules which will be visible to the users assigned to the role, as well as the capabilities the user will have within each module.

SUGARCRM.
REPLACE WITH YOUR COMPANY LOGO

My Account | Employees | Admin | Logout | About

SUGAR SUITE.

| Home | My Portal | Calendar | Activities | Contacts | Accounts | Leads | Opportunities | Cases | Bug Tracker | Documents | Emails |

Welcome admin

Search [   ] 🔍

Last Viewed: Base Implementa.. Base Implementa.. Base Implementa.. 🔊 Portal User 📇 2 Big Consolida.. 🍴 Lunch with Maggie 🌐 Superfior Campaign 📄 Superfior Targets

Shortcuts
- 🍃 List Roles
- 🍃 List Roles By User
- 🍃 Create Role

Role: Management

[Edit] [Duplicate] [Delete]

	Name:	Management
	Description:	For senior management

	Access	Delete	Edit	Export	Import	List	View
Accounts	Enabled	All	All	All	All	All	All
Bug Tracker	Enabled	All	All	All	All	All	All
Calls	Enabled	All	All	All	All	All	All
Campaigns	Enabled	All	All	All	All	All	All
Cases	Enabled	All	All	All	All	All	All
Contacts	Enabled	All	All	All	All	All	All
Documents	Enabled	All	All	All	All	All	All
Email Marketing	Enabled	All	All	All	All	All	All
Emails	Enabled	All	All	All	All	All	All
Email Templates	Enabled	All	All	All	All	All	All
Leads	Enabled	All	All	All	All	All	All
Meetings	Enabled	All	All	All	All	All	All
Notes	Enabled	All	All	All	All	All	All
Opportunities	Enabled	All	All	All	All	All	All
Projects	Enabled	All	All	All	All	All	All
Project Tasks	Enabled	All	All	All	All	All	All
Target Lists	Enabled	All	All	All	All	All	All
Targets	Enabled	All	All	All	All	All	All
Tasks	Enabled	All	All	All	All	All	All

⊻ Users

Hide ⌃

[Select]

⤒ Start ◁ Previous (1 - 1 of 1) Next ▷ End ⤓

Name ⬦	User Name ⬦	Email ⬦	Phone ⬦
Doc Newhart	Doc Newhart		🗑 rem

Role Detail View

To create a role, click the Create Role shortcut, type a name and a description for the role, adjust the modules the role can access and the functions that may be performed within each module, and then save the role. To assign users to a role, use the detail view for that role. In the Users sub-panel, click the Select button to display a list of users. You can check the user names that you want to assign to this role. Note that when a module is excluded from a role, access is also removed to the sub-panels in other modules that relate to the excluded module. Also note that if a user belongs to multiple roles, their access in each module is defined by the most restrictive access any of their roles are assigned.

Configuring System Tabs

Both system administrators and users can easily configure which tabs appear at the top of the application. In the Configure Tabs administration option, administrators can define which menu tabs will be available for all users, and which will effectively not be part of the installation.

Users can then modify their own personal tab settings in the My Account screen. Any tabs that an administrator removes cannot be added back by a user.

Defining Releases for Bug Tracker

The Releases administration function is used to maintain the set of options available as selections on the Release drop-down box offered to users when reporting a new bug in the Bug Tracker module.

Each release entry consists of a release version, a status (Active or Inactive, where Inactive will remove it from drop-down lists) and the order in which it is to appear in the Release drop-down list.

Adding System Users

To add new users to the system, or to edit user settings, select User Management from the main Administration screen. Note that system users may not be deleted. They may be made Inactive, or be recycled into a new user record, but not deleted. This system is designed this way principally to avoid having data in the system that is associated to a user that does not exist.

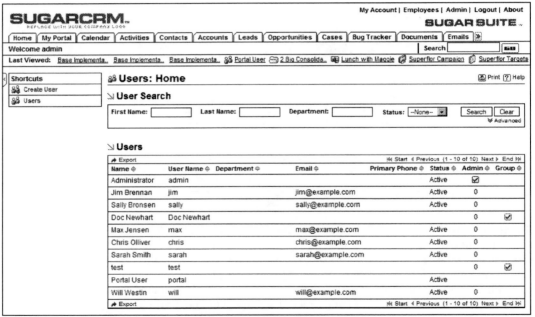

User Management Screen

Use the Create User shortcut to define a new user. Once a new user has been defined, with all the information shown in the screen below, then a new password must be defined for that user, using the Change Password button on the User Detail screen. Then you should send an email to the user giving them the full login information—what URL to use, and their new user name and password. It is also a good idea to tell the user how to change their password, and the procedure to follow when they forget their user name or password.

SUGARCRM.

My Account | Employees | Admin | Logout | About

SUGAR SUITE

| Home | My Portal | Calendar | Activities | Contacts | Accounts | Leads | Opportunities | Cases | Bug Tracker | Documents | Emails |

Welcome admin   Search

Last Viewed: Will Westin   Base Implementa.   Base Implementa.   Base Implementa.   Portal User   2 Big Consolida.   Lunch with Maggie   Superfior Campaign

Shortcuts
- Create User
- Users

Users: Will Westin (will)

Print   Help

| Edit | Change Password | Duplicate |

Reset To Default Preferences

Return to List   Start   Previous   (10 of 10)   Next   End

Name: Will Westin   User Name: will

Status: Active

User Settings

Administrator:		Grants administrator privileges to this user
Group User:		Act as a group user. This user cannot login through the Sugar Suite web interface. This user is only used for assigning items to a group via Inbound Email functionality.
Portal Only User:		Act as a portal user. This user cannot login through the Sugar Suite web interface. This user is only used for portal web services. Normal users cannot be used for portal web services.
Assignment Notification:		Receive an e-mail notification when a record is assigned to you.
Date Format:	2006-12-23	Set the display format for date stamps
Time Format:	23:00	Set the display format for time stamps
Timezone:	(GMT+6) (+DST)	
Show Gridlines:		Controls gridlines on detail views
Currency:	US Dollar : $	Select the default currency
Default Reminder:		Default time to remind a person of an upcoming call or meeting
Mail Merge:		Enable Mail Merge (Mail Merge must also be enabled by the system administrator in Configure Settings)
URL:	http://sugaros40.longreach.net	Use this URL when establishing login settings for the Sugar Plug-In for Microsoft Outlook and the Sugar Plug-In for Microsoft Word.

User Information

Employee Status:	Active		
Title:	Sales Manager East	Office Phone:	
Department:		Mobile Phone:	
Reports to:	Jim Brennan	Other:	
		Fax:	
Email:	will@example.com	Home Phone:	
Other Email:			
IM Type:			
IM Name:			
Address:			
Notes:			

E-mail Options

"From" Name:		"From" Address:	
Mail Transfer Agent:			

Calendar Options

Publish Key:	Choose a key to prevent unauthorized publishing of your calendar
Publish at my location:	http://sugaros40.longreach.net/vcal_server.php/type=vfb&user_name=will&source=outlook&key=
Search location:	http://sugaros40.longreach.net/vcal_server.php/type=vfb&email=%NAME%@%SERVER%

Access	Delete	Edit	Export	Import	List	View
Enabled	All	All	All	All	All	All
Enabled	All	All	All	All	All	All
Enabled	All	All	All	All	All	All
Enabled	All	All	All	All	All	All
Enabled	All	All	All	All	All	All
Enabled	All	All	All	All	All	All
Enabled	All	All	All	All	All	All
Enabled	All	All	All	All	All	All
Enabled	All	All	All	All	All	All
Enabled	All	All	All	All	All	All
Enabled	All	All	All	All	All	All
Enabled	All	All	All	All	All	All
Enabled	All	All	All	All	All	All
Enabled	All	All	All	All	All	All
Enabled	All	All	All	All	All	All
Enabled	All	All	All	All	All	All
Enabled	All	All	All	All	All	All

Roles

| Select |

Start   Previous   (0 - 0 of 0)   Next   End

Name	Description

User Edit View Screen

Using Sugar Studio

The Administration home page shows a number of tools grouped together as the Sugar Studio. They include:

- Field layout editor
- Dropdown editor
- Edit Custom fields
- Configure tabs
- Rename tabs

These tools collectively enable administrative users to perform a broad range of customization tasks, reducing the need for custom software development. For more information on these tools, see Chapter 5, which discusses these SugarCRM customization issues in detail.

Enabling the Mass Emailer

The system administrator can manage mass email campaigns that have been created in the Campaigns module. Within SugarCRM, users may create email campaigns targeting large numbers of prospects utilizing an email template. Depending on the send date the creator assigns to the email campaign, the emails then wait in the email queue to be sent at the particular date and time.

As an administrator you can monitor these emails as they are sent. You can also delete emails that are waiting to be sent. You can view information on each email such as **Campaign, Recipient Name, Recipient Email, From Name, From Address, User Name** sending the email, **Send On** date, **Send Attempts,** and **In Progress** status.

You should note that the Mass Emailing Queue Manager only displays emails created through email campaigns, not emails created using the Email module.

To delete an email that is waiting to be sent, click the checkbox next to the email and click the Delete button. Click **Check All** to select all the emails in the list.

The mass email queue manager processes emails that are scheduled to be sent from within Campaigns. The templated emails are sent to their recipients by a PHP script that must be run on regular intervals to send out the emails at the appropriate time. The user specifies the email template in the Campaigns module, as well as the sender name, sender email address (recommended to be no-reply@<your company.com> or something similar), and the time and date to send the email.

When an email is processed, a link is appended to the end of the email for recipients to opt out of receiving emails. This will link back to a page on the same machine as your Sugar instance.

To use the mass email queue manager, you must first correctly configure the email settings covered in the administration section **Configure System Settings.** The mass email queue manager uses the same email server connection settings. Notifications do not necessarily have to be turned on, but the settings must be properly configured for recipients to properly receive emails.

As well, the system administrator must also use the **Mass Emailer Campaign Settings** option to set how many emails may be sent per batch, and the location of the campaign tracking files.

To use email campaigns within SugarCRM, the administrator must first enable the System Scheduler, and configure the Schedule list within the Scheduler option of System section of the administration home page.

The System Scheduler is enabled in two different ways—one for a Linux server, and another for a Windows server. For Microsoft Windows, you can use the Task Scheduler. For Linux, you can use cron.

For Linux, as a root user, type the following command at the shell prompt, replacing the **path-to-sugar** with your own path to the Sugar installation directory and replacing the **apache** with the proper username that the web server runs as (usually defaults to apache or wwwrun):

```
/echo "0,10,20,30,40,50 * * * * cd /<path-to-sugar>;
<path-to-php> ./scheduler.php" | crontab -u apache/
```

This will setup a cron job to check every 10 minutes whether any emails need to be sent out. If any do, the mass email queue manager will process the template and send an email out immediately to the recipient.

For Windows, as a user with Administrator privileges, go to Start > Settings > Control Panel > Scheduled Tasks. Double-click on Add Scheduled Task. When the Scheduled Task Wizard asks you for the program you want Windows to run, browse for the scheduler.php file under your **path-to-sugar** directory. Continue with the rest of the Wizard, making sure you click on the Daily option when asked when to perform this task.

Before you click on the Finish button for the Scheduled Task Wizard, check the box that says, Open advanced properties for this task when I click Finish. A new dialog box displays after you click Finish. Click on the Schedule tab, and then on the Advanced button. Check the box for Repeat task and specify every 10 minutes with duration of 24 hours.

Recurring Administration Duties

This section describes those administrative duties that need to be performed on a regular or ad hoc basis throughout the time that your Sugar Open Source system is installed.

User Management

New users will need to be created, and existing users may need to be marked temporarily as Inactive if they take prolonged breaks such as a maternity leave. You can see how to add a new user earlier in this section.

To mark a user as Inactive, go to the Admin main screen, select User Management, select the user you wish to mark as Inactive, click on the Edit button, mark Status as Inactive (from the dropdown), and then click on Save.

Users may not be removed. Typically, the best solution is to mark a user as Inactive for a period of time (say 6 months) and then rename the user as a new user name you need to create, and mark it as Active once more.

Resetting Passwords

When a user calls in with a need to have their password reset, go to the Admin main screen, select User Management, and then select the user involved. On their detail view screen, click on Change Password, and then enter New Password—and then Confirm Password—then click on Save.

You will then need to email or telephone the user with their new temporary password, plus instructions on how to reset the password themselves to something you do not know.

General Maintenance

There are six topics that fall under general maintenance of the Sugar Open Source CRM system:

- Updating currency rates
- Maintaining Role data
- Checking for Sugar updates
- System Backups
- Data backups
- Checking that available storage is not in danger of running out on the Sugar server

Some of these topics are explained sufficiently in the previous section on *Administration Duties at System Installation Time*, such as the maintenance of currency rates and roles.

Checking for Updates to Sugar Open Source

You can check for updates automatically using the Sugar Open Source administrative function Sugar Updates, as shown here:

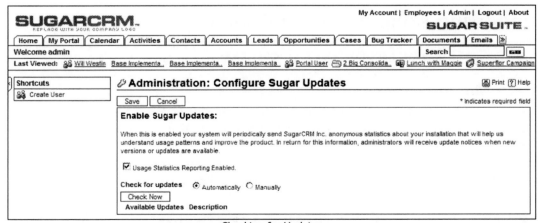

Checking for Updates

You can set the system to automatically check for updates, or you can do it manually. If you do it manually, the system will perform the update check, and will display the name of the most recent update just below the Check Now button.

The only drawback to using this function is that Sugar requests that you agree to its collection of usage statistics from your server. If that does not bother you, then this solution is ideal.

If you do not wish to have Sugar collect usage statistics, you can check manually for newer revisions to the Sugar Open Source software at http://www.sugarcrm.com/crm/download/sugar-suite.html.

Either way, if you find a new update to the Sugar Open Source software, you can apply it using the **Upgrade Wizard**, dealt with in a section coming up shortly.

System Backups

Backing up the system directory, the area where the programs that compose your installation of Sugar Open Source are stored (including any customization you may have installed to the software), is a simple task. Use the Backups function within Admin to perform this backup. You need only enter the name of the directory in which the backup is to be stored, and the filename for the backup file (in Zip format) to be generated.

To restore the system software from the Zip format file produced, a manual re-installation process must be performed, using this Zip file instead of the distribution file you originally used.

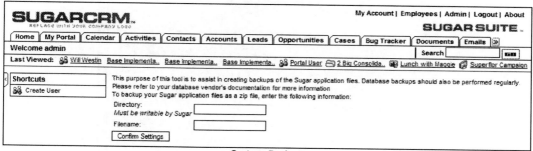

System Backup

Data Backups

To backup your system data from the MySQL database, you should use a MySQL administration tool such as phpMyAdmin—which provides web-based access to all database administration functions. Alternatively, you can simply perform a command-line dump in MySQL. To learn more about phpMyAdmin, and download a copy, please visit http://www.phpmyadmin.net.

Checking Available Storage

Other than completely losing the data on a hard drive, few things are quite as bad as having the drive run out of free space.

You can check for free disk space on a Linux server by using the **df -h** command in a shell, logged in as root.

You can check for free space on a Windows server by simply right-clicking on the hard drive used for data storage within My Computer. This will display a dialog box like this:

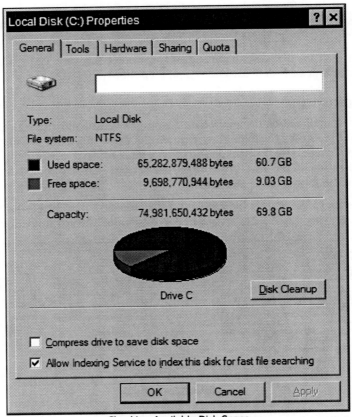

Checking Available Disk Space

As long as there is at least 5 GB of free space on the hard drive, there is not that much to worry about. If that is all there remains, or less, then it is time to be adding a new hard drive, replacing the existing one(s), or replacing the server. Going through system email (and attachments) and the document repository may also be a good idea, as that is where the bulk of disk space is used.

Using the Upgrade Wizard

The Upgrade Wizard is used to upgrade your system software from one revision to the next. Is it a sophisticated piece of software, which can also run SQL scripts to upgrade your database structure from the structure needed for one revision of software to that required for the next revision.

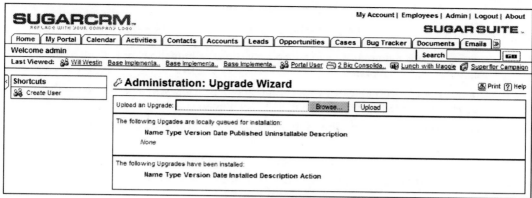

The Upgrade Wizard

The Upgrade Wizard also provides a quick way to upload and install patches to existing versions, as well as language packs and custom themes.

1. You simply browse to select the zip file for the upgrade and click Upload. Uploading the file queues the upgrade files for installation. Next, whenever you like, you can click Install to install the upgrade files.

2. When you do so, a file list will be displayed, with checkboxes to deselect specific files if you don't want them installed.

3. You then click Commit to complete the installation.

4. The Upgrade Wizard automatically unzips and installs the files. A history of all upgrades that have been queued and installed displays in a list on the Upgrade Wizard screen.

5. You can also uninstall language packs and themes using the Upgrade Wizard. Select an item to uninstall and click Uninstall.

Note that you typically cannot uninstall upgrades to new overall versions, or patch updates.

Using the Module Loader

The Module Loader is a remarkably innovative feature, introduced in Sugar Open Source and Pro at version 3.5, which enables independent third-party software modules to be developed for the Sugar application framework, and dynamically installed or uninstalled using the Module Loader.

The Module Loader defines a standard packaging for a third-party module—a zip file that includes a manifest file, which specifies the following information for the module:

- **Acceptable_sugar_versions**: The version of the sugar server that must be present to load this module. The format of the version dependency check can be provided as an exact match, or as a regex comparison.

- **Acceptable_sugar_flavors**: The flavor of sugar server. Currently Sugar supports Open Source, Professional, and Enterprise flavors. If there are elements or dependencies on functionality in a specific flavor this parameter should be used to specify what is required. If there are no restrictions or limitations specify all of the supported sugar flavors.

- **Name**: The user-readable name for the module. This name will be displayed in the Sugar Admin interface when loading and installing the module.

- **Description**: The description of the module that is displayed in the Sugar Admin interface.

- **Author**: The name of the person or company that authored the module.

- **Published Date**: The date the module was published or last revised.

- **Version**: The version of the module.

- **Type**: The type of package that is contained in the zip file. Currently the module loader only supports modules, and the Upgrade Wizard provides support for language packs, themes, patches, and a full upgrade.

- **Icon**: The relative path and name of the icon file in the zip file the Sugar Loader should use to display in the Sugar Admin interface for this module. The system will use default icons if this is left blank.

- **Copy_files**: An array of file copy instructions that specify the From & To source and destination for folders and files. The installation processing simply walks through this tree moving the files as specified. Folders are copied recursively.

To use the Module Loader, simply select that option from the Admin main screen.

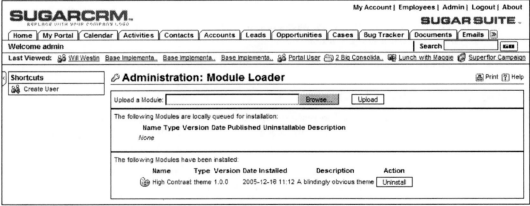

The Module Loader

Just browse for the zip file of the module to be loaded, click on Upload, and the module will be queued for installation. Once this step is complete, at any time you may click on Install to install the software, or Delete Package to remove the queued software. The figure above shows the High Contrast theme installed—the theme we have used in this book to make captured screenshots more readable.

Index

F

features, CRM, 9
feedback, CRM deployment, 219
Field Layout Editor, 141
Filter tab, Reporting module, 183
Filter user restriction setting, 154
Firefox support, SugarCRM, 58
firewall, security measures, 52
Forecast History shortcut, Forecasts module, 181
Forecasts module, Sugar Pro add-ons
    forecast commitment, 181
    forecast history screen, 180
    Forecast History shortcut, 181
    Forecasts tab, 179
Forecasts tab, 179
form factor, server hardware, 48
front office applications, 172
functional areas slide, CRM training materials, 216

G

goals, CRM implementation, 208
graphical dashboard, 81
Group Inbox, SugarCRM email features, 98
Group tab, Reporting module, 184
groupware application, 17

H

hard disk speed, server hardware, 48
hard disk technology, server hardware, 48
hardware, server requirements, 48
help, documentation, 101
Hide Controls for each sub-panel, details view, 67
History sub-panel, 91
home page, 282
home screen, SugarCRM, 11
Home tab, 60, 90
home tab slide, CRM training materials, 217
home-based business, 6
hosted application pack model, CRM deployment, 16
HR module, add-ons, 160

human resources management, commercial add-ons, 159

I

IDE, 49
IDE disk drives, server hardware, 49
implementing a CRM, 203
Import Accounts function, 285
Import and Export Wizard dialog box, 284
Import Contacts function, Contacts module, 287
Import restriction setting, 154
Import vCard button, 104
importing, 283
importing data
    about, 108, 283
    accounts, 284
    contacts, 287
    leads and opportunities, 287
importing data, CRM implementation, 211
inactive users, user management, 299
inbound traffic, server bandwidth, 53
input business card, 103
installation, SugarCRM
    Linux, 255
    Mambo components, 241
    Mambo portal, 229
    Windows Server, 271
integration, CRM customization, 36
interface consolidation, 133
interface consolidation, business activities, 30
Internal Drive Electronics (IDE), 49
international offices, requirements, 35
Internet Explorer support, SugarCRM, 58
invitees, add, 87, 88
issue management, CRM training, 212

J

junior administrator, enhanced role management, 192

K

Konqueror support, SugarCRM, 58

308

V

vCard, 104
VCR controls, details view, 67
video, server hardware, 49
View Change Log, details view, 68

W

web based application platforms, server
requirements, 47

web-based CRM, 8
Wireless Contact List View, Sugar Pro, 194

X

XE, 6, 255

Z

ZuckerMail module, commercial add-ons, 167

9 781904 811688